CAPTAIN MARVEL

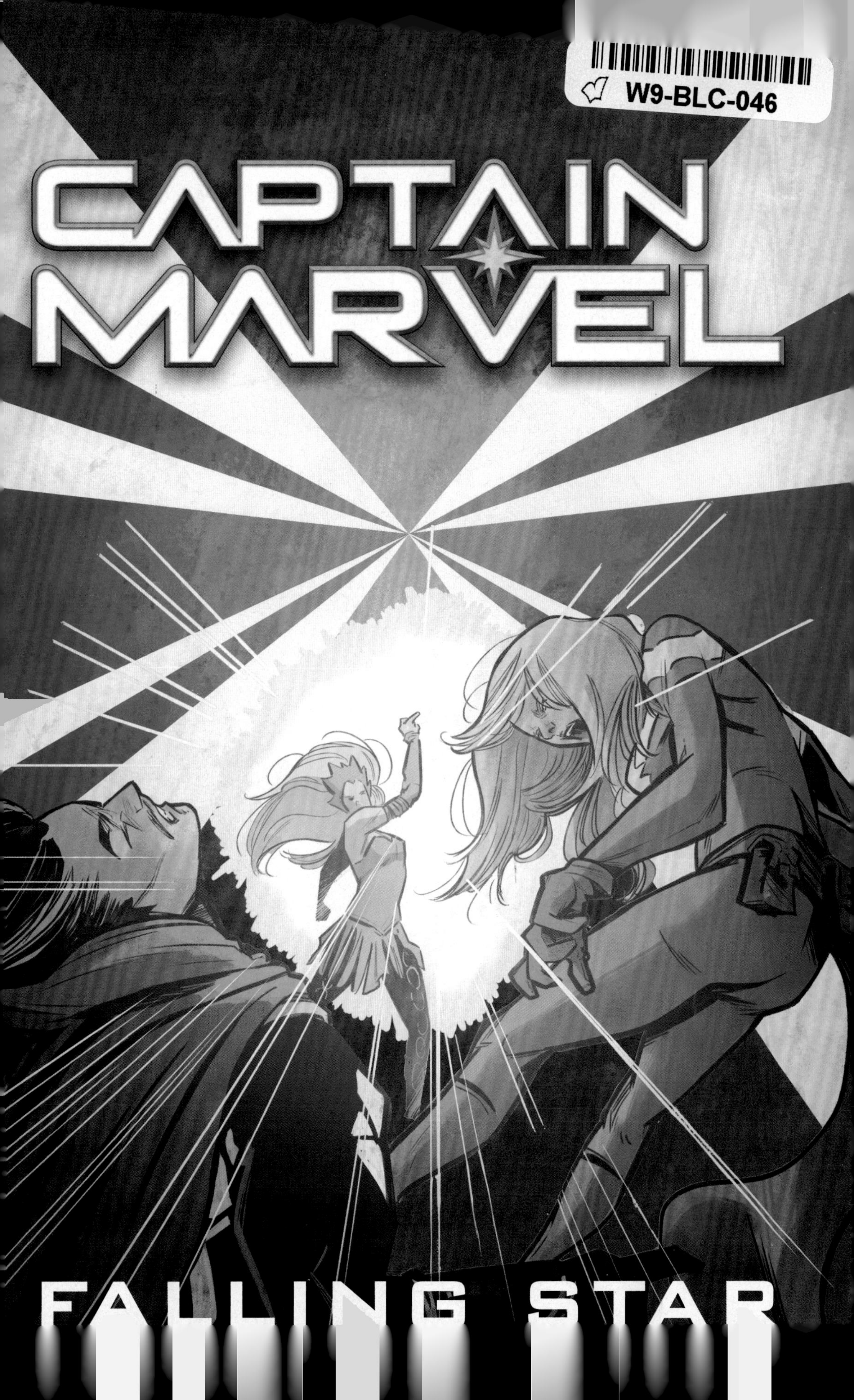

FALLING STAR

Born to a Kree mother and human father, former U.S. Air Force pilot **CAROL DANVERS** became a super hero when a Kree device activated her latent powers. Now, she's an Avenger and Earth's Mightiest Hero.

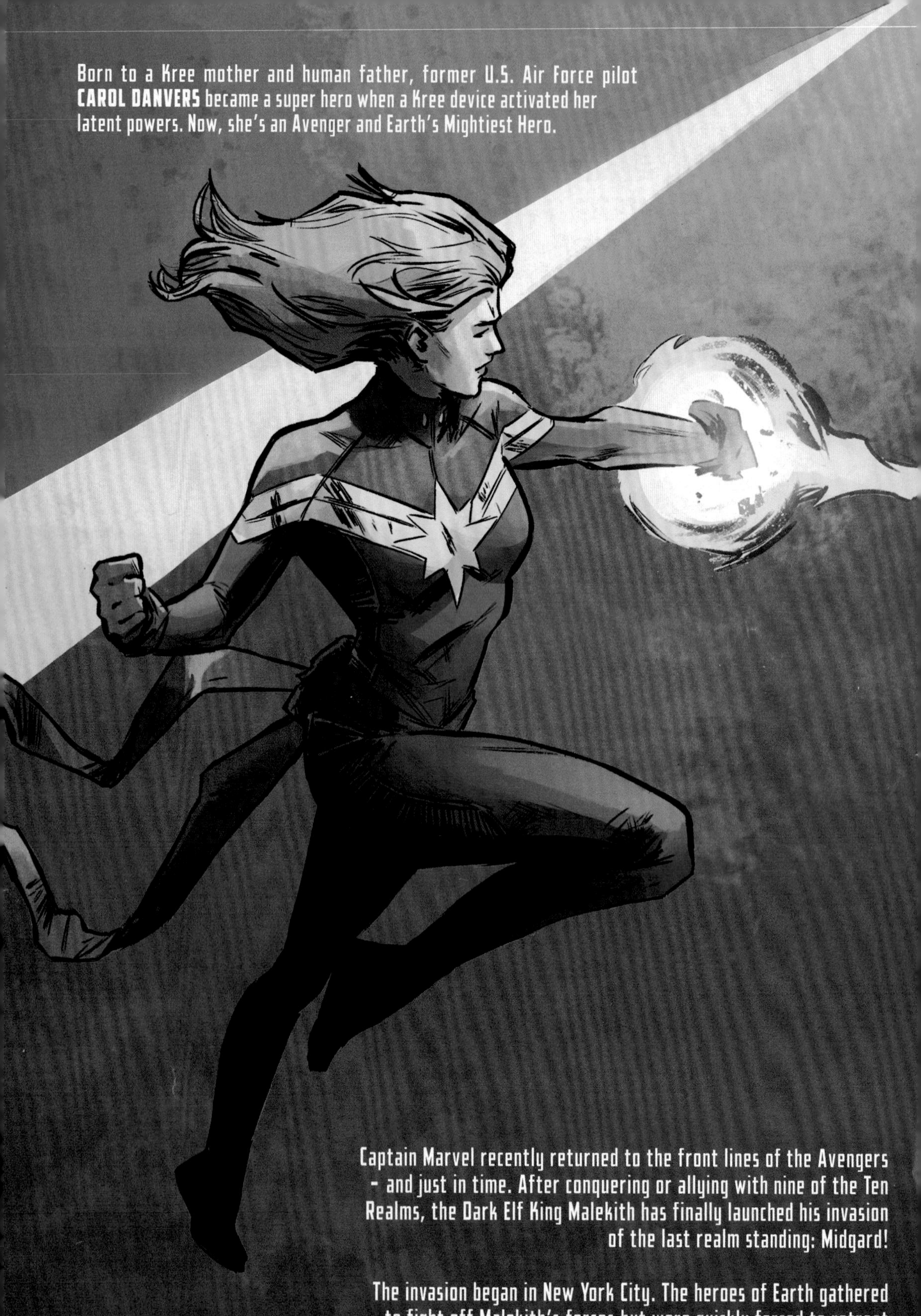

Captain Marvel recently returned to the front lines of the Avengers – and just in time. After conquering or allying with nine of the Ten Realms, the Dark Elf King Malekith has finally launched his invasion of the last realm standing: Midgard!

The invasion began in New York City. The heroes of Earth gathered to fight off Malekith's forces but were quickly forced to retreat after evacuating civilians. Now Malekith's army has spread across the globe, each of his allies claiming a continent to themselves.

Captain Marvel is leading the strike teams to defend Earth

CAPTAIN MARVEL

FALLING STAR

KELLY THOMPSON
Writer

ANNAPAOLA MARTELLO [#6-7] &
CARMEN CARNERO [#8-11]
Artists

TAMRA BONVILLAIN
Color Artist

VC's CLAYTON COWLES
Letterer

AMANDA CONNER & PAUL MOUNTS [#6, #8],
AMANDA CONNER & DAVE JOHNSON [#7]
AND MARK BROOKS [#9-11]
Cover Art

SARAH BRUNSTAD
Editor

WIL MOSS
Consulting Editor

Special thanks to
VITA AYALA

Collection Editor JENNIFER GRÜNWALD
Assistant Editor CAITLIN O'CONNELL
Associate Managing Editor KATERI WOODY
Editor, Special Projects MARK D. BEAZLEY
VP Production & Special Projects JEFF YOUNGQUIST
Book Designers STACIE ZUCKER AND ADAM DEL RE with
CLAYTON COWLES and NICK RUSSELL

SVP Print, Sales & Marketing DAVID GABRIEL
Director, Licensed Publishing SVEN LARSEN
Editor in Chief C.B. CEBULSKI
Chief Creative Officer JOE QUESADA
President DAN BUCKLEY
Executive Producer ALAN FINE

CAPTAIN MARVEL VOL. 2: FALLING STAR. Contains material originally published in magazine form as CAPTAIN MARVEL #6-11. First printing 2019. ISBN 978-1-302-91688-6. Published by MARVEL WORLDWIDE, INC., a subsidiary of MARVEL ENTERTAINMENT, LLC. OFFICE OF PUBLICATION: 135 West 50th Street, New York, NY 10020. © 2019 MARVEL No similarity between any of the names, characters, persons, and/or institutions in this magazine with those of any living or dead person or institution is intended, and any such similarity which may exist is purely coincidental. **Printed in Canada.** DAN BUCKLEY, President, Marvel Entertainment; JOHN NEE, Publisher; JOE QUESADA, Chief Creative Officer; TOM BREVOORT, SVP of Publishing; DAVID BOGART, Associate Publisher & SVP of Talent Affairs; DAVID GABRIEL, VP of Print & Digital Publishing; JEFF YOUNGQUIST, VP of Production & Special Projects; DAN CARR, Executive Director of Publishing Technology; ALEX MORALES, Director of Publishing Operations; DAN EDINGTON, Managing Editor; SUSAN CRESPI, Production Manager; STAN LEE, Chairman Emeritus. For information regarding advertising in Marvel Comics or on Marvel.com, please contact Vit DeBellis, Custom Solutions & Integrated Advertising Manager, at vdebellis@marvel.com. For Marvel subscription inquiries, please call 888-511-5480. **Manufactured between 11/15/2019 and 12/17/2019 by SOLISCO PRINTERS, SCOTT, QC, CANADA.**

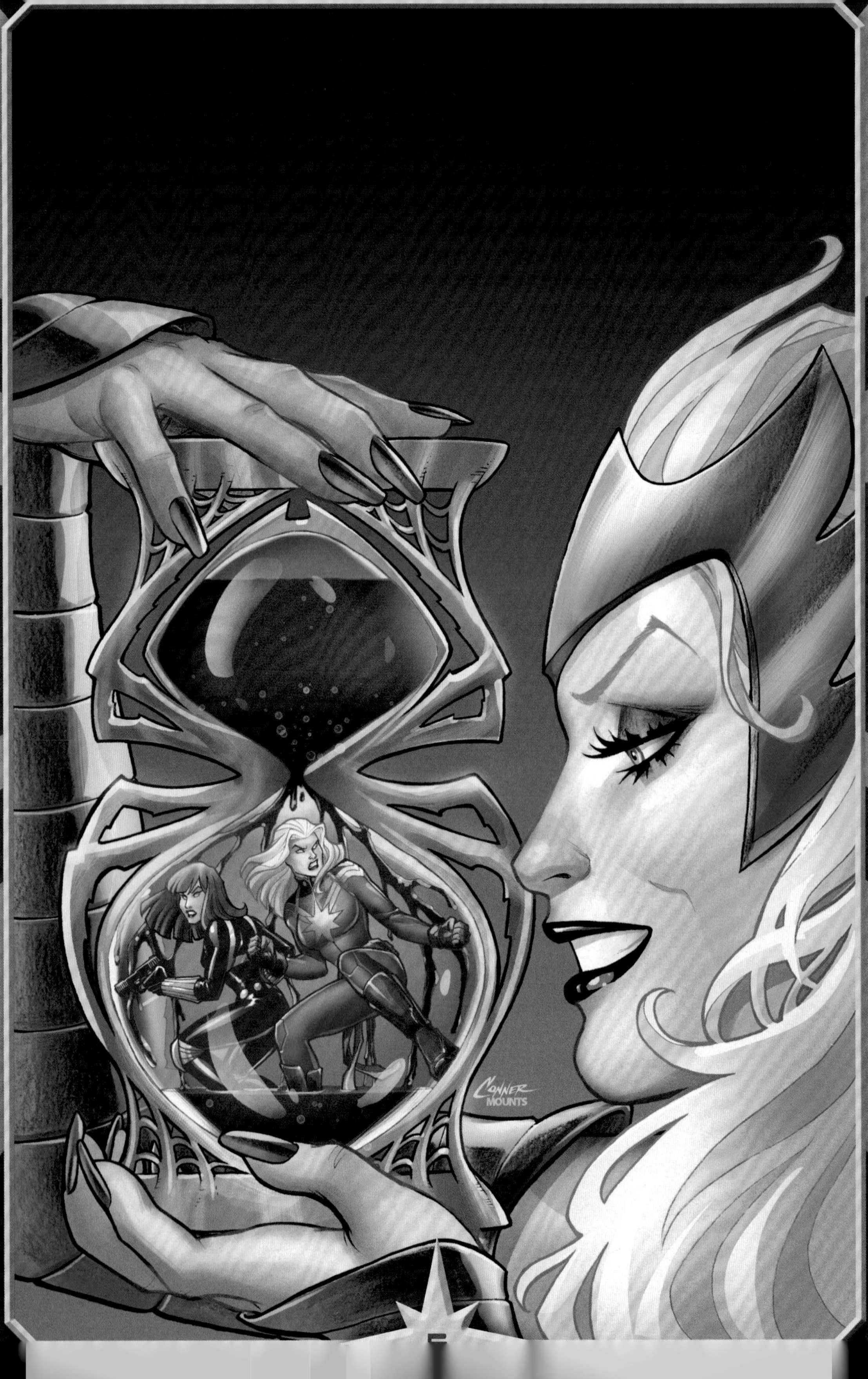
CONNER
MOUNTS

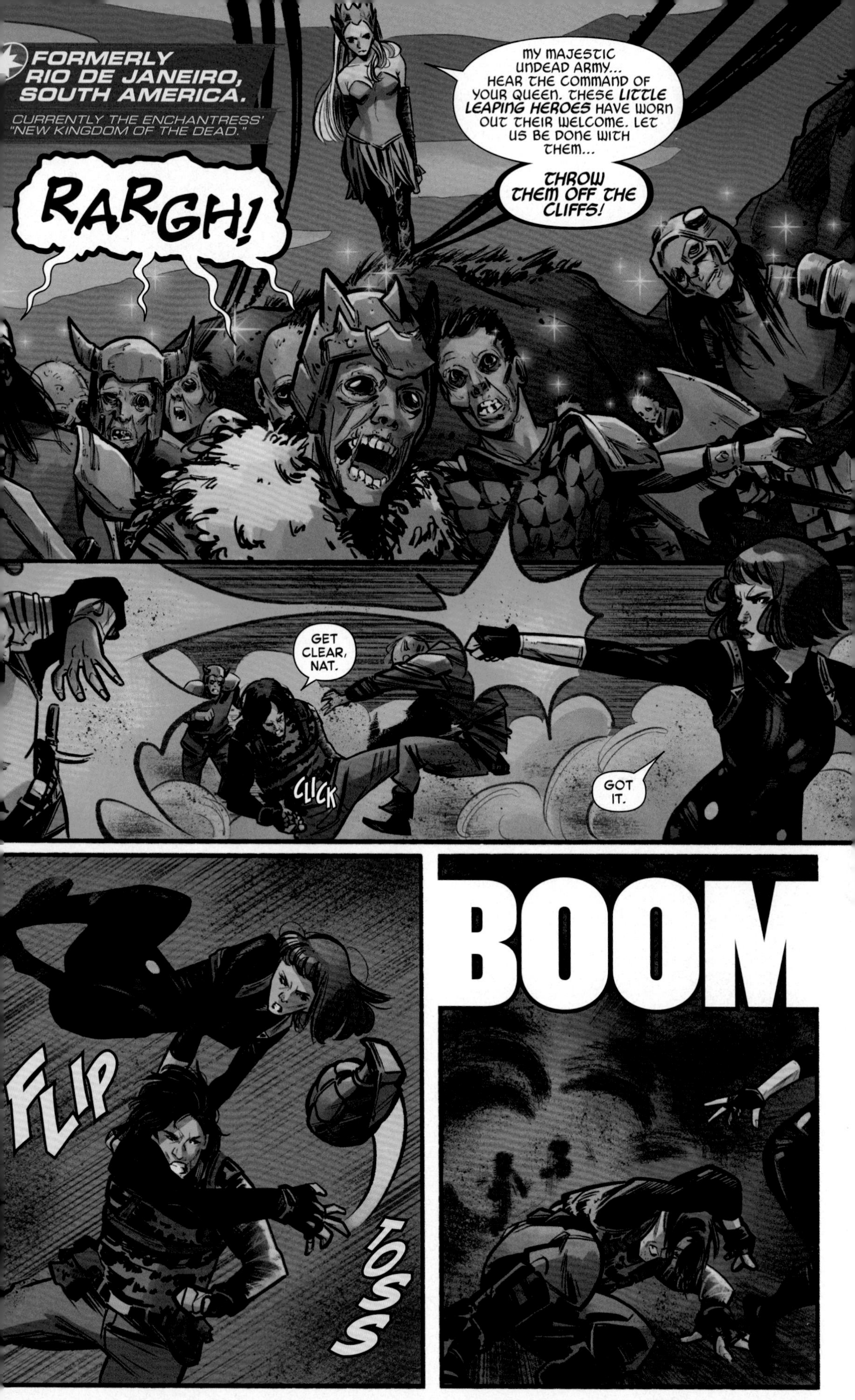
FORMERLY RIO DE JANEIRO, SOUTH AMERICA.
CURRENTLY THE ENCHANTRESS' "NEW KINGDOM OF THE DEAD."
RARGH!
MY MAJESTIC UNDEAD ARMY... HEAR THE COMMAND OF YOUR QUEEN. THESE LITTLE LEAPING HEROES HAVE WORN OUT THEIR WELCOME. LET US BE DONE WITH THEM...
THROW THEM OFF THE CLIFFS!
GET CLEAR, NAT.
CLICK
GOT IT.
FLIP
TOSS
BOOM

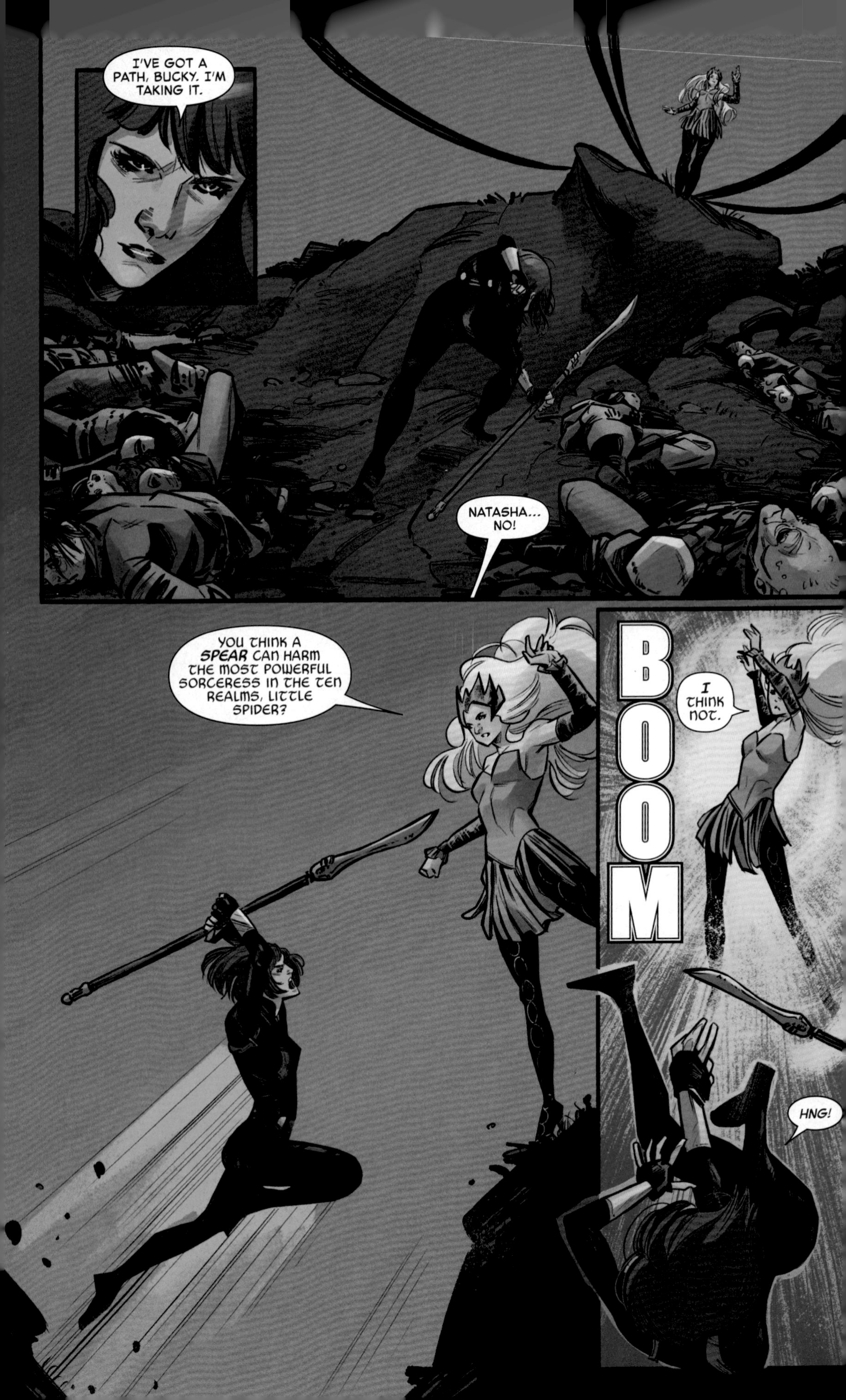
I'VE GOT A PATH, BUCKY. I'M TAKING IT.
NATASHA... NO!
YOU THINK A SPEAR CAN HARM THE MOST POWERFUL SORCERESS IN THE TEN REALMS, LITTLE SPIDER?
BOOM
I THINK NOT.
HNG!

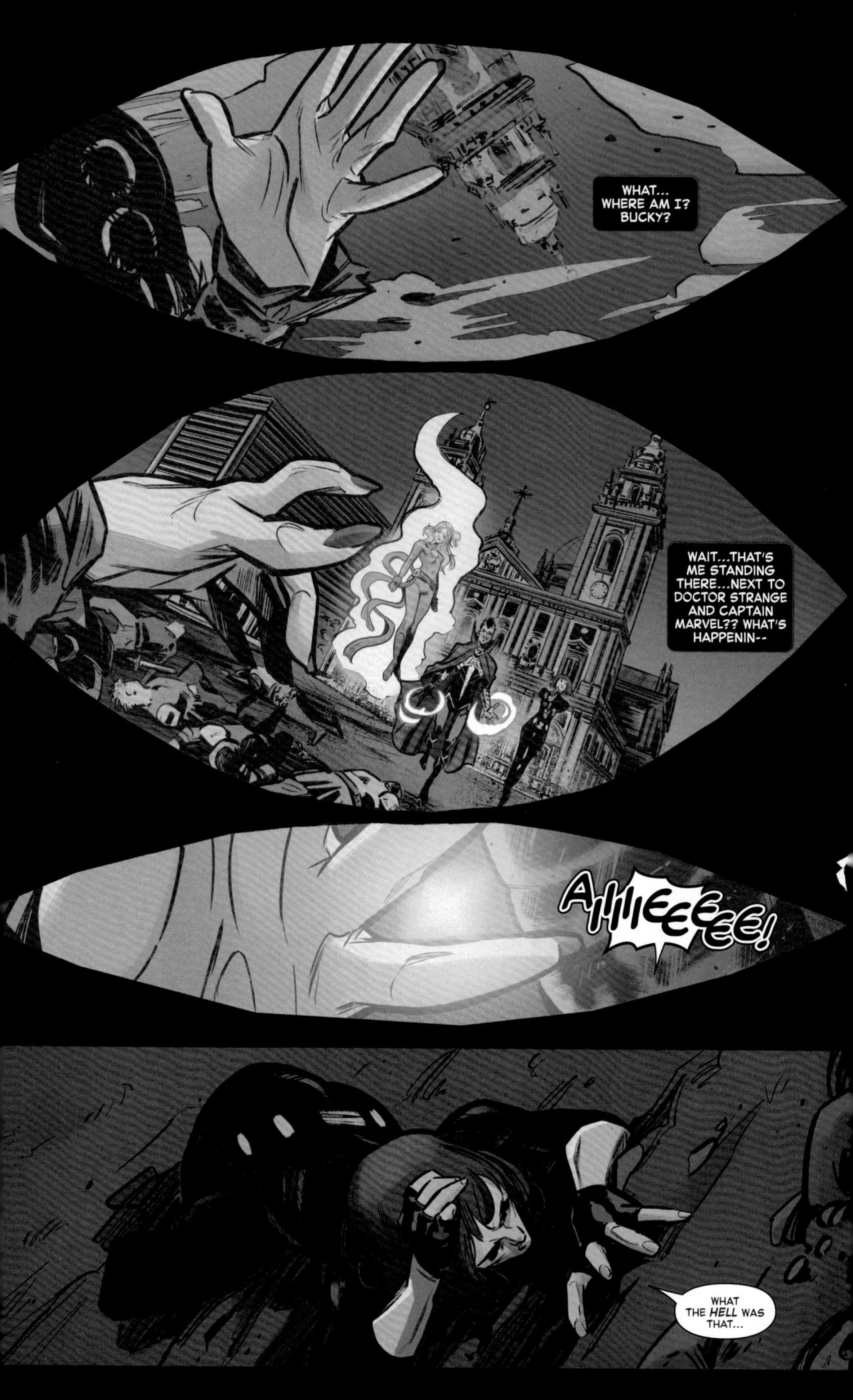
WHAT... WHERE AM I? BUCKY?
WAIT...THAT'S ME STANDING THERE...NEXT TO DOCTOR STRANGE AND CAPTAIN MARVEL?? WHAT'S HAPPENIN--
AIIIIEEEEEE!
WHAT THE *HELL* WAS THAT...

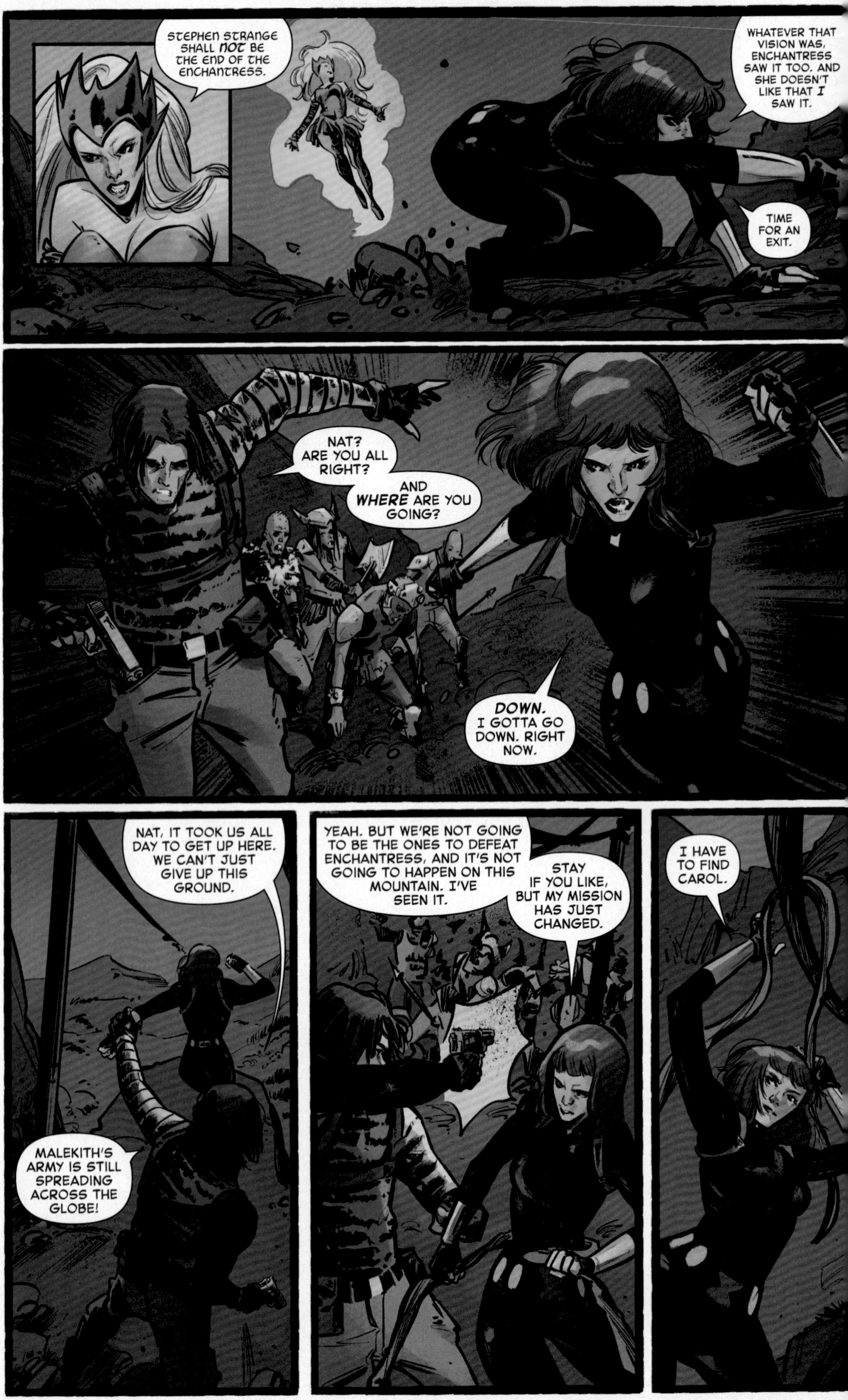
STEPHEN STRANGE SHALL NOT BE THE END OF THE ENCHANTRESS.
WHATEVER THAT VISION WAS, ENCHANTRESS SAW IT TOO. AND SHE DOESN'T LIKE THAT I SAW IT.
TIME FOR AN EXIT.
NAT? ARE YOU ALL RIGHT?
AND WHERE ARE YOU GOING?
DOWN. I GOTTA GO DOWN. RIGHT NOW.
NAT, IT TOOK US ALL DAY TO GET UP HERE. WE CAN'T JUST GIVE UP THIS GROUND.
MALEKITH'S ARMY IS STILL SPREADING ACROSS THE GLOBE!
YEAH. BUT WE'RE NOT GOING TO BE THE ONES TO DEFEAT ENCHANTRESS, AND IT'S NOT GOING TO HAPPEN ON THIS MOUNTAIN. I'VE SEEN IT.
STAY IF YOU LIKE, BUT MY MISSION HAS JUST CHANGED.
I HAVE TO FIND CAROL.

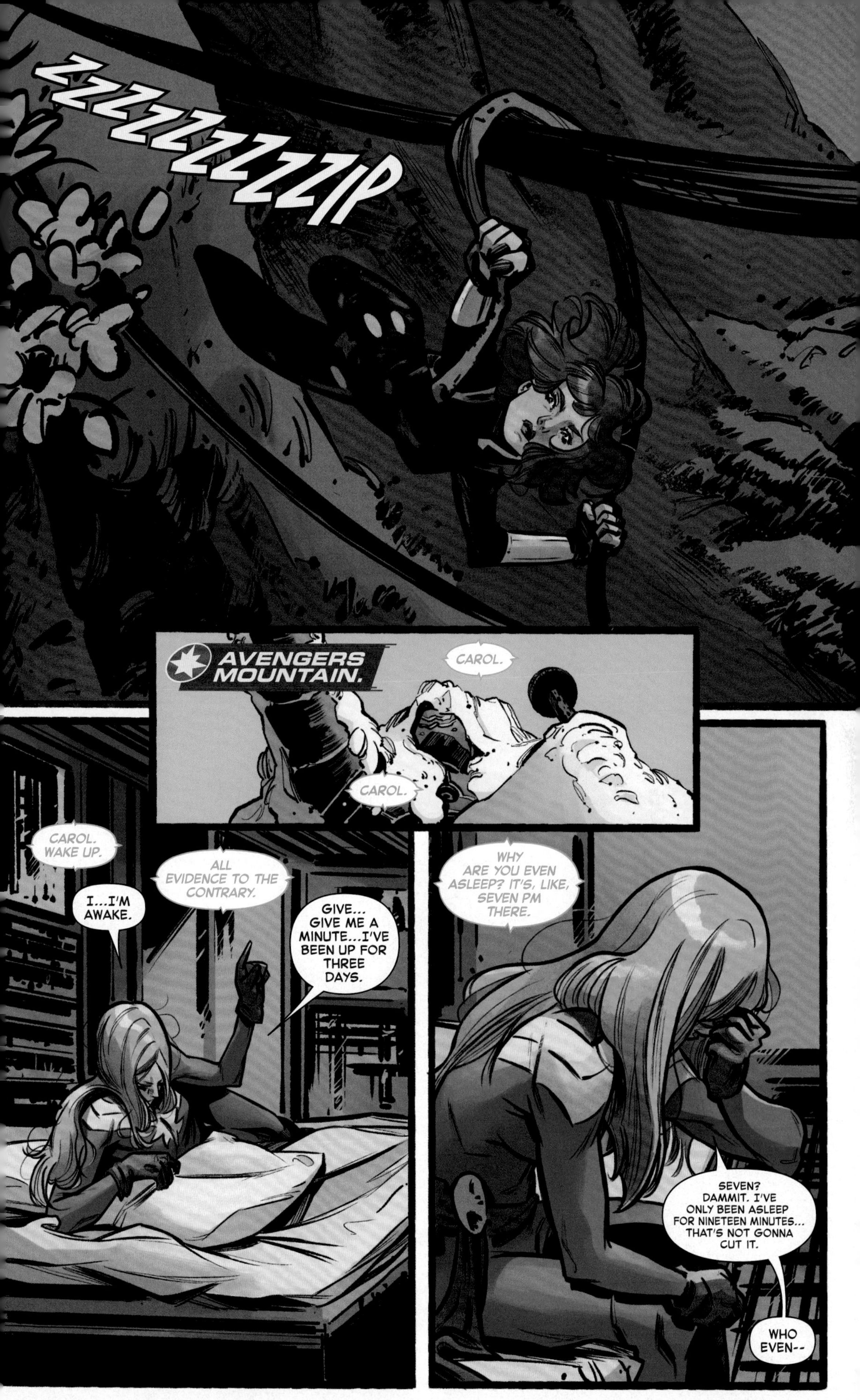
ZZZZZZZZZZIP
AVENGERS MOUNTAIN.
CAROL.
CAROL.
CAROL. WAKE UP.
I...I'M AWAKE.
ALL EVIDENCE TO THE CONTRARY.
GIVE... GIVE ME A MINUTE...I'VE BEEN UP FOR THREE DAYS.
WHY ARE YOU EVEN ASLEEP? IT'S, LIKE, SEVEN PM THERE.
SEVEN? DAMMIT. I'VE ONLY BEEN ASLEEP FOR NINETEEN MINUTES... THAT'S NOT GONNA CUT IT.
WHO EVEN--

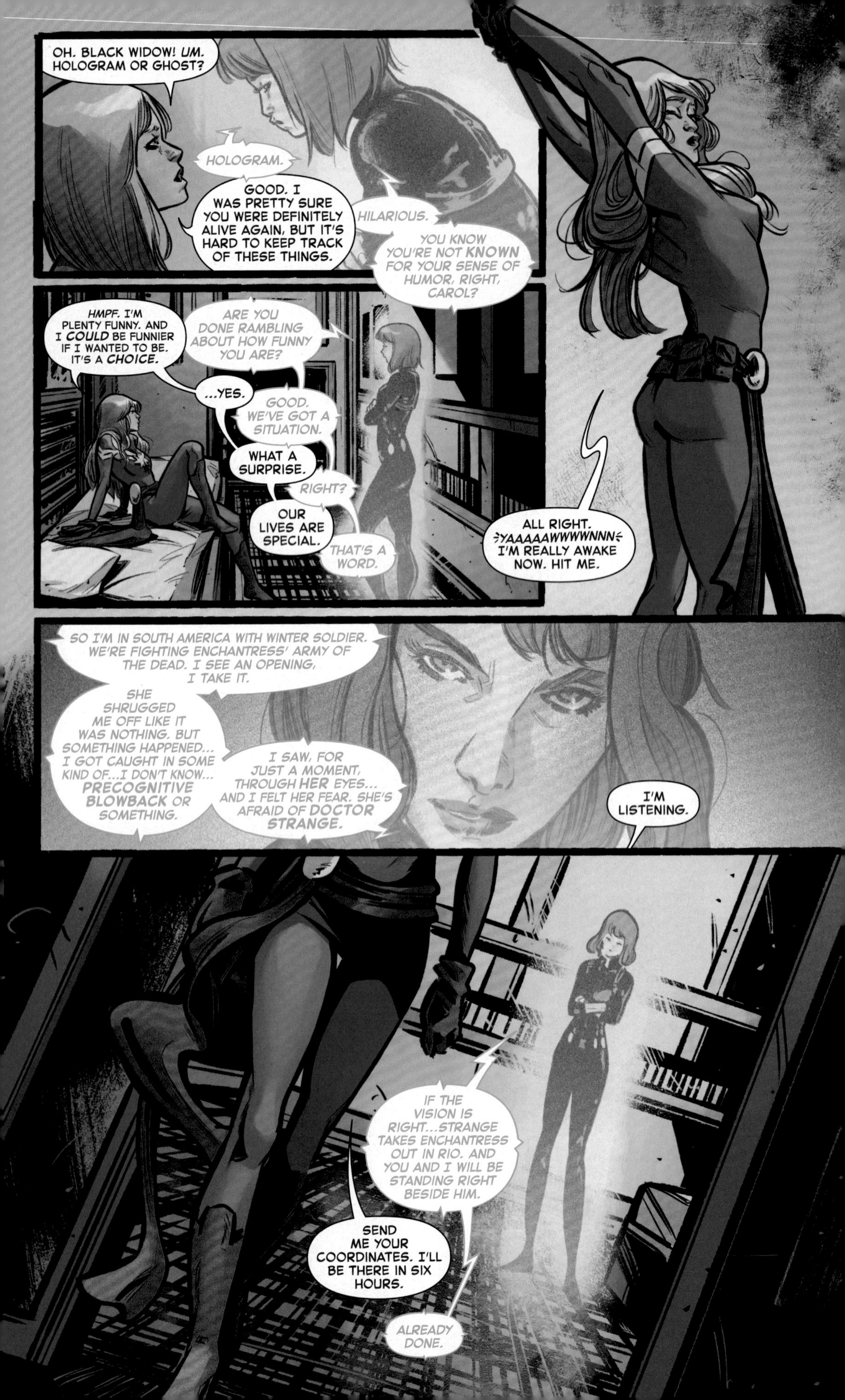

OH. BLACK WIDOW! UM. HOLOGRAM OR GHOST?
HOLOGRAM.
GOOD. I WAS PRETTY SURE YOU WERE DEFINITELY ALIVE AGAIN, BUT IT'S HARD TO KEEP TRACK OF THESE THINGS.
HILARIOUS.
YOU KNOW YOU'RE NOT KNOWN FOR YOUR SENSE OF HUMOR, RIGHT, CAROL?
HMPF. I'M PLENTY FUNNY. AND I COULD BE FUNNIER IF I WANTED TO BE. IT'S A CHOICE.
ARE YOU DONE RAMBLING ABOUT HOW FUNNY YOU ARE?
...YES.
GOOD. WE'VE GOT A SITUATION.
WHAT A SURPRISE.
RIGHT?
OUR LIVES ARE SPECIAL.
THAT'S A WORD.
ALL RIGHT. YAAAAAWWWWNNN I'M REALLY AWAKE NOW. HIT ME.
SO I'M IN SOUTH AMERICA WITH WINTER SOLDIER. WE'RE FIGHTING ENCHANTRESS' ARMY OF THE DEAD. I SEE AN OPENING, I TAKE IT.
SHE SHRUGGED ME OFF LIKE IT WAS NOTHING. BUT SOMETHING HAPPENED... I GOT CAUGHT IN SOME KIND OF...I DON'T KNOW... PRECOGNITIVE BLOWBACK OR SOMETHING.
I SAW, FOR JUST A MOMENT, THROUGH HER EYES... AND I FELT HER FEAR. SHE'S AFRAID OF DOCTOR STRANGE.
I'M LISTENING.
IF THE VISION IS RIGHT...STRANGE TAKES ENCHANTRESS OUT IN RIO. AND YOU AND I WILL BE STANDING RIGHT BESIDE HIM.
SEND ME YOUR COORDINATES. I'LL BE THERE IN SIX HOURS.
ALREADY DONE.

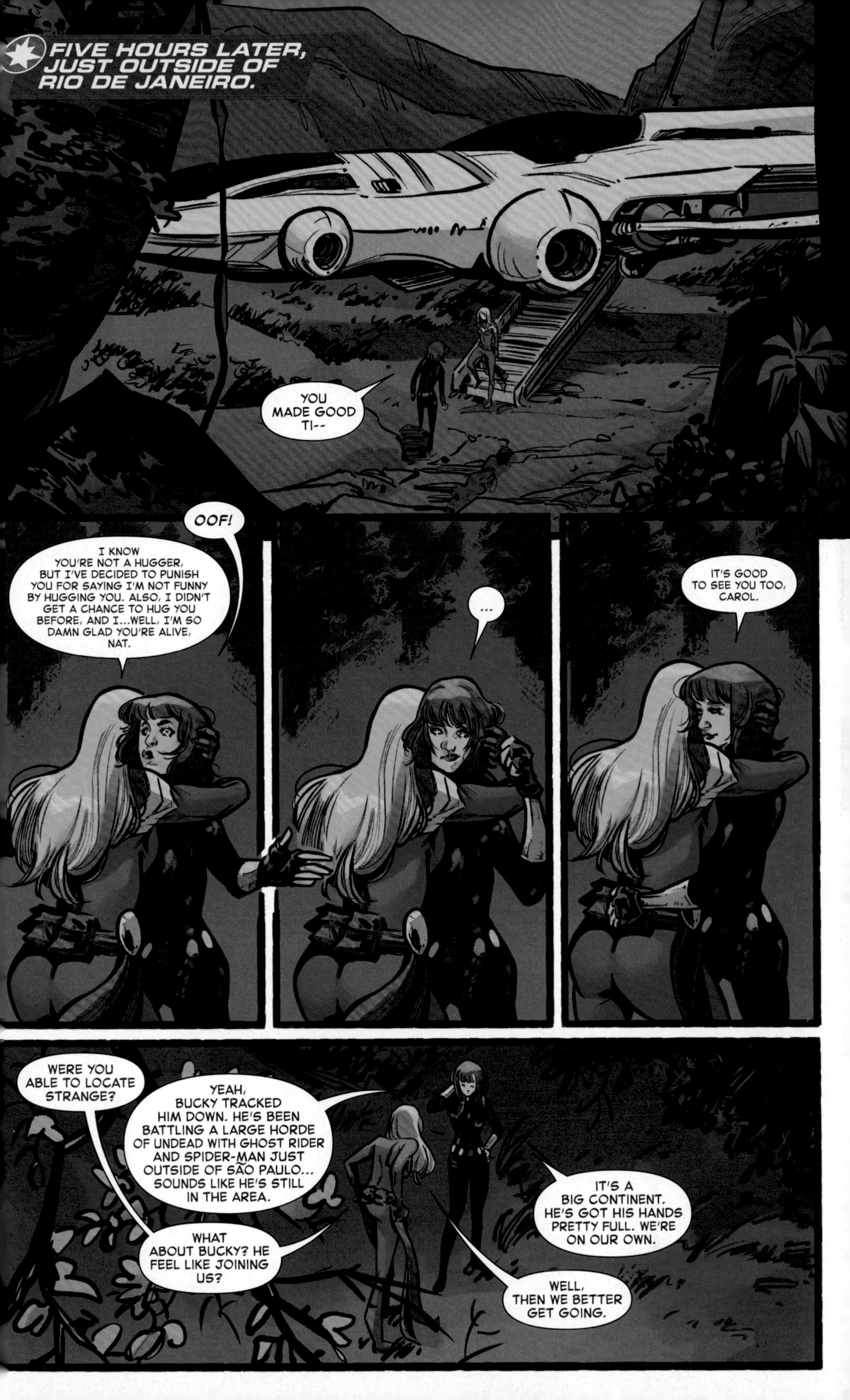
FIVE HOURS LATER, JUST OUTSIDE OF RIO DE JANEIRO.
YOU MADE GOOD TI--
OOF!
I KNOW YOU'RE NOT A HUGGER, BUT I'VE DECIDED TO PUNISH YOU FOR SAYING I'M NOT FUNNY BY HUGGING YOU. ALSO, I DIDN'T GET A CHANCE TO HUG YOU BEFORE, AND I...WELL, I'M SO DAMN GLAD YOU'RE ALIVE, NAT.
...
IT'S GOOD TO SEE YOU TOO, CAROL.
WERE YOU ABLE TO LOCATE STRANGE?
YEAH, BUCKY TRACKED HIM DOWN. HE'S BEEN BATTLING A LARGE HORDE OF UNDEAD WITH GHOST RIDER AND SPIDER-MAN JUST OUTSIDE OF SÃO PAULO... SOUNDS LIKE HE'S STILL IN THE AREA.
WHAT ABOUT BUCKY? HE FEEL LIKE JOINING US?
IT'S A BIG CONTINENT. HE'S GOT HIS HANDS PRETTY FULL. WE'RE ON OUR OWN.
WELL, THEN WE BETTER GET GOING.

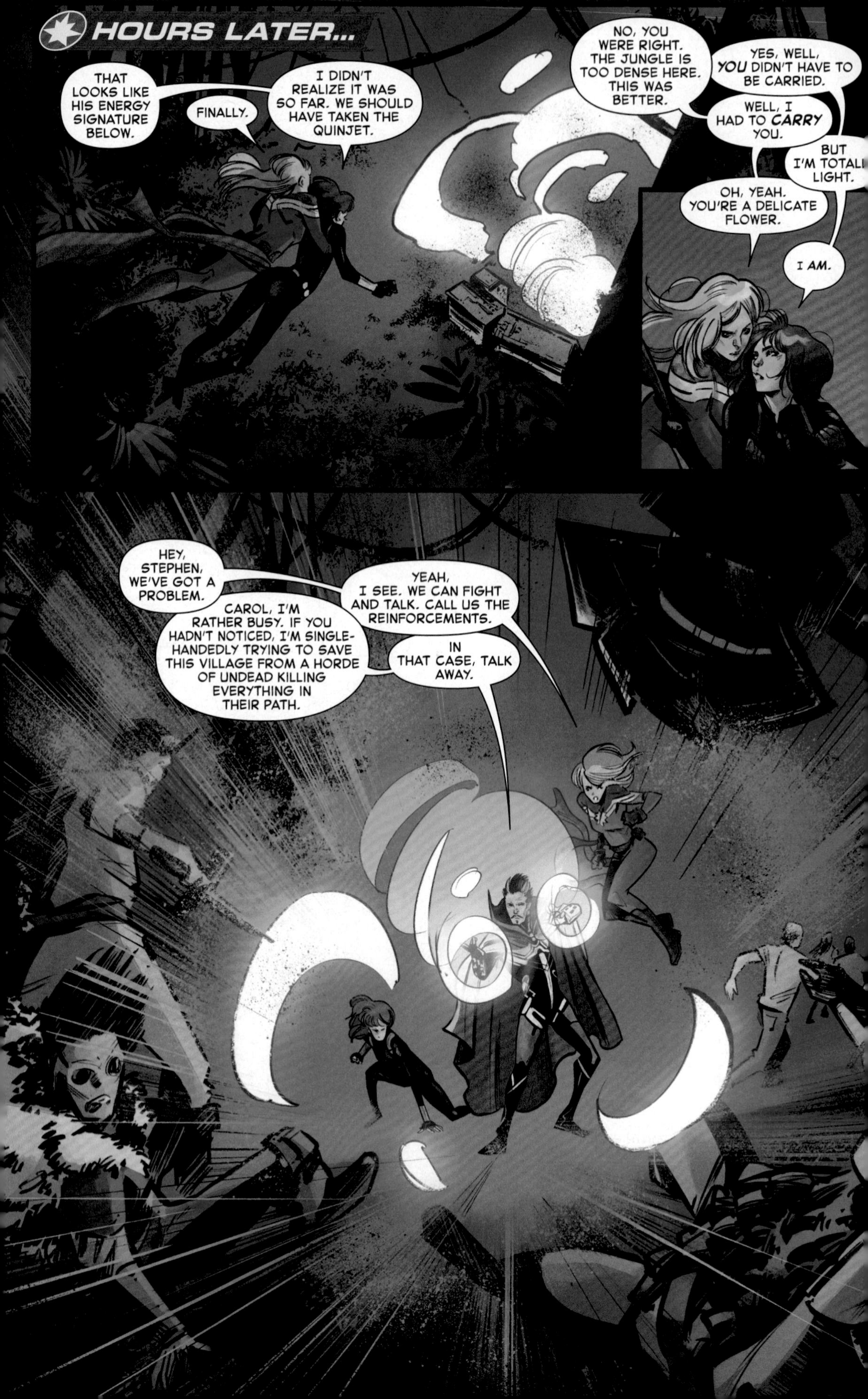

HOURS LATER...
THAT LOOKS LIKE HIS ENERGY SIGNATURE BELOW.
FINALLY.
I DIDN'T REALIZE IT WAS SO FAR. WE SHOULD HAVE TAKEN THE QUINJET.
NO, YOU WERE RIGHT. THE JUNGLE IS TOO DENSE HERE. THIS WAS BETTER.
YES, WELL, YOU DIDN'T HAVE TO BE CARRIED.
WELL, I HAD TO CARRY YOU.
BUT I'M TOTALL LIGHT.
OH, YEAH. YOU'RE A DELICATE FLOWER.
I AM.
HEY, STEPHEN, WE'VE GOT A PROBLEM.
CAROL, I'M RATHER BUSY. IF YOU HADN'T NOTICED, I'M SINGLE-HANDEDLY TRYING TO SAVE THIS VILLAGE FROM A HORDE OF UNDEAD KILLING EVERYTHING IN THEIR PATH.
YEAH, I SEE. WE CAN FIGHT AND TALK. CALL US THE REINFORCEMENTS.
IN THAT CASE, TALK AWAY.

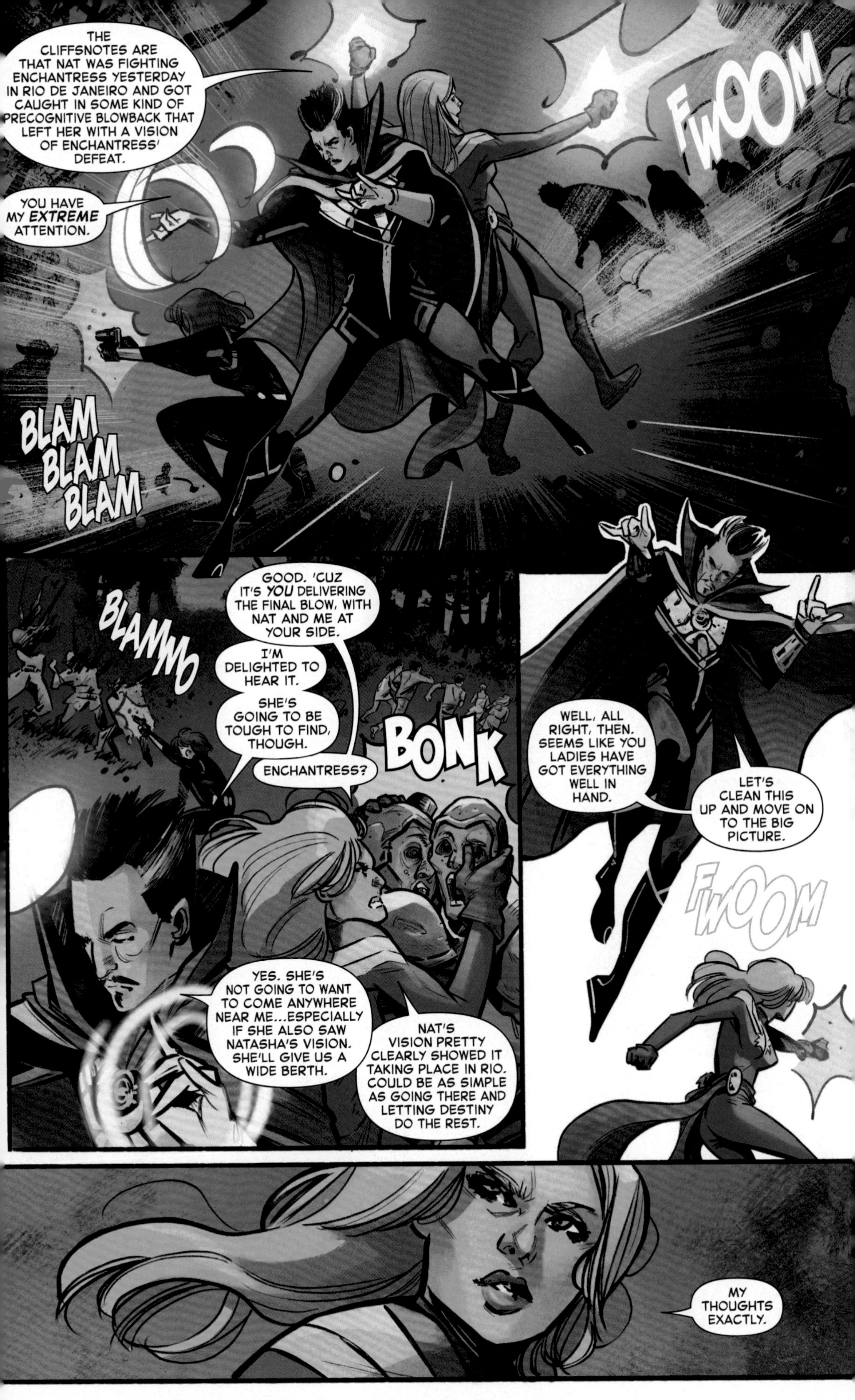
THE CLIFFSNOTES ARE THAT NAT WAS FIGHTING ENCHANTRESS YESTERDAY IN RIO DE JANEIRO AND GOT CAUGHT IN SOME KIND OF PRECOGNITIVE BLOWBACK THAT LEFT HER WITH A VISION OF ENCHANTRESS' DEFEAT.
FWOOM
YOU HAVE MY *EXTREME* ATTENTION.
BLAM BLAM BLAM
BLAMMO
GOOD. 'CUZ IT'S *YOU* DELIVERING THE FINAL BLOW, WITH NAT AND ME AT YOUR SIDE.
I'M DELIGHTED TO HEAR IT.
SHE'S GOING TO BE TOUGH TO FIND, THOUGH.
ENCHANTRESS?
BONK
YES. SHE'S NOT GOING TO WANT TO COME ANYWHERE NEAR ME...ESPECIALLY IF SHE ALSO SAW NATASHA'S VISION. SHE'LL GIVE US A WIDE BERTH.
NAT'S VISION PRETTY CLEARLY SHOWED IT TAKING PLACE IN RIO. COULD BE AS SIMPLE AS GOING THERE AND LETTING DESTINY DO THE REST.
WELL, ALL RIGHT, THEN. SEEMS LIKE YOU LADIES HAVE GOT EVERYTHING WELL IN HAND.
LET'S CLEAN THIS UP AND MOVE ON TO THE BIG PICTURE.
FWOOM
MY THOUGHTS EXACTLY.

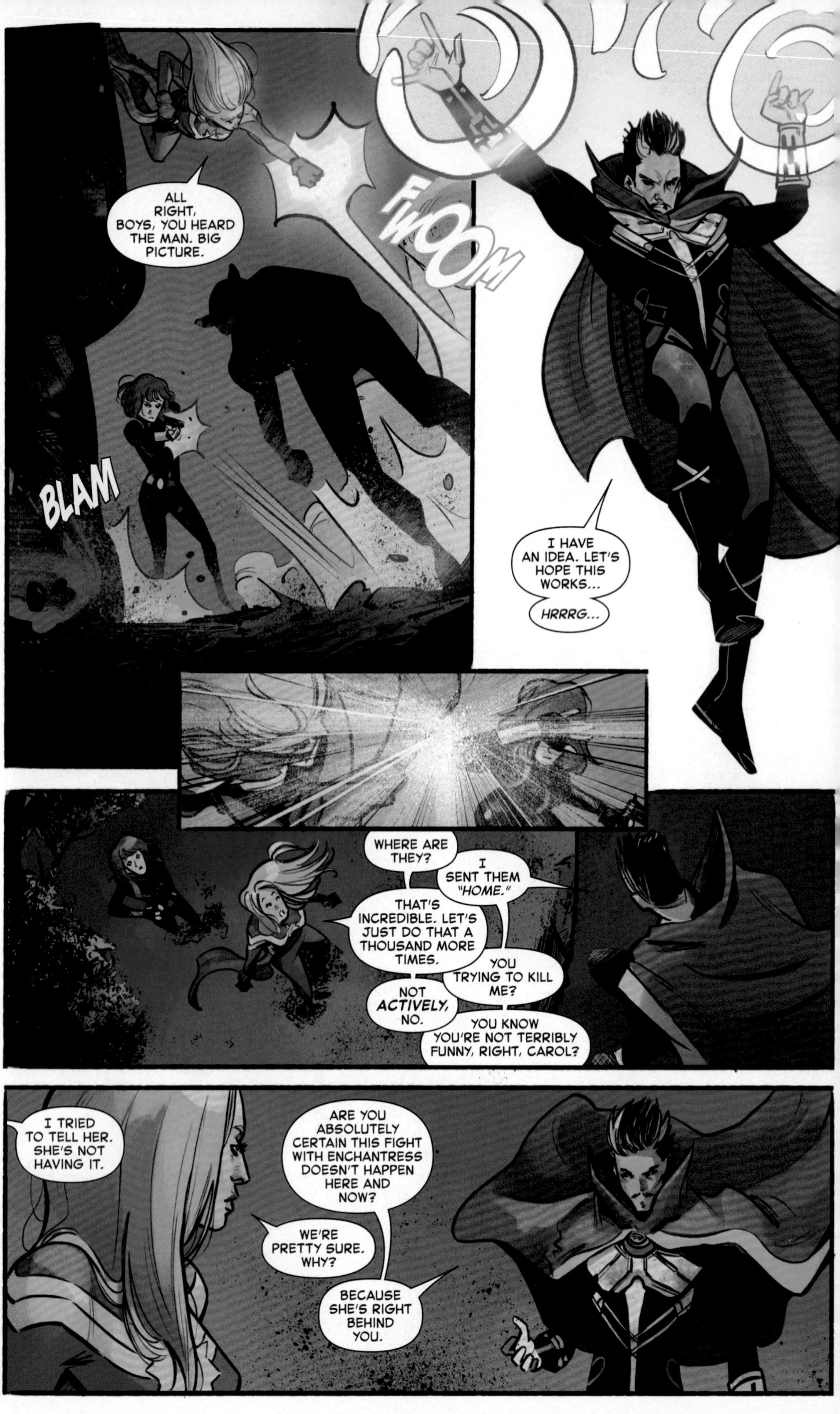

ALL RIGHT, BOYS, YOU HEARD THE MAN. BIG PICTURE.
FWOOM
BLAM
I HAVE AN IDEA. LET'S HOPE THIS WORKS...
HRRRG...
WHERE ARE THEY?
I SENT THEM "HOME."
THAT'S INCREDIBLE. LET'S JUST DO THAT A THOUSAND MORE TIMES.
YOU TRYING TO KILL ME?
NOT ACTIVELY, NO.
YOU KNOW YOU'RE NOT TERRIBLY FUNNY, RIGHT, CAROL?
I TRIED TO TELL HER. SHE'S NOT HAVING IT.
ARE YOU ABSOLUTELY CERTAIN THIS FIGHT WITH ENCHANTRESS DOESN'T HAPPEN HERE AND NOW?
WE'RE PRETTY SURE. WHY?
BECAUSE SHE'S RIGHT BEHIND YOU.

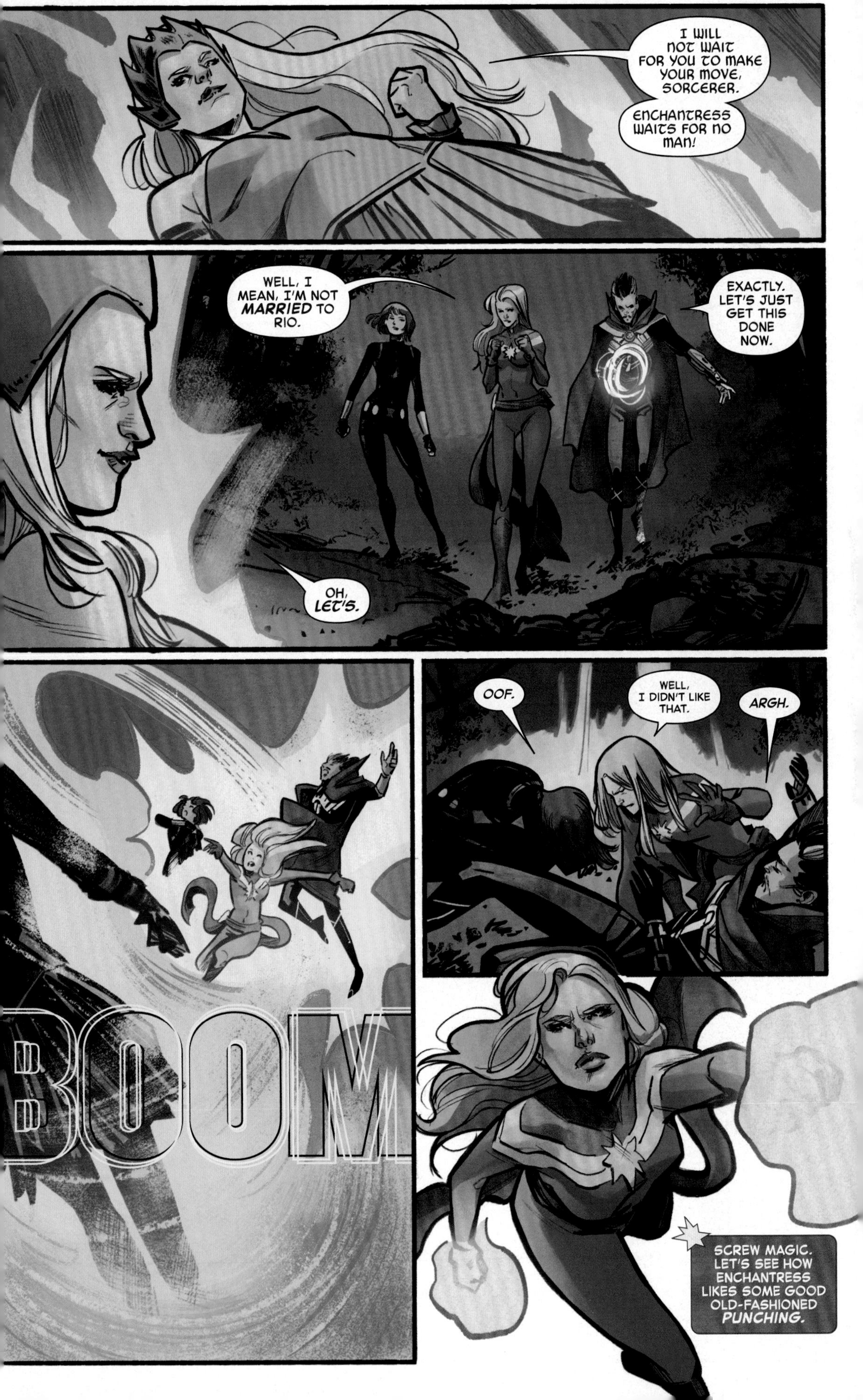
I WILL NOT WAIT FOR YOU TO MAKE YOUR MOVE, SORCERER.
ENCHANTRESS WAITS FOR NO MAN!
WELL, I MEAN, I'M NOT MARRIED TO RIO.
EXACTLY. LET'S JUST GET THIS DONE NOW.
OH, LET'S.
BOOM
OOF.
WELL, I DIDN'T LIKE THAT.
ARGH.
SCREW MAGIC. LET'S SEE HOW ENCHANTRESS LIKES SOME GOOD OLD-FASHIONED PUNCHING.

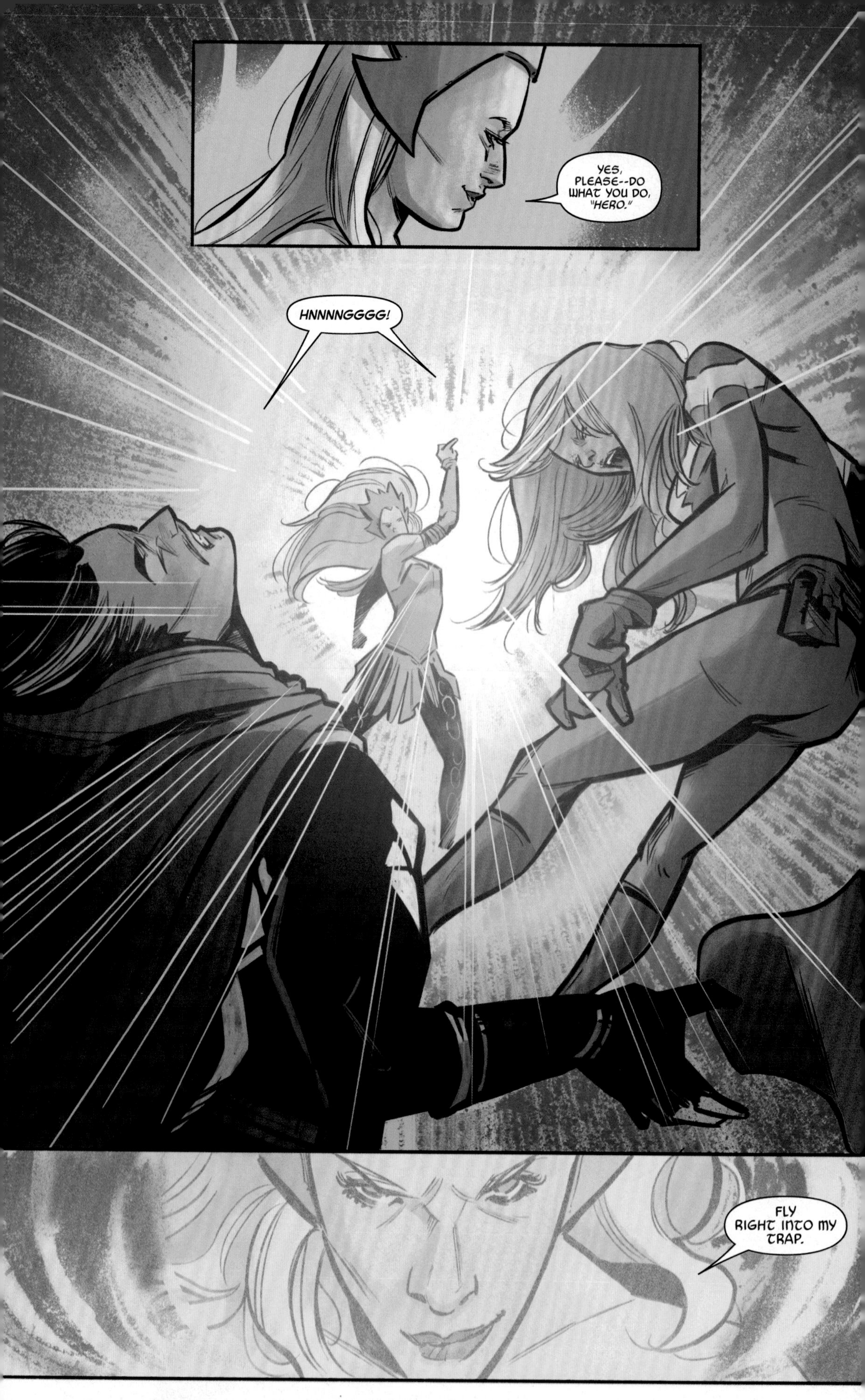
YES, PLEASE--DO WHAT YOU DO, "HERO."
HNNNNGGGG!
FLY RIGHT INTO MY TRAP.

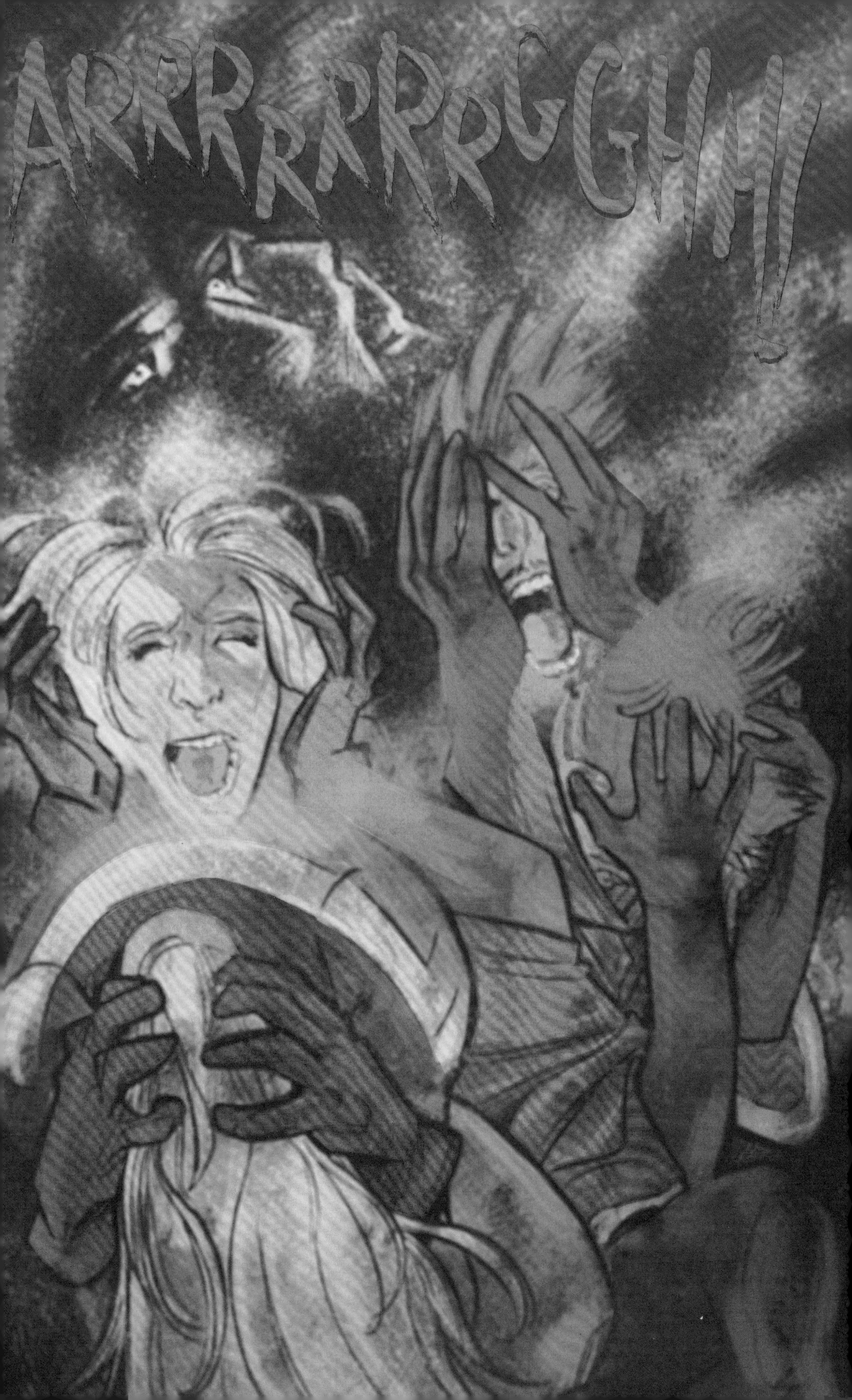
ARRRRRRRRGGHH!!

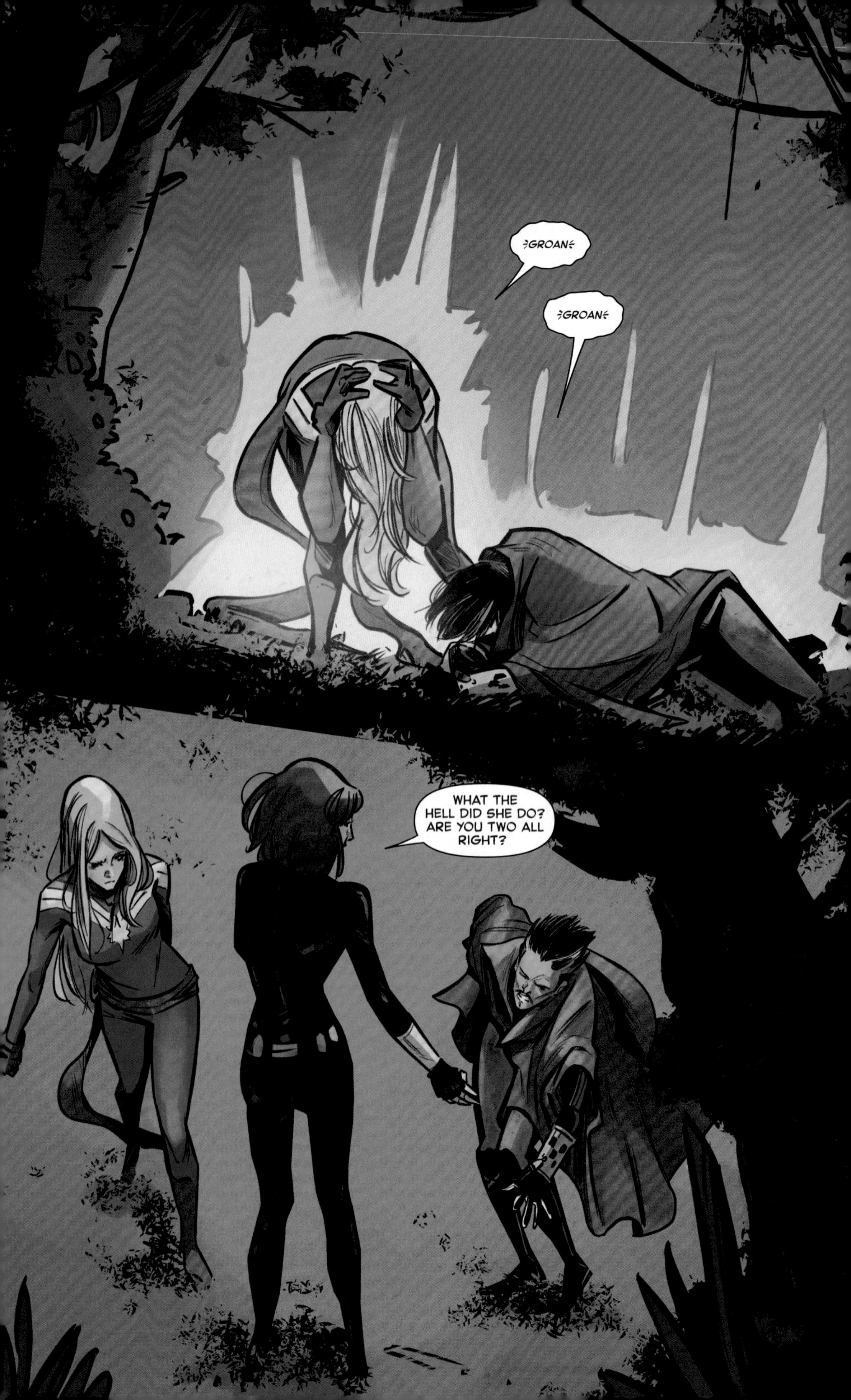
GROAN
GROAN
WHAT THE HELL DID SHE DO? ARE YOU TWO ALL RIGHT?

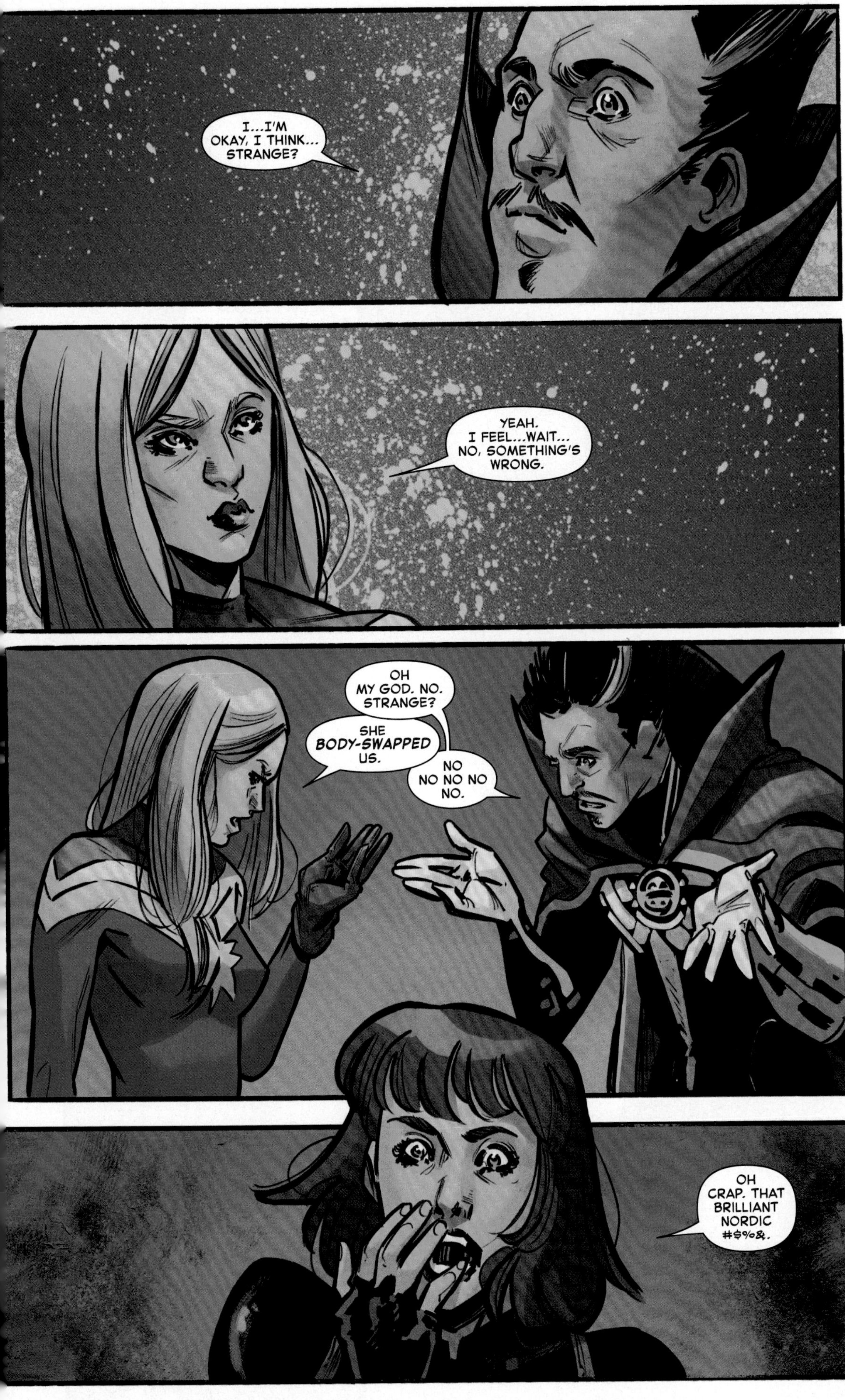
I...I'M OKAY, I THINK... STRANGE?
YEAH. I FEEL...WAIT... NO, SOMETHING'S WRONG.
OH MY GOD. NO. STRANGE?
SHE BODY-SWAPPED US.
NO NO NO NO NO.
OH CRAP. THAT BRILLIANT NORDIC #$%&.

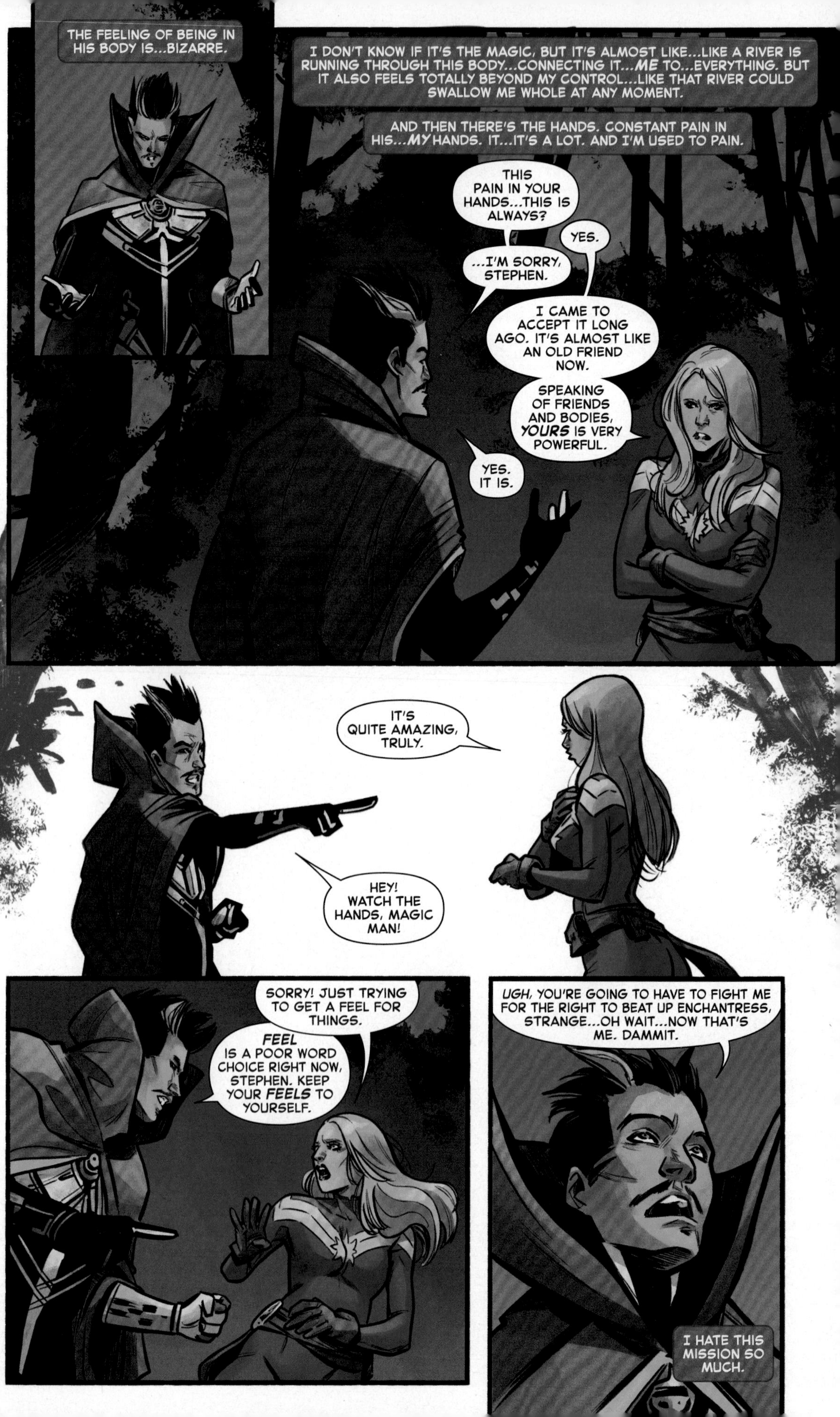
THE FEELING OF BEING IN HIS BODY IS...BIZARRE.
I DON'T KNOW IF IT'S THE MAGIC, BUT IT'S ALMOST LIKE...LIKE A RIVER IS RUNNING THROUGH THIS BODY...CONNECTING IT...ME TO...EVERYTHING. BUT IT ALSO FEELS TOTALLY BEYOND MY CONTROL...LIKE THAT RIVER COULD SWALLOW ME WHOLE AT ANY MOMENT.
AND THEN THERE'S THE HANDS. CONSTANT PAIN IN HIS...MY HANDS. IT...IT'S A LOT. AND I'M USED TO PAIN.
THIS PAIN IN YOUR HANDS...THIS IS ALWAYS?
YES.
...I'M SORRY, STEPHEN.
I CAME TO ACCEPT IT LONG AGO. IT'S ALMOST LIKE AN OLD FRIEND NOW.
SPEAKING OF FRIENDS AND BODIES, YOURS IS VERY POWERFUL.
YES. IT IS.
IT'S QUITE AMAZING, TRULY.
HEY! WATCH THE HANDS, MAGIC MAN!
SORRY! JUST TRYING TO GET A FEEL FOR THINGS.
FEEL IS A POOR WORD CHOICE RIGHT NOW, STEPHEN. KEEP YOUR FEELS TO YOURSELF.
UGH, YOU'RE GOING TO HAVE TO FIGHT ME FOR THE RIGHT TO BEAT UP ENCHANTRESS, STRANGE...OH WAIT...NOW THAT'S ME. DAMMIT.
I HATE THIS MISSION SO MUCH.

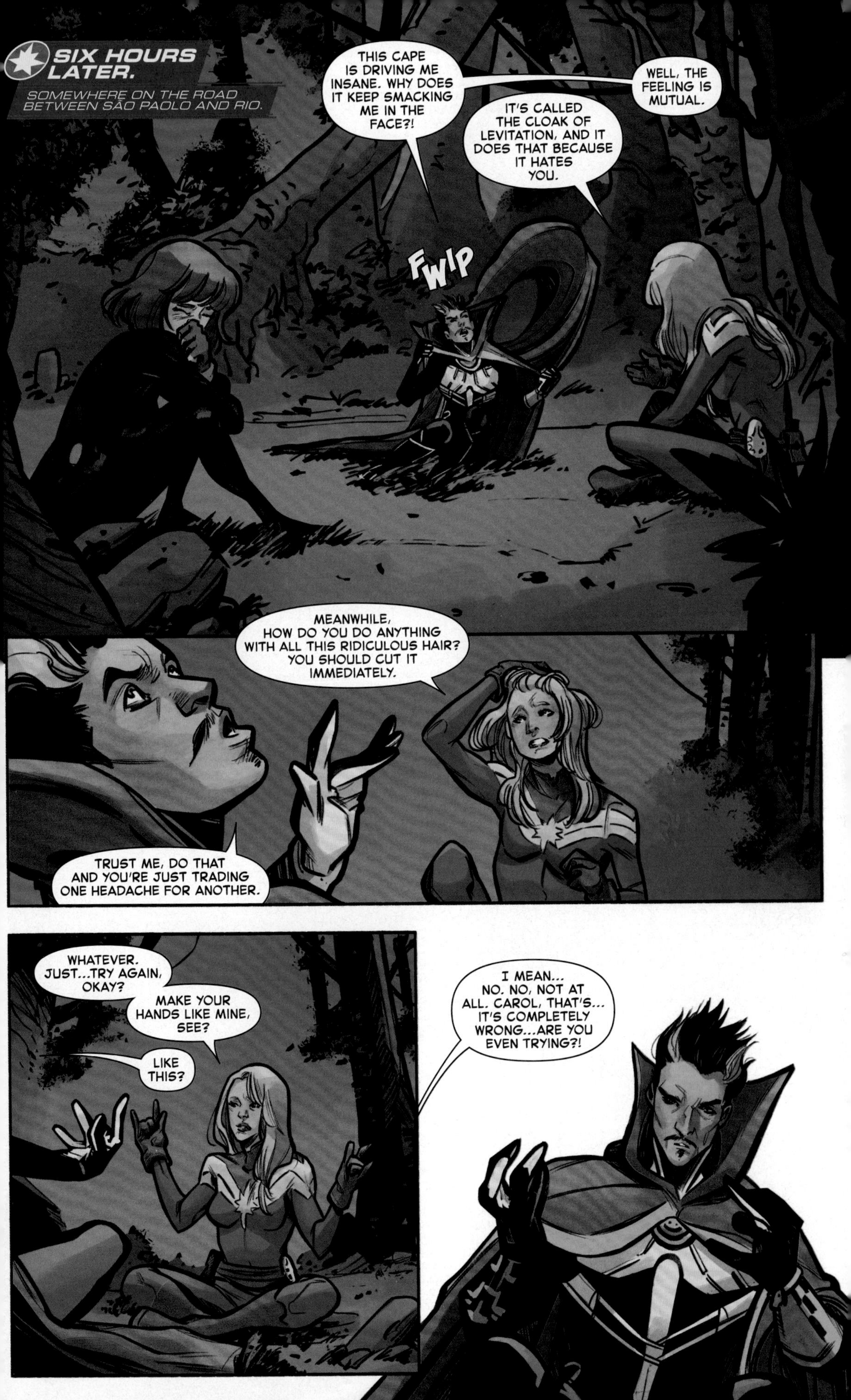
SIX HOURS LATER.
SOMEWHERE ON THE ROAD BETWEEN SÃO PAOLO AND RIO.
THIS CAPE IS DRIVING ME INSANE. WHY DOES IT KEEP SMACKING ME IN THE FACE?!
WELL, THE FEELING IS MUTUAL.
IT'S CALLED THE CLOAK OF LEVITATION, AND IT DOES THAT BECAUSE IT HATES YOU.
FWIP
MEANWHILE, HOW DO YOU DO ANYTHING WITH ALL THIS RIDICULOUS HAIR? YOU SHOULD CUT IT IMMEDIATELY.
TRUST ME, DO THAT AND YOU'RE JUST TRADING ONE HEADACHE FOR ANOTHER.
WHATEVER. JUST...TRY AGAIN, OKAY?
MAKE YOUR HANDS LIKE MINE, SEE?
LIKE THIS?
I MEAN... NO. NO, NOT AT ALL. CAROL, THAT'S... IT'S COMPLETELY WRONG...ARE YOU EVEN TRYING?!

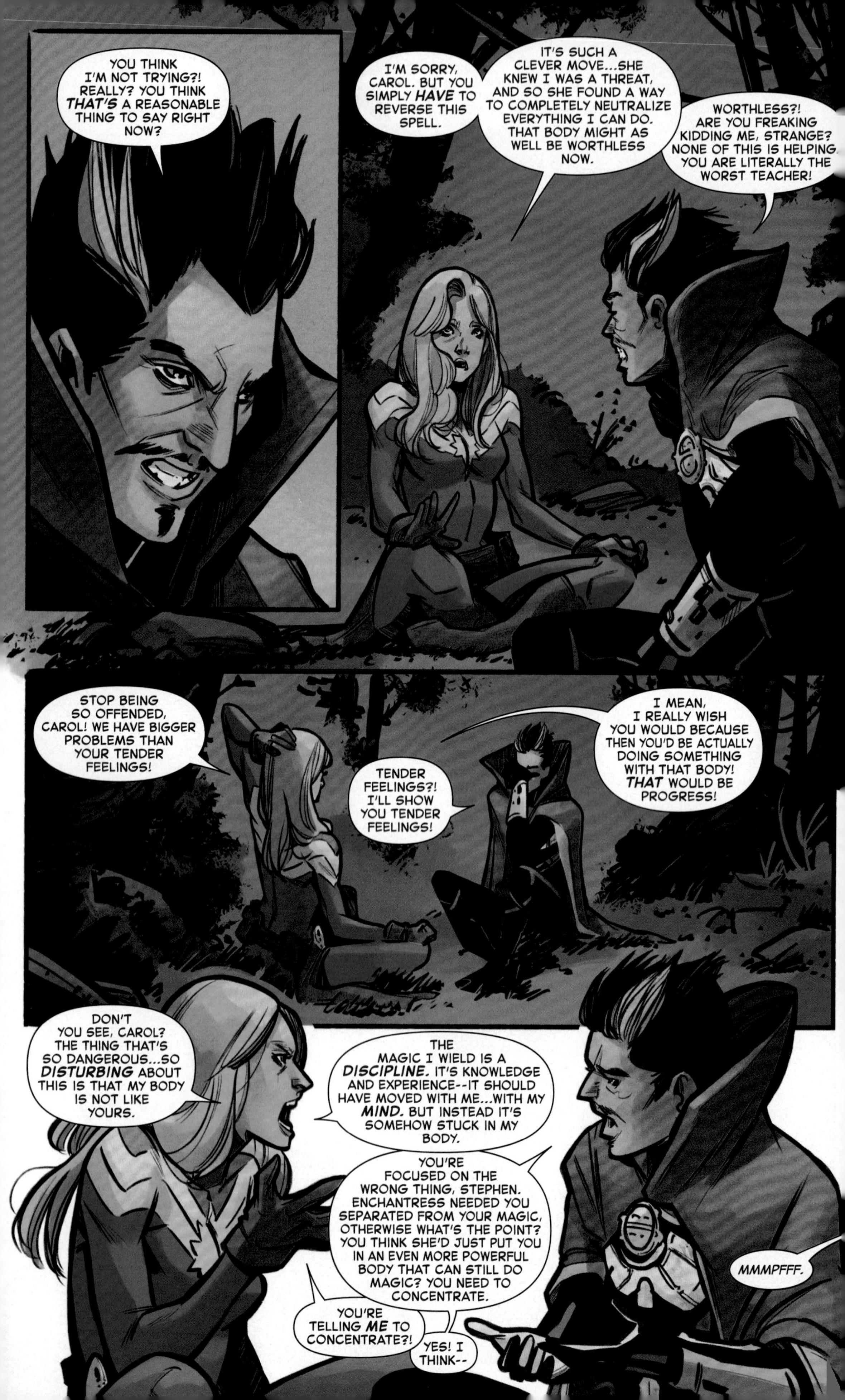

YOU THINK I'M NOT TRYING?! REALLY? YOU THINK THAT'S A REASONABLE THING TO SAY RIGHT NOW?
I'M SORRY, CAROL. BUT YOU SIMPLY HAVE TO REVERSE THIS SPELL.
IT'S SUCH A CLEVER MOVE...SHE KNEW I WAS A THREAT, AND SO SHE FOUND A WAY TO COMPLETELY NEUTRALIZE EVERYTHING I CAN DO. THAT BODY MIGHT AS WELL BE WORTHLESS NOW.
WORTHLESS?! ARE YOU FREAKING KIDDING ME, STRANGE? NONE OF THIS IS HELPING. YOU ARE LITERALLY THE WORST TEACHER!
STOP BEING SO OFFENDED, CAROL! WE HAVE BIGGER PROBLEMS THAN YOUR TENDER FEELINGS!
TENDER FEELINGS?! I'LL SHOW YOU TENDER FEELINGS!
I MEAN, I REALLY WISH YOU WOULD BECAUSE THEN YOU'D BE ACTUALLY DOING SOMETHING WITH THAT BODY! THAT WOULD BE PROGRESS!
DON'T YOU SEE, CAROL? THE THING THAT'S SO DANGEROUS...SO DISTURBING ABOUT THIS IS THAT MY BODY IS NOT LIKE YOURS.
THE MAGIC I WIELD IS A DISCIPLINE. IT'S KNOWLEDGE AND EXPERIENCE--IT SHOULD HAVE MOVED WITH ME...WITH MY MIND. BUT INSTEAD IT'S SOMEHOW STUCK IN MY BODY.
YOU'RE FOCUSED ON THE WRONG THING, STEPHEN. ENCHANTRESS NEEDED YOU SEPARATED FROM YOUR MAGIC, OTHERWISE WHAT'S THE POINT? YOU THINK SHE'D JUST PUT YOU IN AN EVEN MORE POWERFUL BODY THAT CAN STILL DO MAGIC? YOU NEED TO CONCENTRATE.
YOU'RE TELLING ME TO CONCENTRATE?!
YES! I THINK--
MMMPFFF.

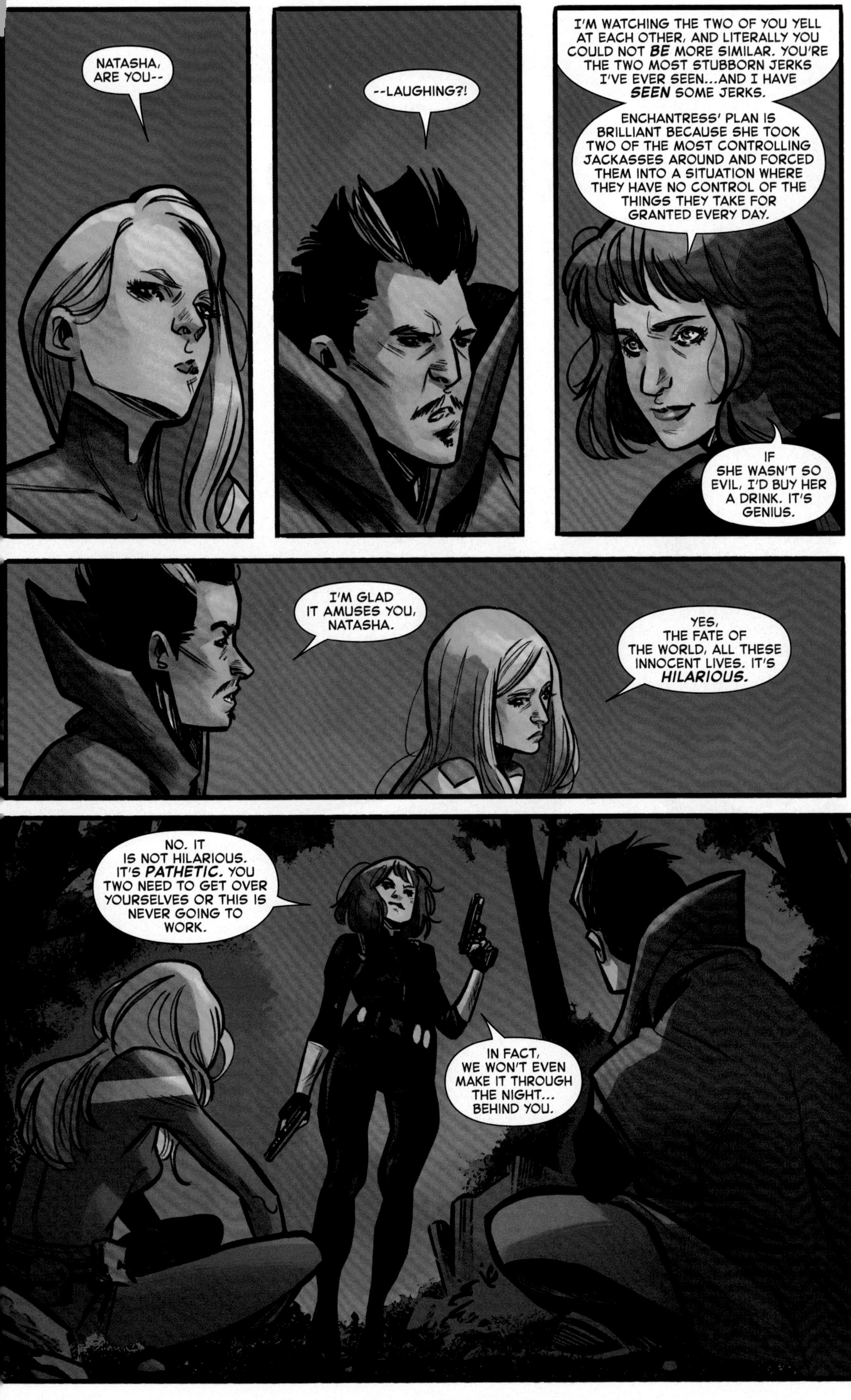
NATASHA, ARE YOU--
--LAUGHING?!
I'M WATCHING THE TWO OF YOU YELL AT EACH OTHER, AND LITERALLY YOU COULD NOT BE MORE SIMILAR. YOU'RE THE TWO MOST STUBBORN JERKS I'VE EVER SEEN...AND I HAVE SEEN SOME JERKS.
ENCHANTRESS' PLAN IS BRILLIANT BECAUSE SHE TOOK TWO OF THE MOST CONTROLLING JACKASSES AROUND AND FORCED THEM INTO A SITUATION WHERE THEY HAVE NO CONTROL OF THE THINGS THEY TAKE FOR GRANTED EVERY DAY.
IF SHE WASN'T SO EVIL, I'D BUY HER A DRINK. IT'S GENIUS.
I'M GLAD IT AMUSES YOU, NATASHA.
YES, THE FATE OF THE WORLD, ALL THESE INNOCENT LIVES. IT'S HILARIOUS.
NO. IT IS NOT HILARIOUS. IT'S PATHETIC. YOU TWO NEED TO GET OVER YOURSELVES OR THIS IS NEVER GOING TO WORK.
IN FACT, WE WON'T EVEN MAKE IT THROUGH THE NIGHT... BEHIND YOU.

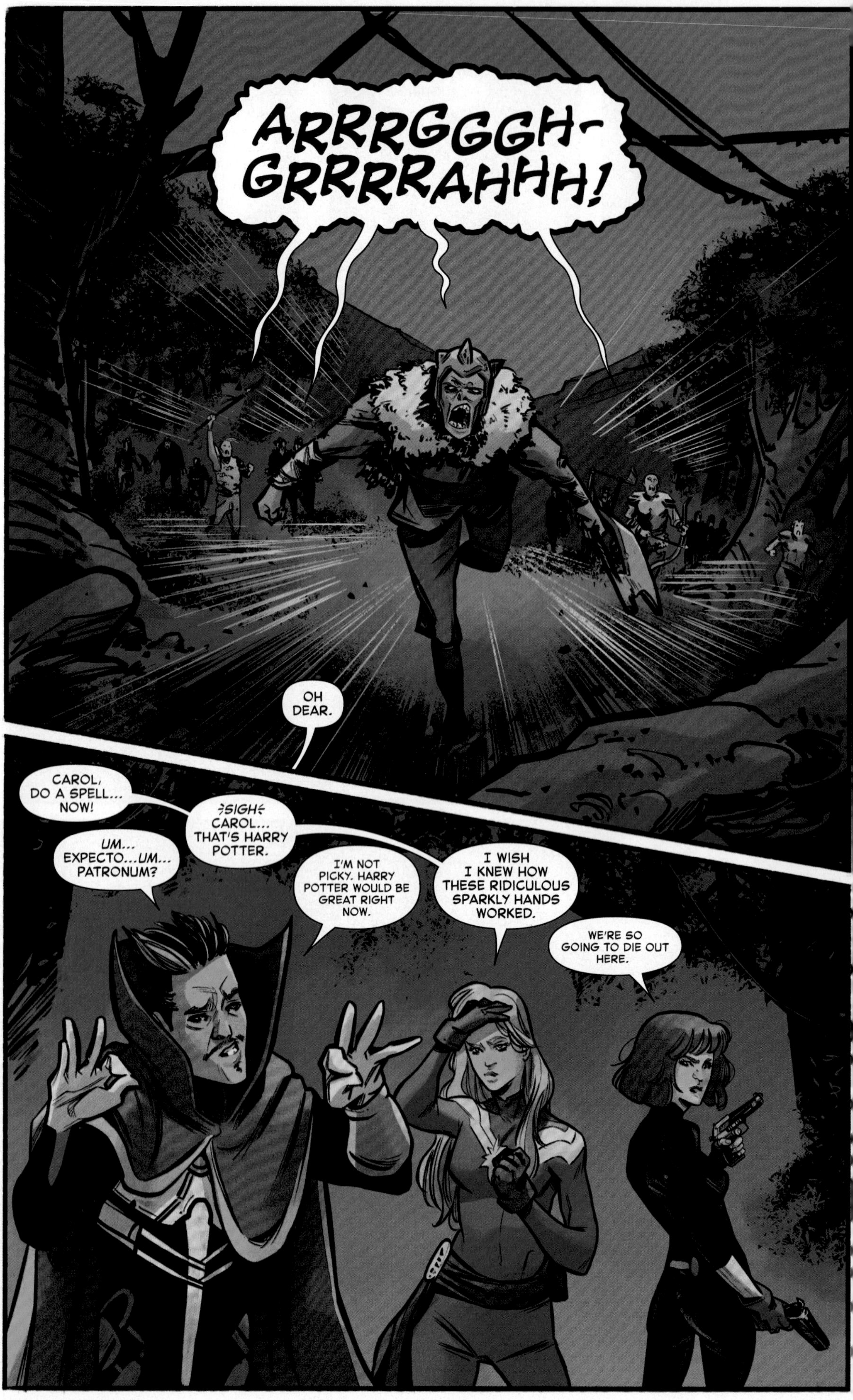
ARRRGGGH-GRRRRAHHH!
OH DEAR.
CAROL, DO A SPELL... NOW!
UM... EXPECTO...UM... PATRONUM?
⋟SIGH⋞ CAROL... THAT'S HARRY POTTER.
I'M NOT PICKY. HARRY POTTER WOULD BE GREAT RIGHT NOW.
I WISH I KNEW HOW THESE RIDICULOUS SPARKLY HANDS WORKED.
WE'RE SO GOING TO DIE OUT HERE.

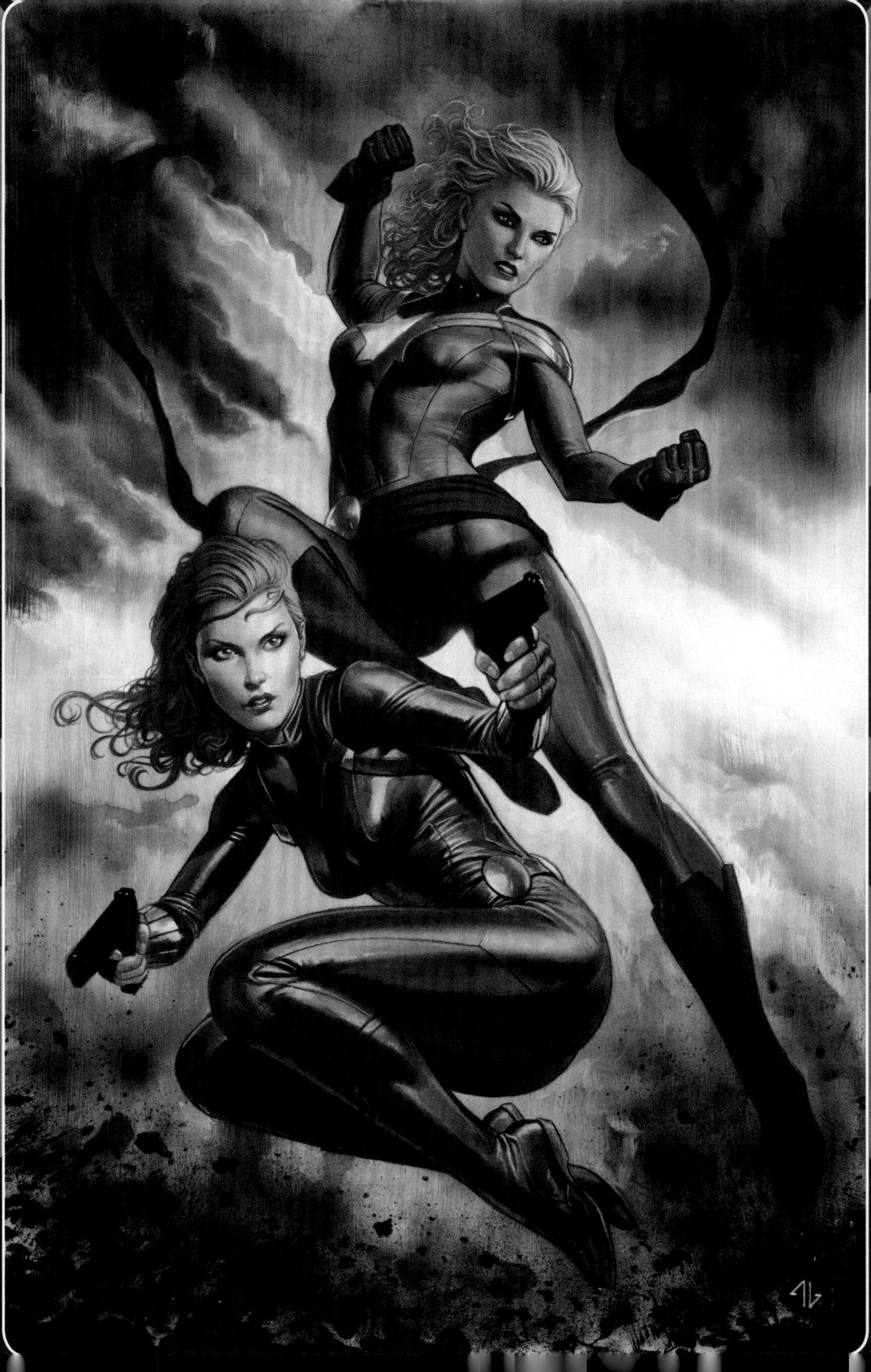

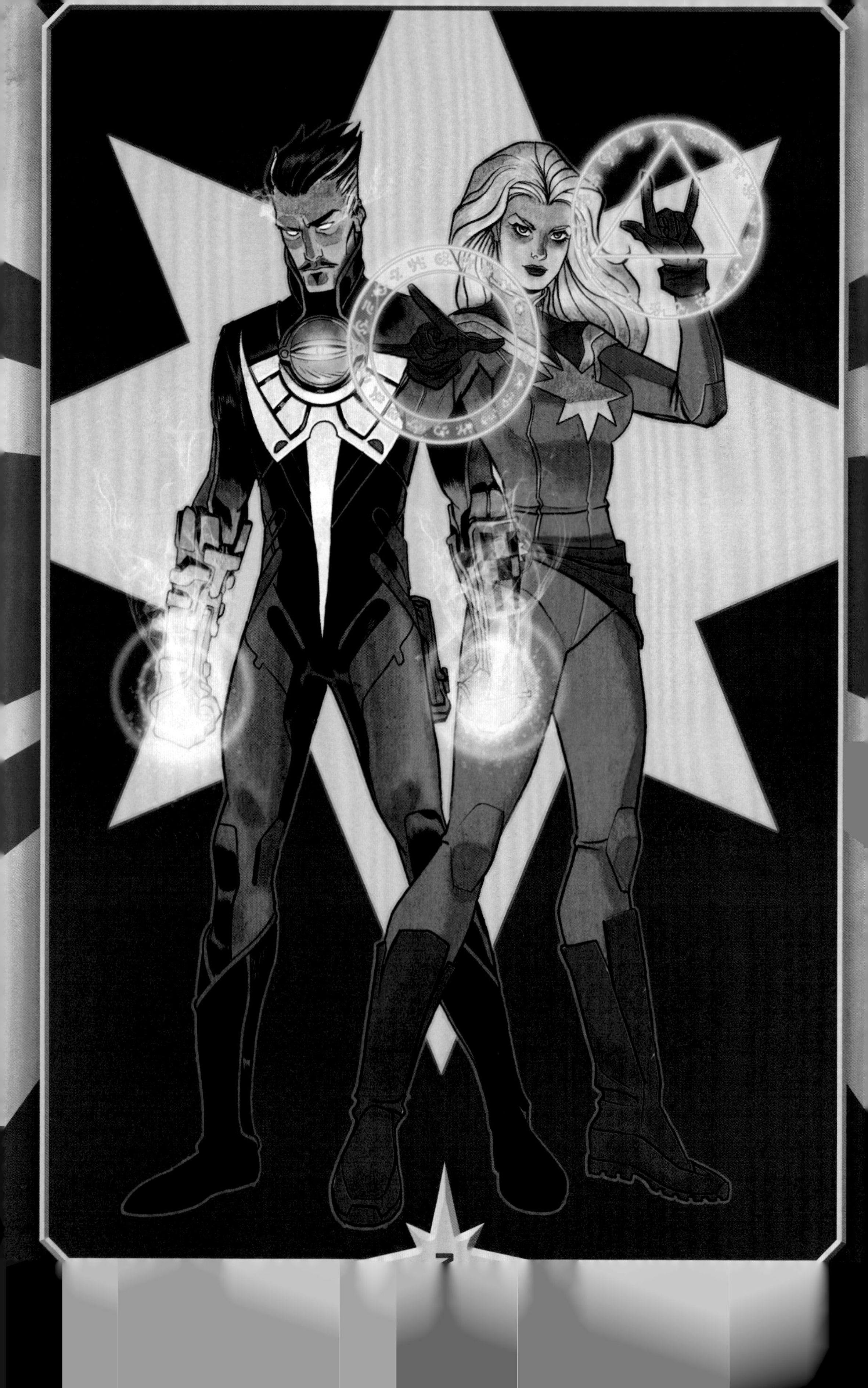

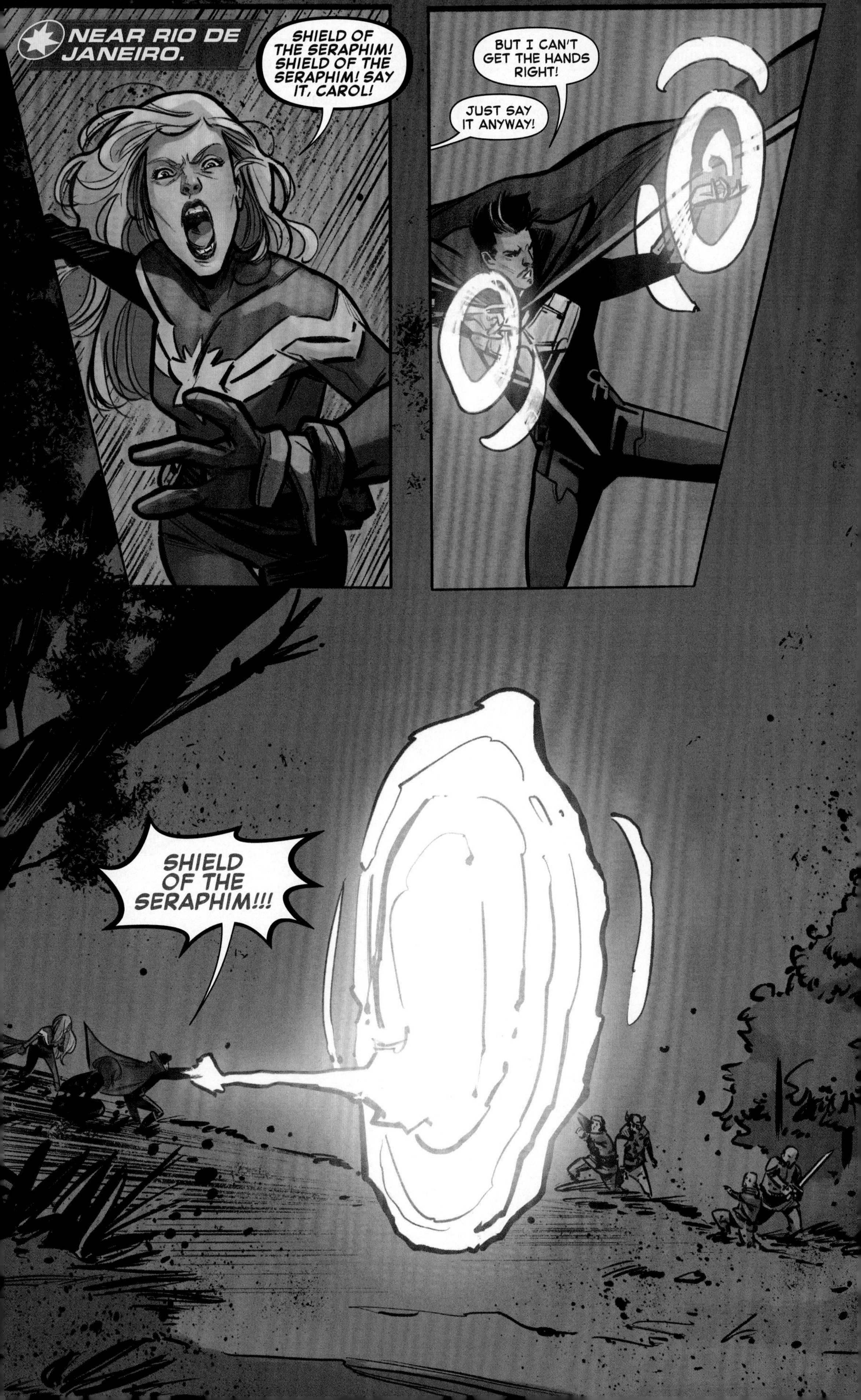
NEAR RIO DE JANEIRO.
SHIELD OF THE SERAPHIM! SHIELD OF THE SERAPHIM! SAY IT, CAROL!
BUT I CAN'T GET THE HANDS RIGHT!
JUST SAY IT ANYWAY!
SHIELD OF THE SERAPHIM!!!

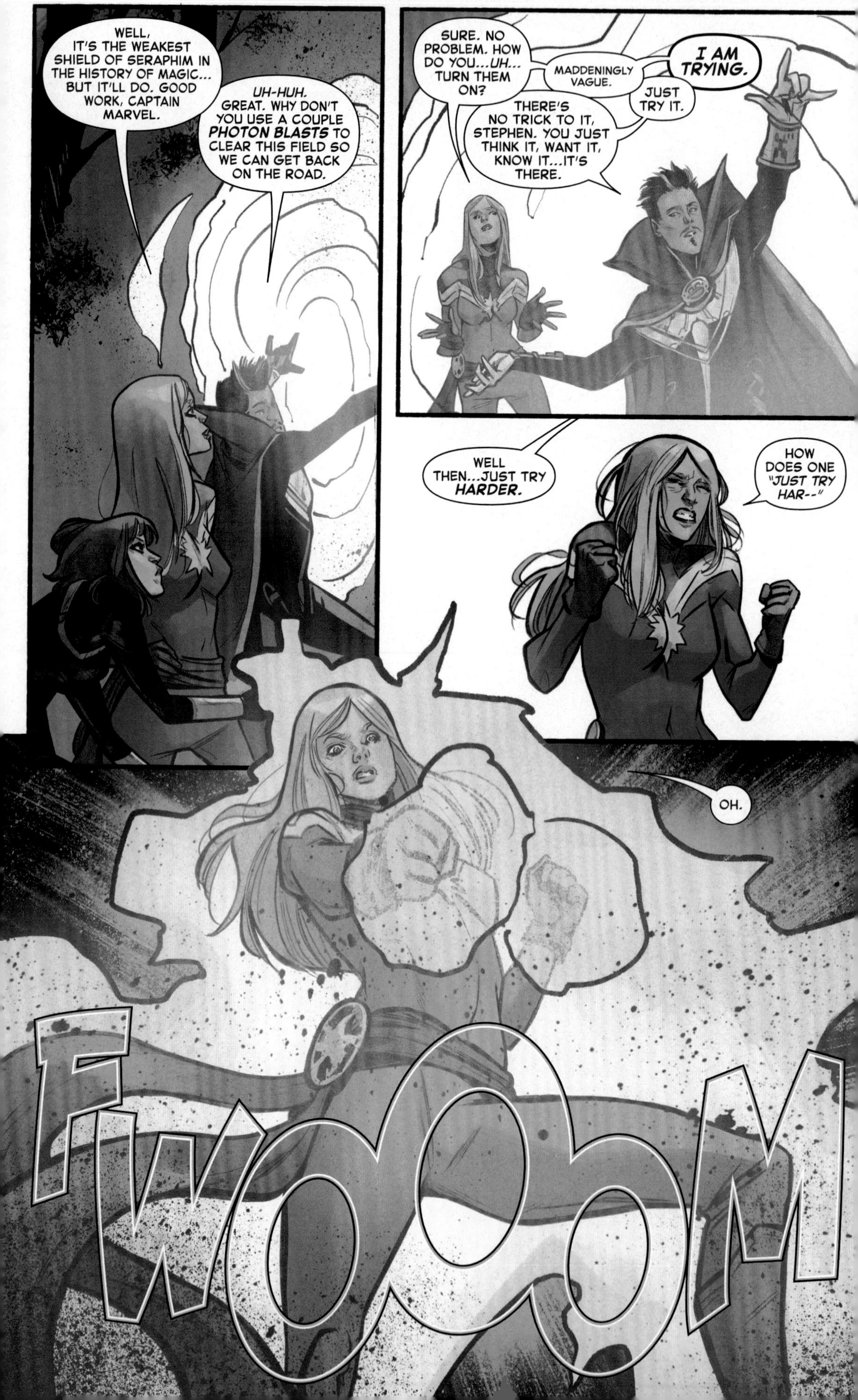

WELL, IT'S THE WEAKEST SHIELD OF SERAPHIM IN THE HISTORY OF MAGIC... BUT IT'LL DO. GOOD WORK, CAPTAIN MARVEL.
UH-HUH. GREAT. WHY DON'T YOU USE A COUPLE PHOTON BLASTS TO CLEAR THIS FIELD SO WE CAN GET BACK ON THE ROAD.
SURE. NO PROBLEM. HOW DO YOU...UH... TURN THEM ON?
THERE'S NO TRICK TO IT, STEPHEN. YOU JUST THINK IT, WANT IT, KNOW IT...IT'S THERE.
MADDENINGLY VAGUE.
JUST TRY IT.
I AM TRYING.
WELL THEN...JUST TRY HARDER.
HOW DOES ONE "JUST TRY HAR--"
OH.
FWOOOM

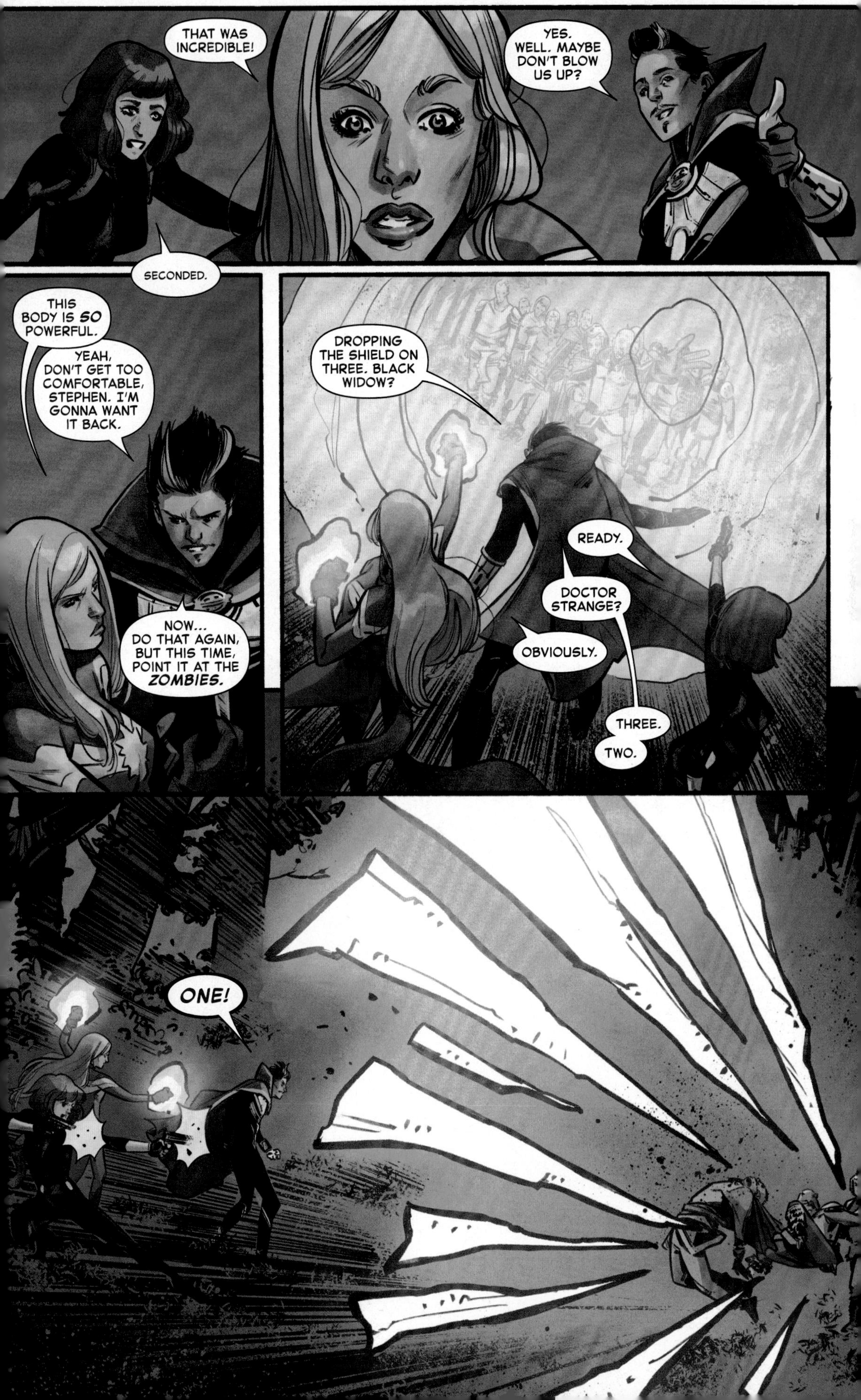
THAT WAS INCREDIBLE!
YES. WELL. MAYBE DON'T BLOW US UP?
SECONDED.
THIS BODY IS SO POWERFUL.
YEAH, DON'T GET TOO COMFORTABLE, STEPHEN. I'M GONNA WANT IT BACK.
NOW... DO THAT AGAIN, BUT THIS TIME, POINT IT AT THE ZOMBIES.
DROPPING THE SHIELD ON THREE. BLACK WIDOW?
READY.
DOCTOR STRANGE?
OBVIOUSLY.
THREE.
TWO.
ONE!

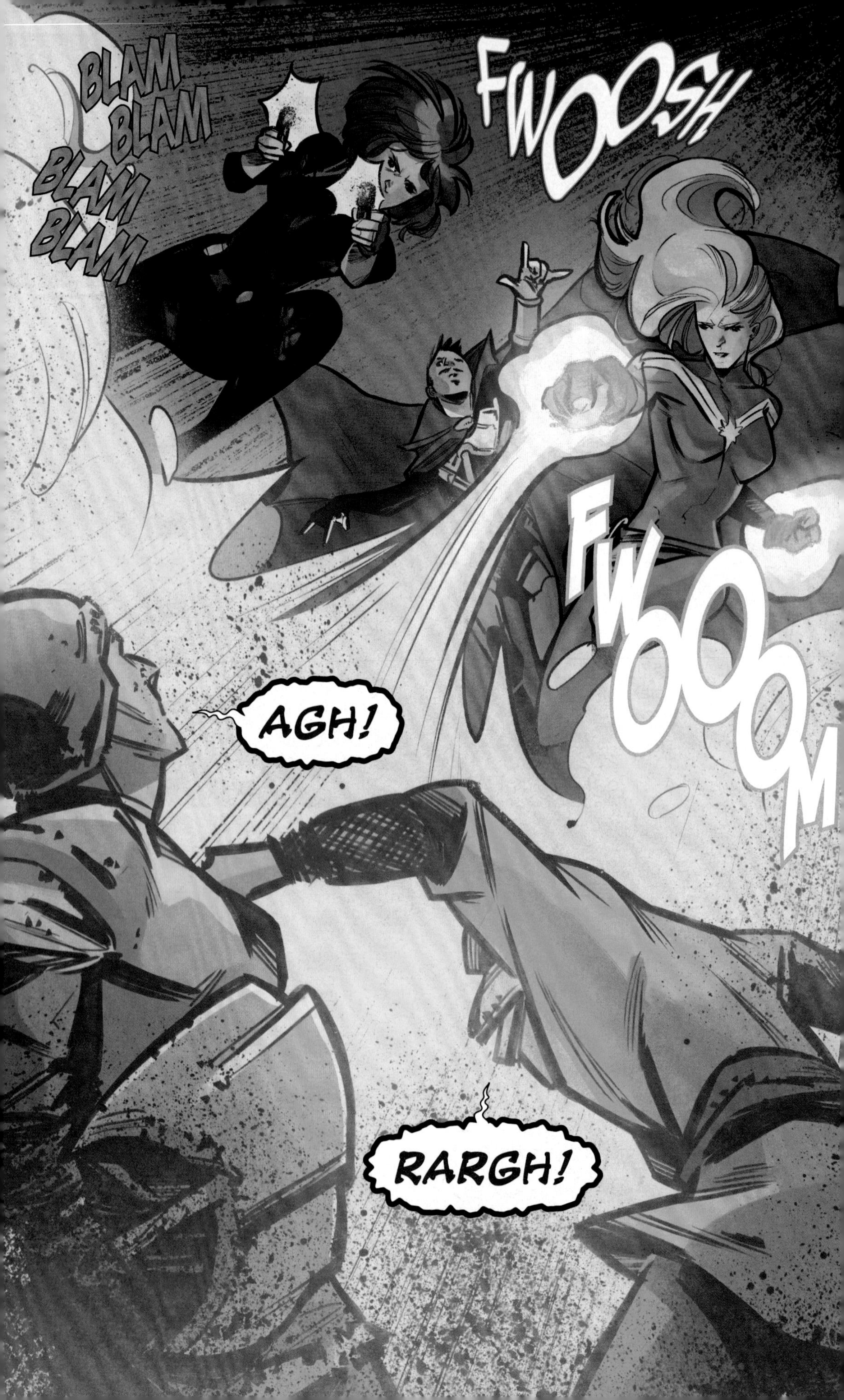
BLAM BLAM BLAM BLAM
FWOOSH
FWOOOM
AGH!
RARGH!

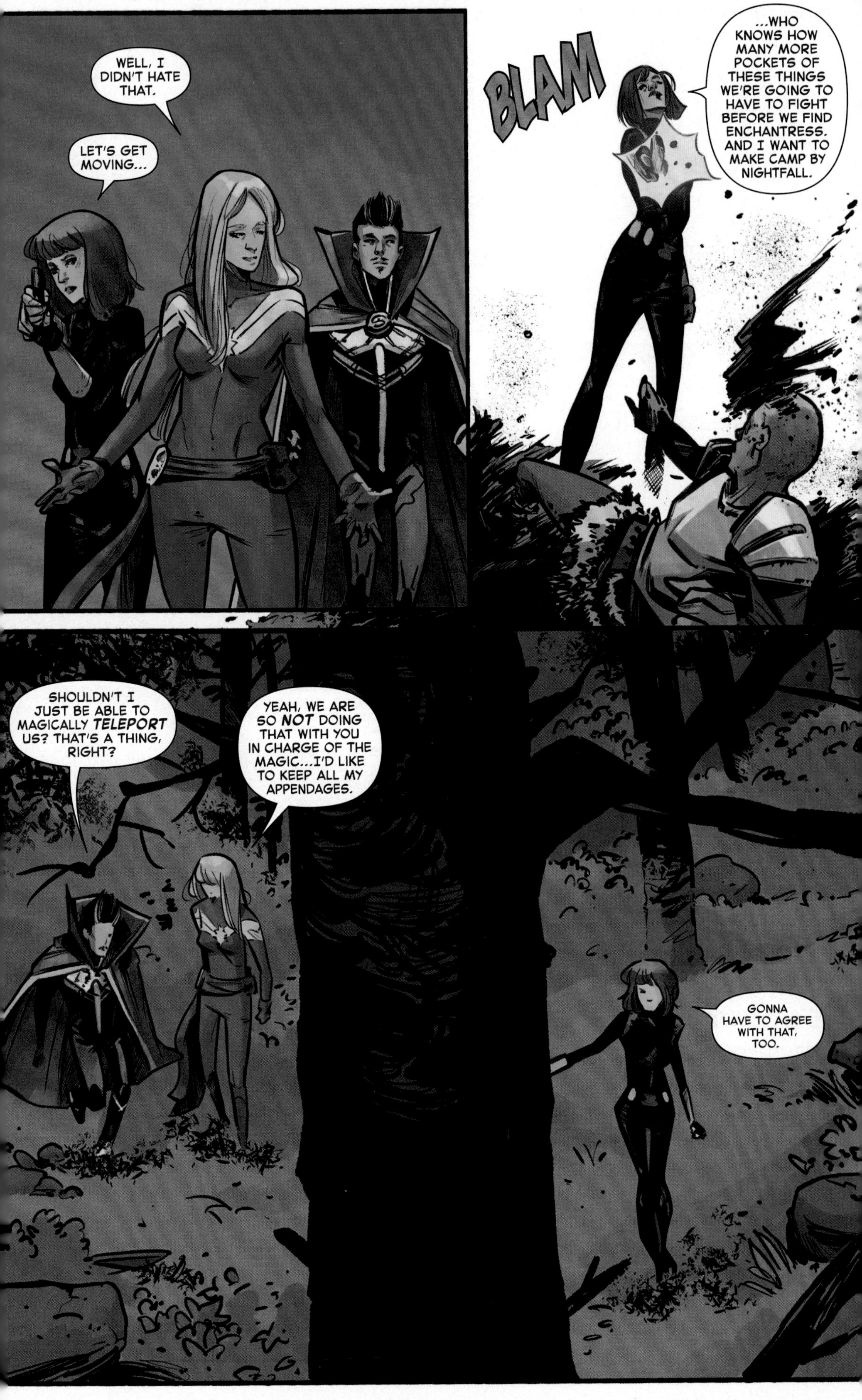

WELL, I DIDN'T HATE THAT.
LET'S GET MOVING...
BLAM
...WHO KNOWS HOW MANY MORE POCKETS OF THESE THINGS WE'RE GOING TO HAVE TO FIGHT BEFORE WE FIND ENCHANTRESS. AND I WANT TO MAKE CAMP BY NIGHTFALL.
SHOULDN'T I JUST BE ABLE TO MAGICALLY *TELEPORT* US? THAT'S A THING, RIGHT?
YEAH, WE ARE SO *NOT* DOING THAT WITH YOU IN CHARGE OF THE MAGIC...I'D LIKE TO KEEP ALL MY APPENDAGES.
GONNA HAVE TO AGREE WITH THAT, TOO.

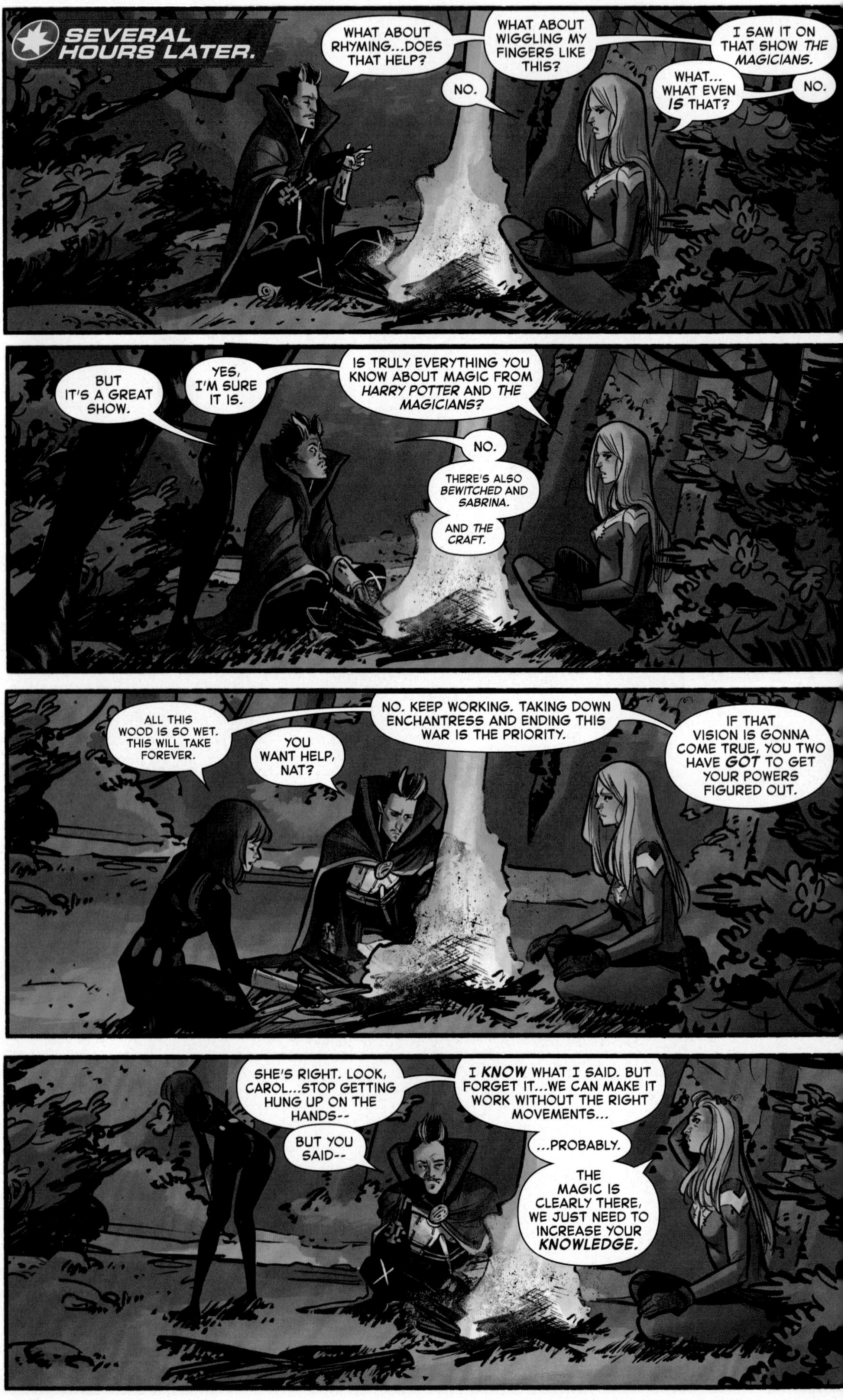
SEVERAL HOURS LATER.
WHAT ABOUT RHYMING...DOES THAT HELP?
NO.
WHAT ABOUT WIGGLING MY FINGERS LIKE THIS?
I SAW IT ON THAT SHOW *THE MAGICIANS.*
WHAT... WHAT EVEN *IS* THAT?
NO.
IS TRULY EVERYTHING YOU KNOW ABOUT MAGIC FROM *HARRY POTTER* AND *THE MAGICIANS?*
YES, I'M SURE IT IS.
BUT IT'S A GREAT SHOW.
NO.
THERE'S ALSO *BEWITCHED* AND *SABRINA.*
AND *THE CRAFT.*
ALL THIS WOOD IS SO WET. THIS WILL TAKE FOREVER.
YOU WANT HELP, NAT?
NO. KEEP WORKING. TAKING DOWN ENCHANTRESS AND ENDING THIS WAR IS THE PRIORITY.
IF THAT VISION IS GONNA COME TRUE, YOU TWO HAVE **GOT** TO GET YOUR POWERS FIGURED OUT.
SHE'S RIGHT. LOOK, CAROL...STOP GETTING HUNG UP ON THE HANDS--
BUT YOU SAID--
I ***KNOW*** WHAT I SAID. BUT FORGET IT...WE CAN MAKE IT WORK WITHOUT THE RIGHT MOVEMENTS...
...PROBABLY.
THE MAGIC IS CLEARLY THERE, WE JUST NEED TO INCREASE YOUR ***KNOWLEDGE.***

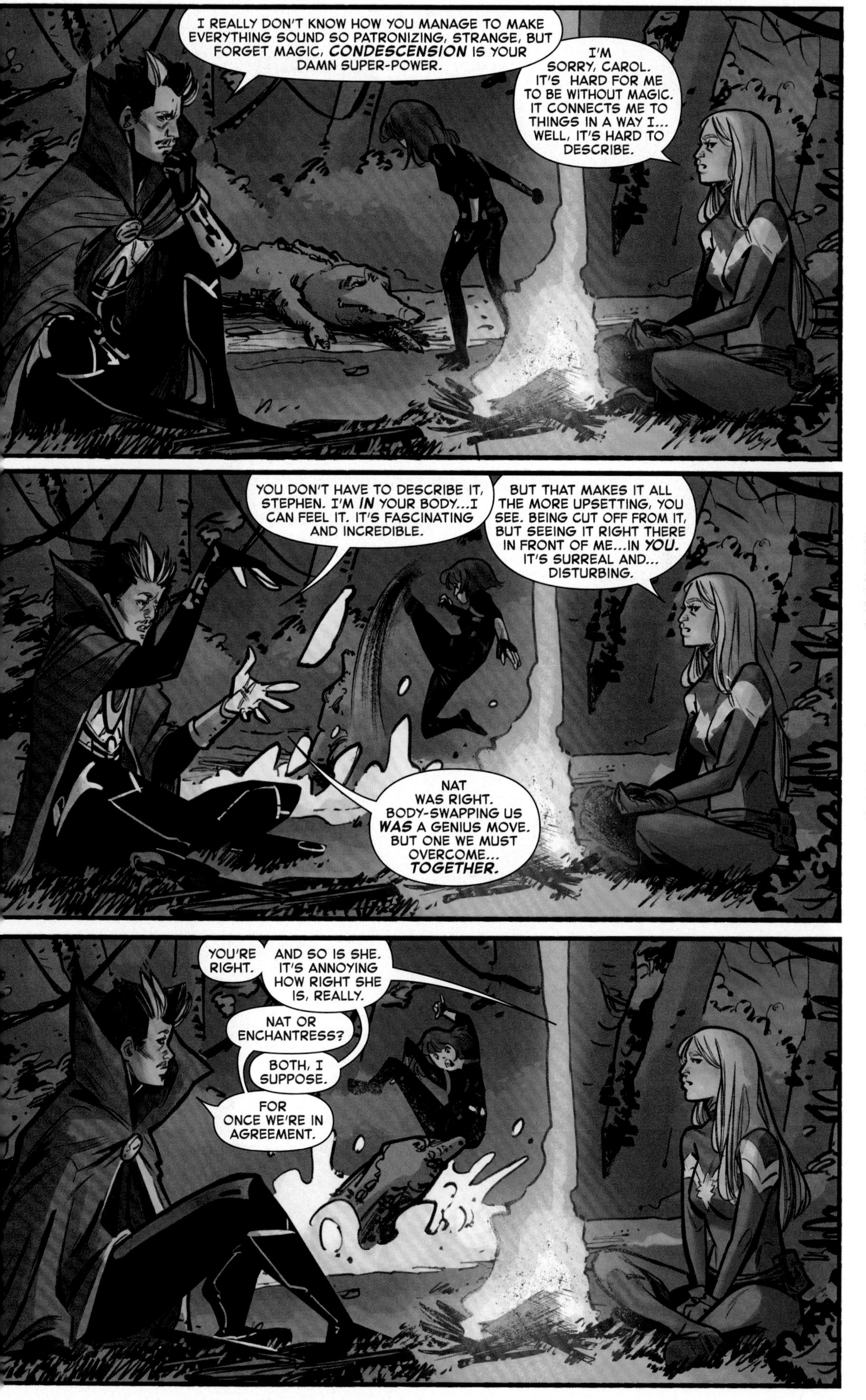
I REALLY DON'T KNOW HOW YOU MANAGE TO MAKE EVERYTHING SOUND SO PATRONIZING, STRANGE, BUT FORGET MAGIC, CONDESCENSION IS YOUR DAMN SUPER-POWER.
I'M SORRY, CAROL. IT'S HARD FOR ME TO BE WITHOUT MAGIC. IT CONNECTS ME TO THINGS IN A WAY I... WELL, IT'S HARD TO DESCRIBE.
YOU DON'T HAVE TO DESCRIBE IT, STEPHEN. I'M IN YOUR BODY...I CAN FEEL IT. IT'S FASCINATING AND INCREDIBLE.
BUT THAT MAKES IT ALL THE MORE UPSETTING, YOU SEE. BEING CUT OFF FROM IT, BUT SEEING IT RIGHT THERE IN FRONT OF ME...IN YOU. IT'S SURREAL AND... DISTURBING.
NAT WAS RIGHT. BODY-SWAPPING US WAS A GENIUS MOVE. BUT ONE WE MUST OVERCOME... TOGETHER.
YOU'RE RIGHT.
AND SO IS SHE. IT'S ANNOYING HOW RIGHT SHE IS, REALLY.
NAT OR ENCHANTRESS?
BOTH, I SUPPOSE.
FOR ONCE WE'RE IN AGREEMENT.

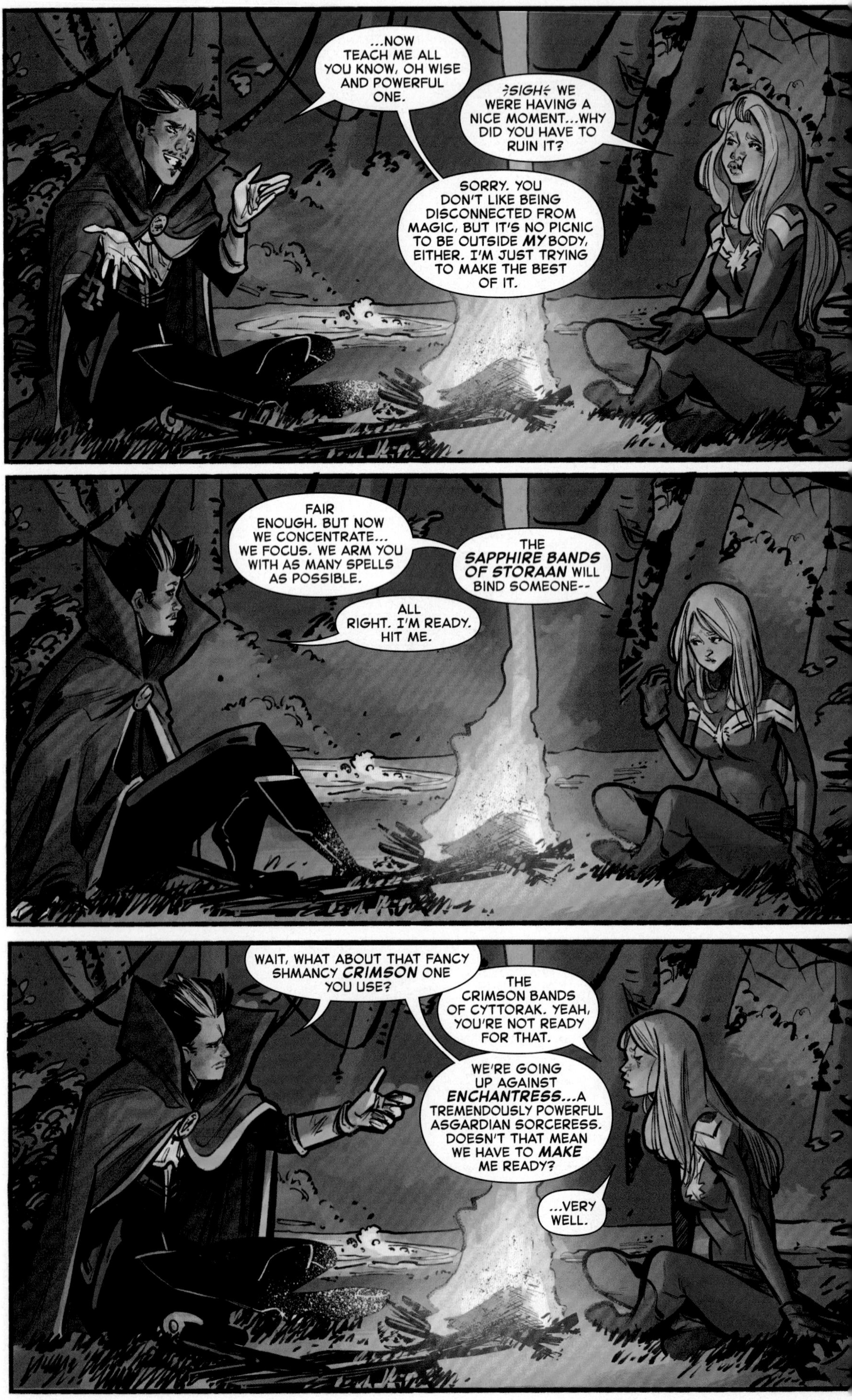
...NOW TEACH ME ALL YOU KNOW, OH WISE AND POWERFUL ONE.
⋟SIGH⋞ WE WERE HAVING A NICE MOMENT...WHY DID YOU HAVE TO RUIN IT?
SORRY. YOU DON'T LIKE BEING DISCONNECTED FROM MAGIC, BUT IT'S NO PICNIC TO BE OUTSIDE *MY* BODY, EITHER. I'M JUST TRYING TO MAKE THE BEST OF IT.
FAIR ENOUGH. BUT NOW WE CONCENTRATE... WE FOCUS. WE ARM YOU WITH AS MANY SPELLS AS POSSIBLE.
THE ***SAPPHIRE BANDS OF STORAAN*** WILL BIND SOMEONE--
ALL RIGHT. I'M READY. HIT ME.
WAIT, WHAT ABOUT THAT FANCY SHMANCY ***CRIMSON*** ONE YOU USE?
THE CRIMSON BANDS OF CYTTORAK. YEAH, YOU'RE NOT READY FOR THAT.
WE'RE GOING UP AGAINST ***ENCHANTRESS***...A TREMENDOUSLY POWERFUL ASGARDIAN SORCERESS. DOESN'T THAT MEAN WE HAVE TO ***MAKE*** ME READY?
...VERY WELL.

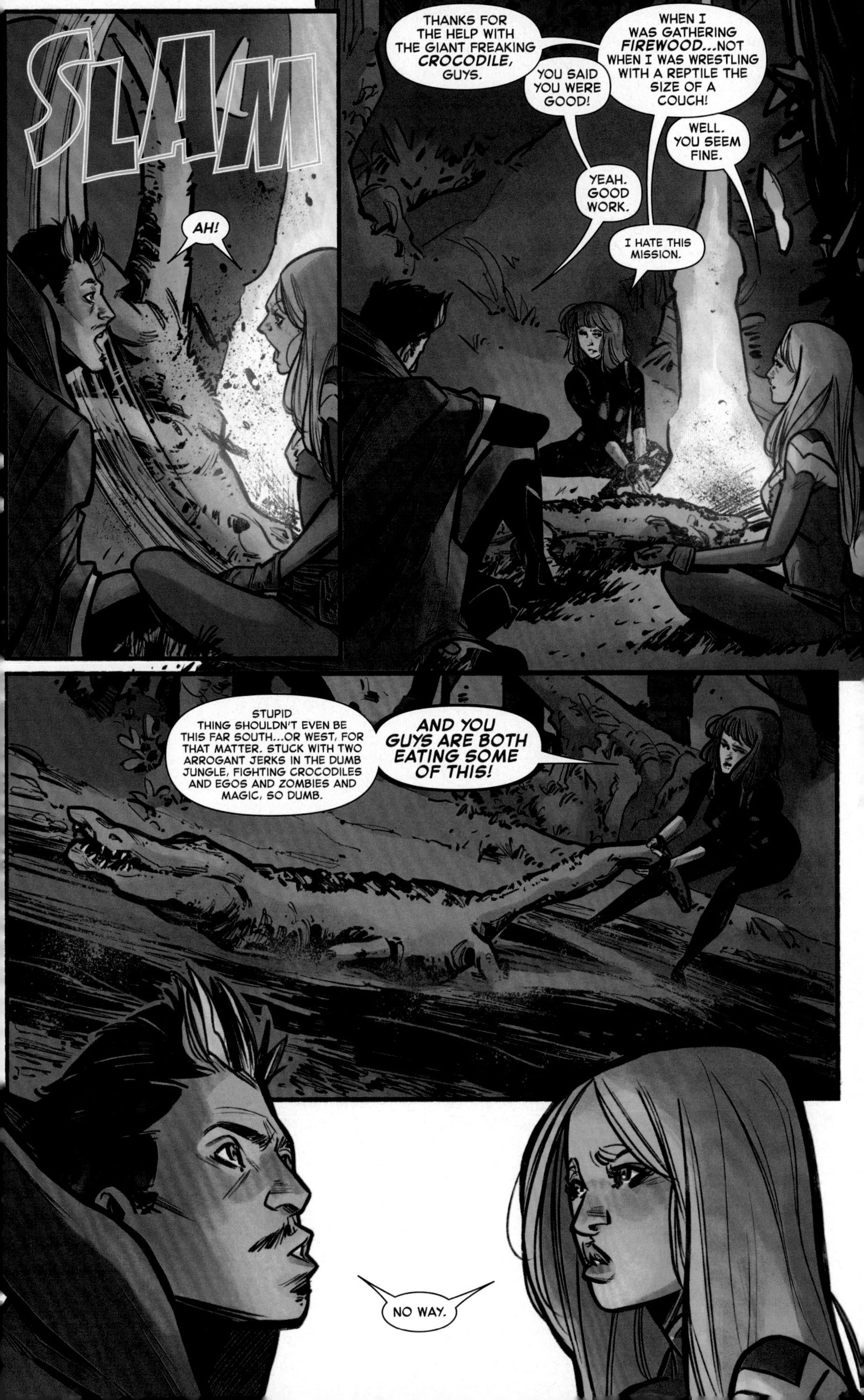
SLAM
AH!
THANKS FOR THE HELP WITH THE GIANT FREAKING CROCODILE, GUYS.
YOU SAID YOU WERE GOOD!
WHEN I WAS GATHERING FIREWOOD...NOT WHEN I WAS WRESTLING WITH A REPTILE THE SIZE OF A COUCH!
WELL. YOU SEEM FINE.
YEAH. GOOD WORK.
I HATE THIS MISSION.
STUPID THING SHOULDN'T EVEN BE THIS FAR SOUTH...OR WEST, FOR THAT MATTER. STUCK WITH TWO ARROGANT JERKS IN THE DUMB JUNGLE, FIGHTING CROCODILES AND EGOS AND ZOMBIES AND MAGIC, SO DUMB.
AND YOU GUYS ARE BOTH EATING SOME OF THIS!
NO WAY.

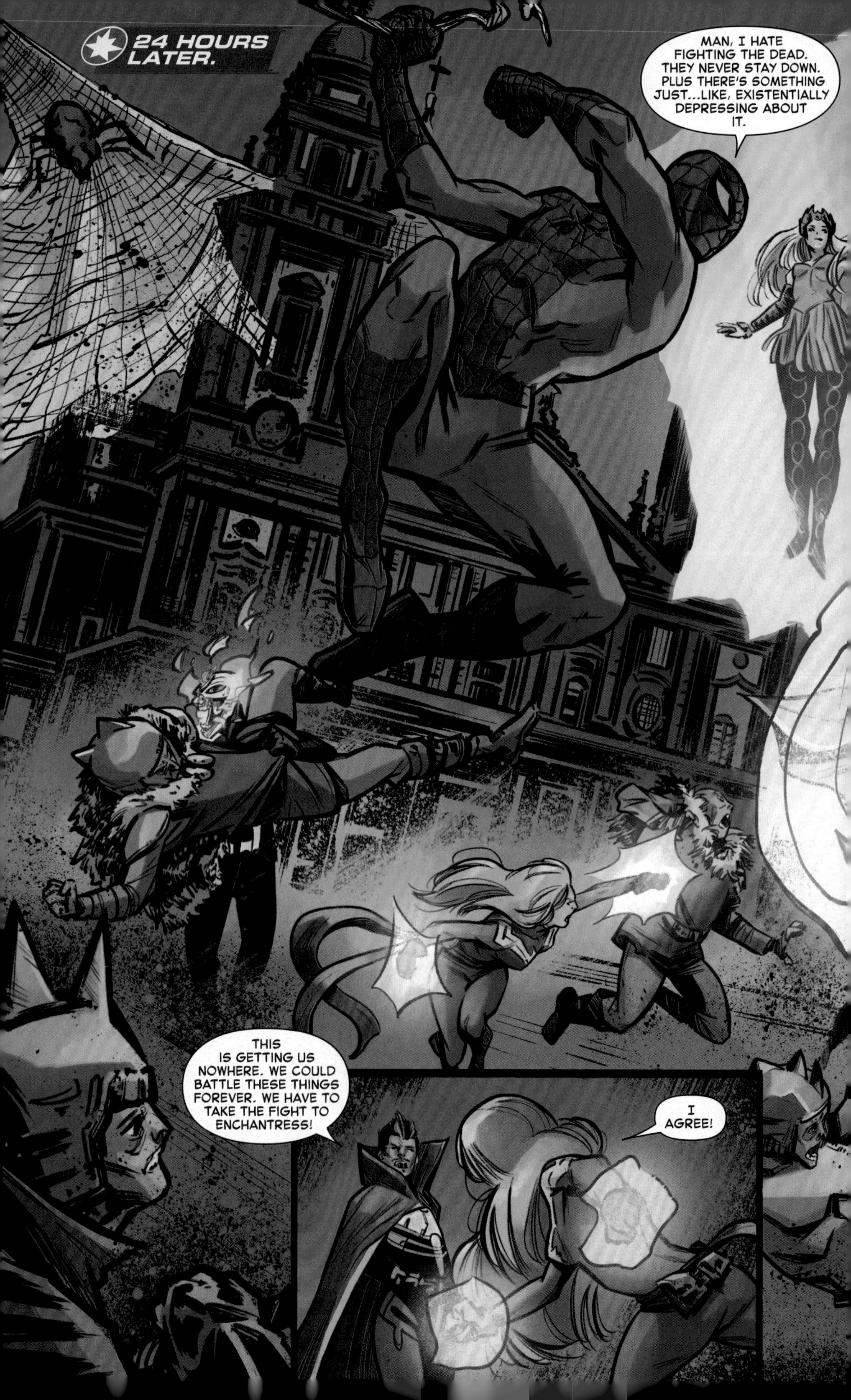
24 HOURS LATER.
MAN, I HATE FIGHTING THE DEAD. THEY NEVER STAY DOWN. PLUS THERE'S SOMETHING JUST...LIKE, EXISTENTIALLY DEPRESSING ABOUT IT.
THIS IS GETTING US NOWHERE. WE COULD BATTLE THESE THINGS FOREVER. WE HAVE TO TAKE THE FIGHT TO ENCHANTRESS!
I AGREE!

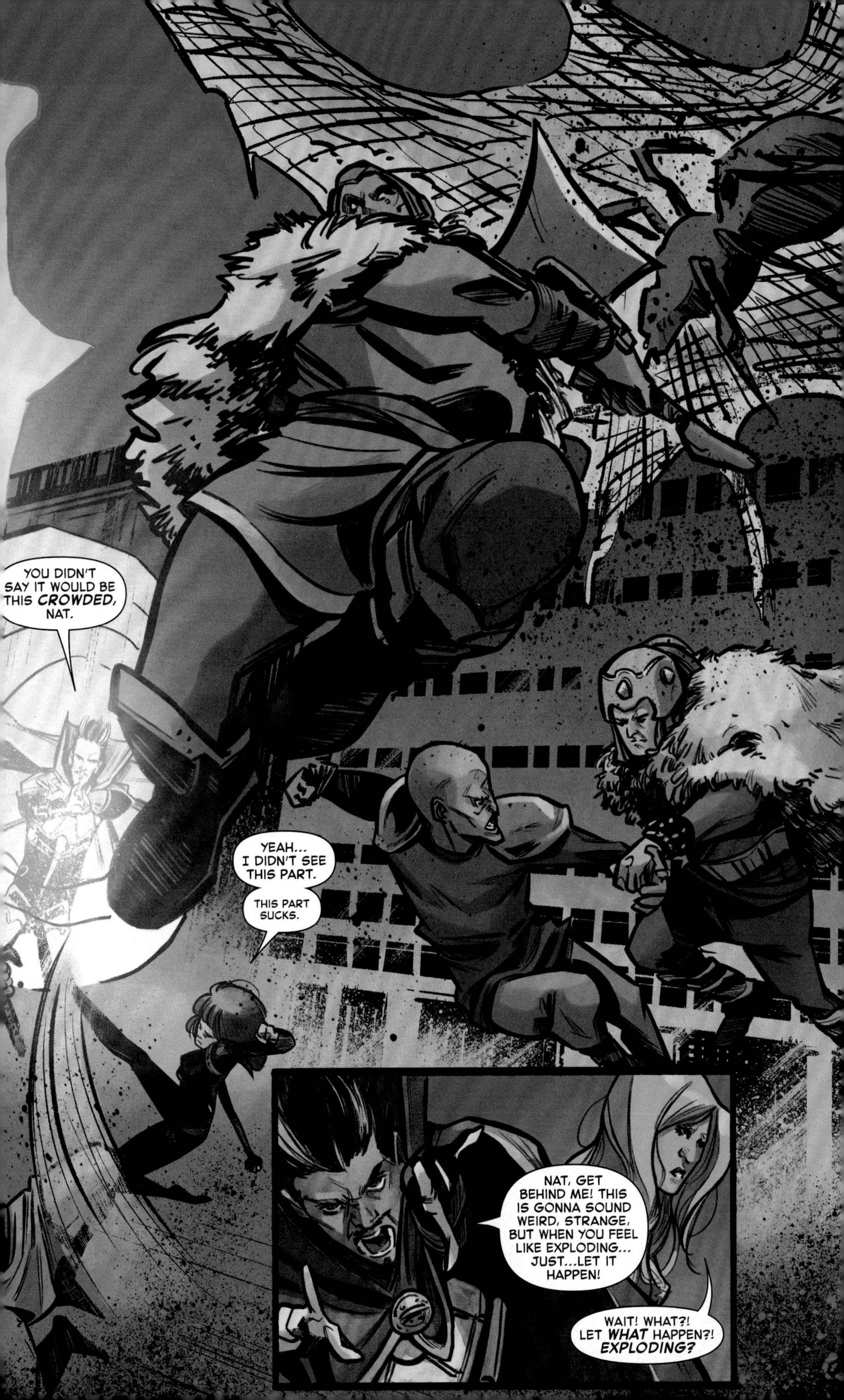
YOU DIDN'T SAY IT WOULD BE THIS CROWDED, NAT.
YEAH... I DIDN'T SEE THIS PART.
THIS PART SUCKS.
NAT, GET BEHIND ME! THIS IS GONNA SOUND WEIRD, STRANGE, BUT WHEN YOU FEEL LIKE EXPLODING... JUST...LET IT HAPPEN!
WAIT! WHAT?! LET WHAT HAPPEN?! EXPLODING?

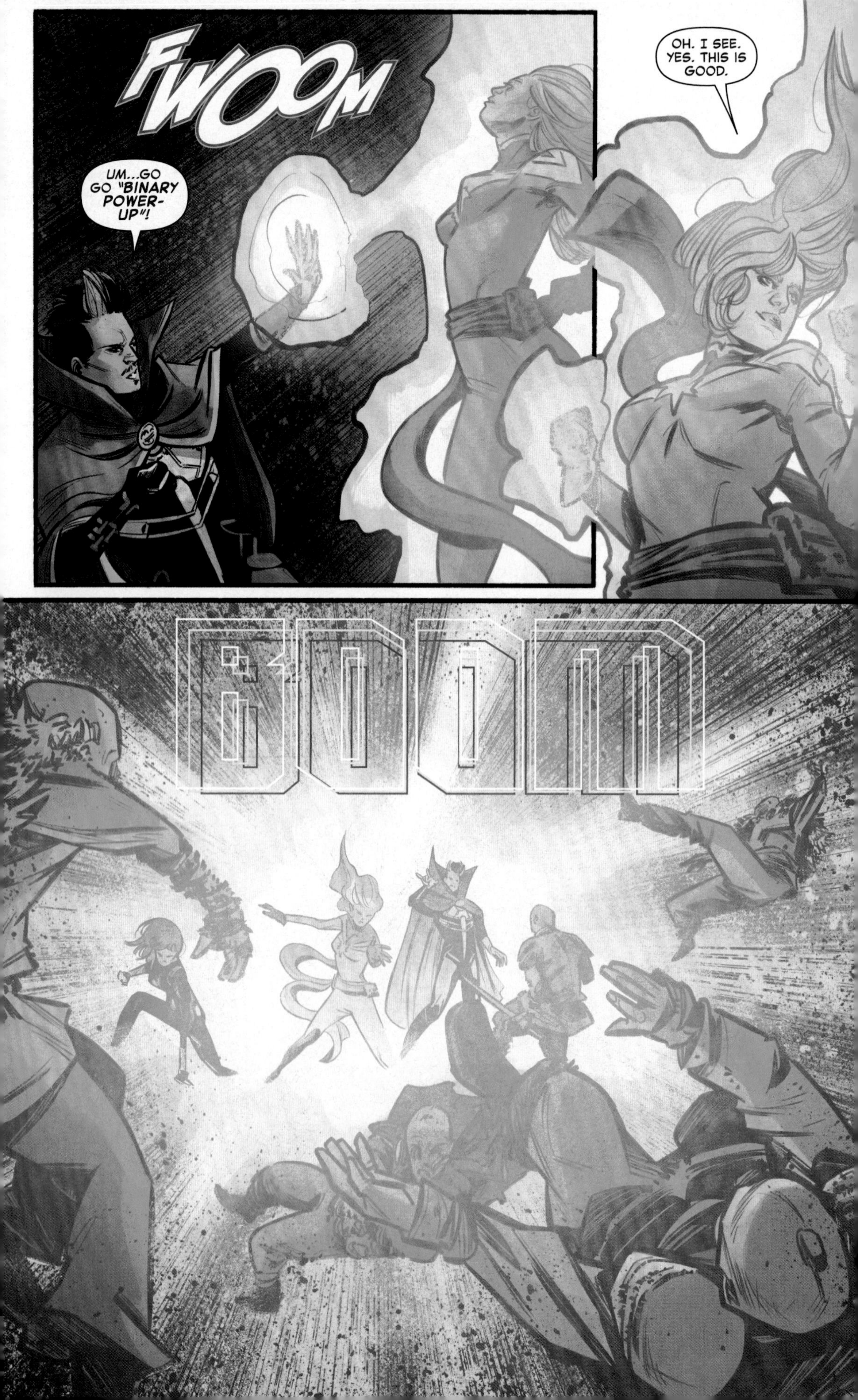
FWOOM
UM...GO GO "BINARY POWER-UP"!
OH. I SEE. YES. THIS IS GOOD.
BOOM

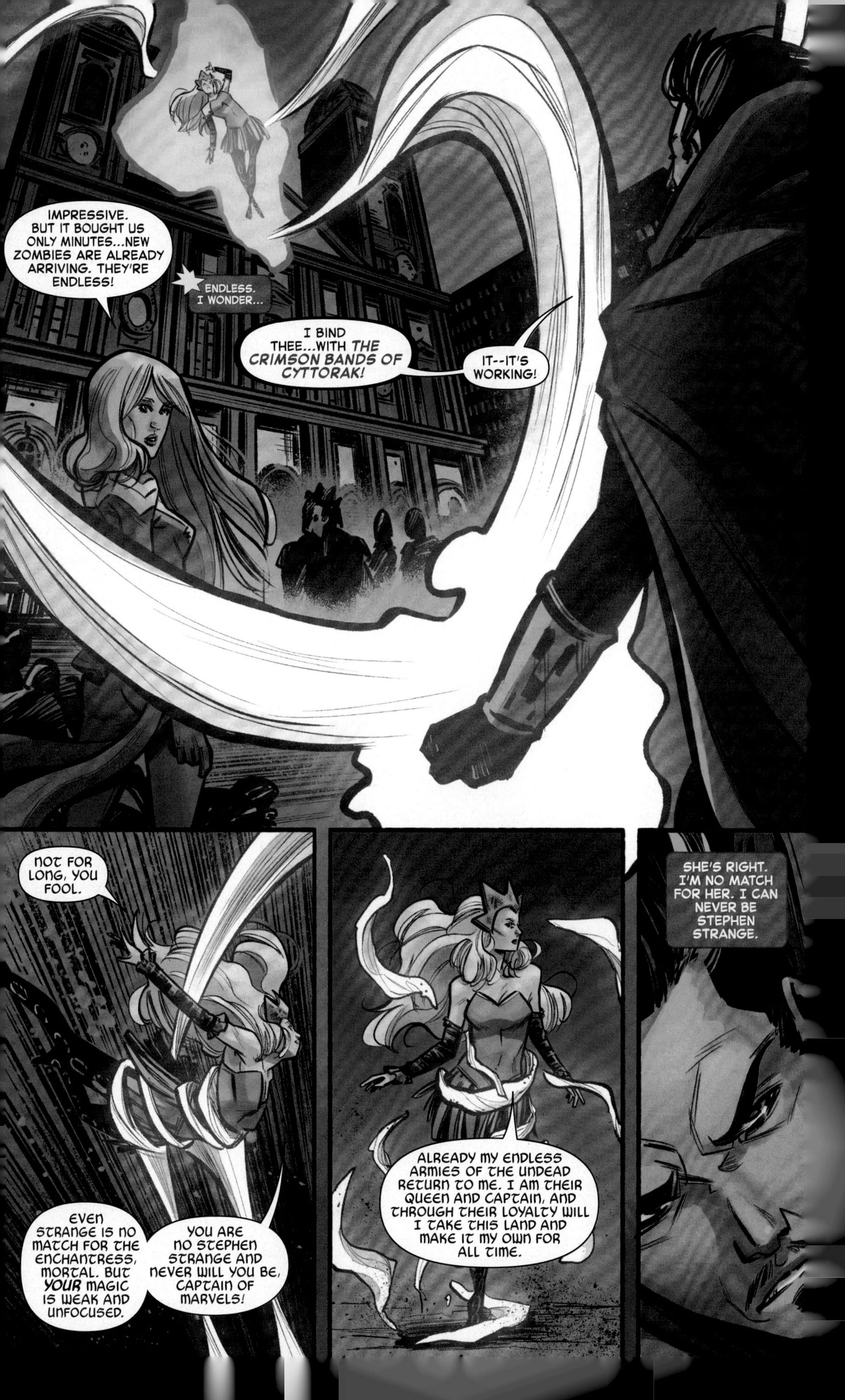
IMPRESSIVE. BUT IT BOUGHT US ONLY MINUTES...NEW ZOMBIES ARE ALREADY ARRIVING. THEY'RE ENDLESS!
ENDLESS. I WONDER...
I BIND THEE...WITH THE CRIMSON BANDS OF CYTTORAK!
IT--IT'S WORKING!
NOT FOR LONG, YOU FOOL.
EVEN STRANGE IS NO MATCH FOR THE ENCHANTRESS, MORTAL. BUT YOUR MAGIC IS WEAK AND UNFOCUSED.
YOU ARE NO STEPHEN STRANGE AND NEVER WILL YOU BE, CAPTAIN OF MARVELS!
ALREADY MY ENDLESS ARMIES OF THE UNDEAD RETURN TO ME. I AM THEIR QUEEN AND CAPTAIN, AND THROUGH THEIR LOYALTY WILL I TAKE THIS LAND AND MAKE IT MY OWN FOR ALL TIME.
SHE'S RIGHT. I'M NO MATCH FOR HER. I CAN NEVER BE STEPHEN STRANGE.

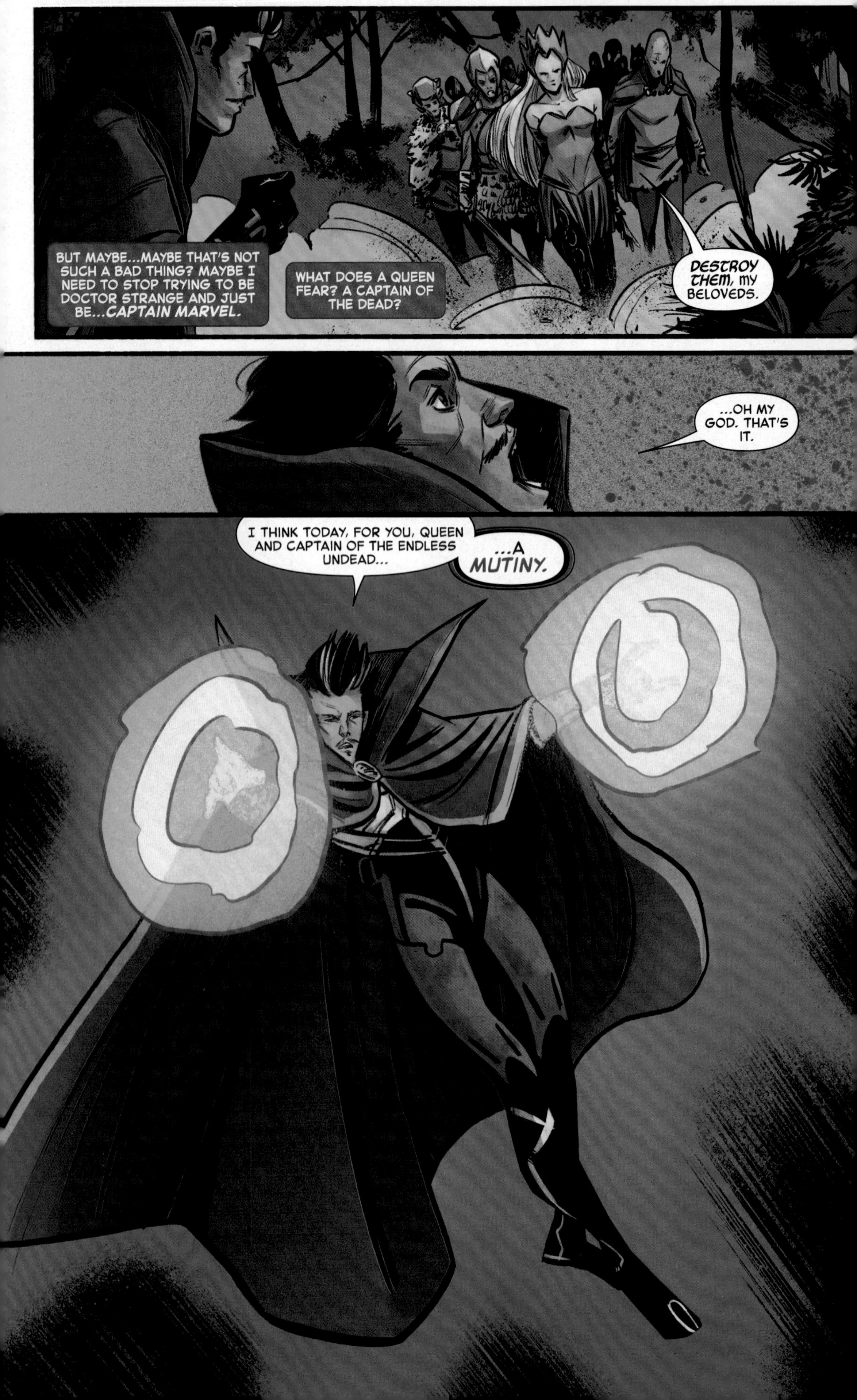
BUT MAYBE...MAYBE THAT'S NOT SUCH A BAD THING? MAYBE I NEED TO STOP TRYING TO BE DOCTOR STRANGE AND JUST BE...CAPTAIN MARVEL.
WHAT DOES A QUEEN FEAR? A CAPTAIN OF THE DEAD?
DESTROY THEM, MY BELOVEDS.
...OH MY GOD. THAT'S IT.
I THINK TODAY, FOR YOU, QUEEN AND CAPTAIN OF THE ENDLESS UNDEAD...
...A MUTINY.

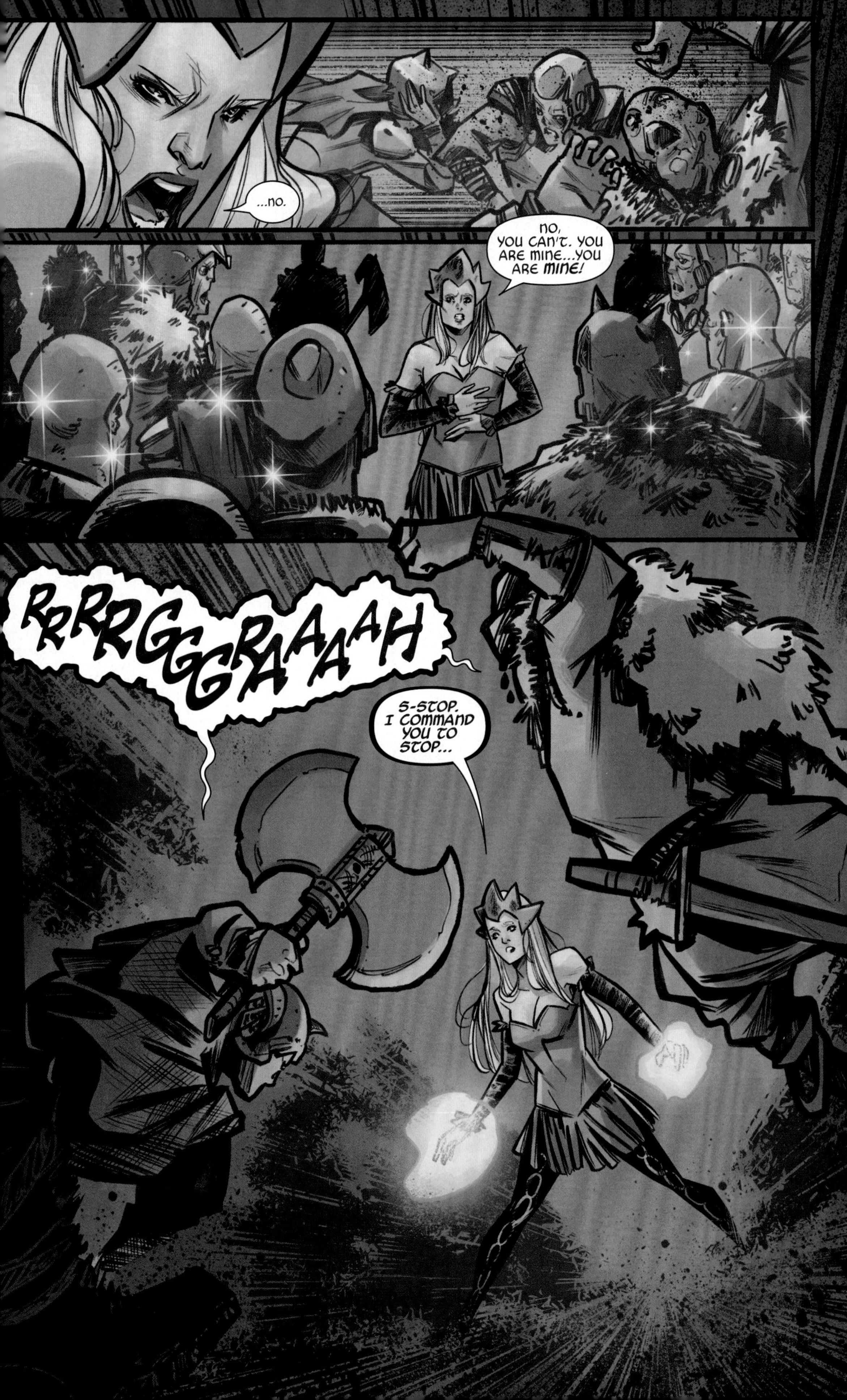
...no.
no, you can't. you are mine...you are mine!
RRRRGGGRAAAAH
S-STOP. I COMMAND YOU TO STOP...

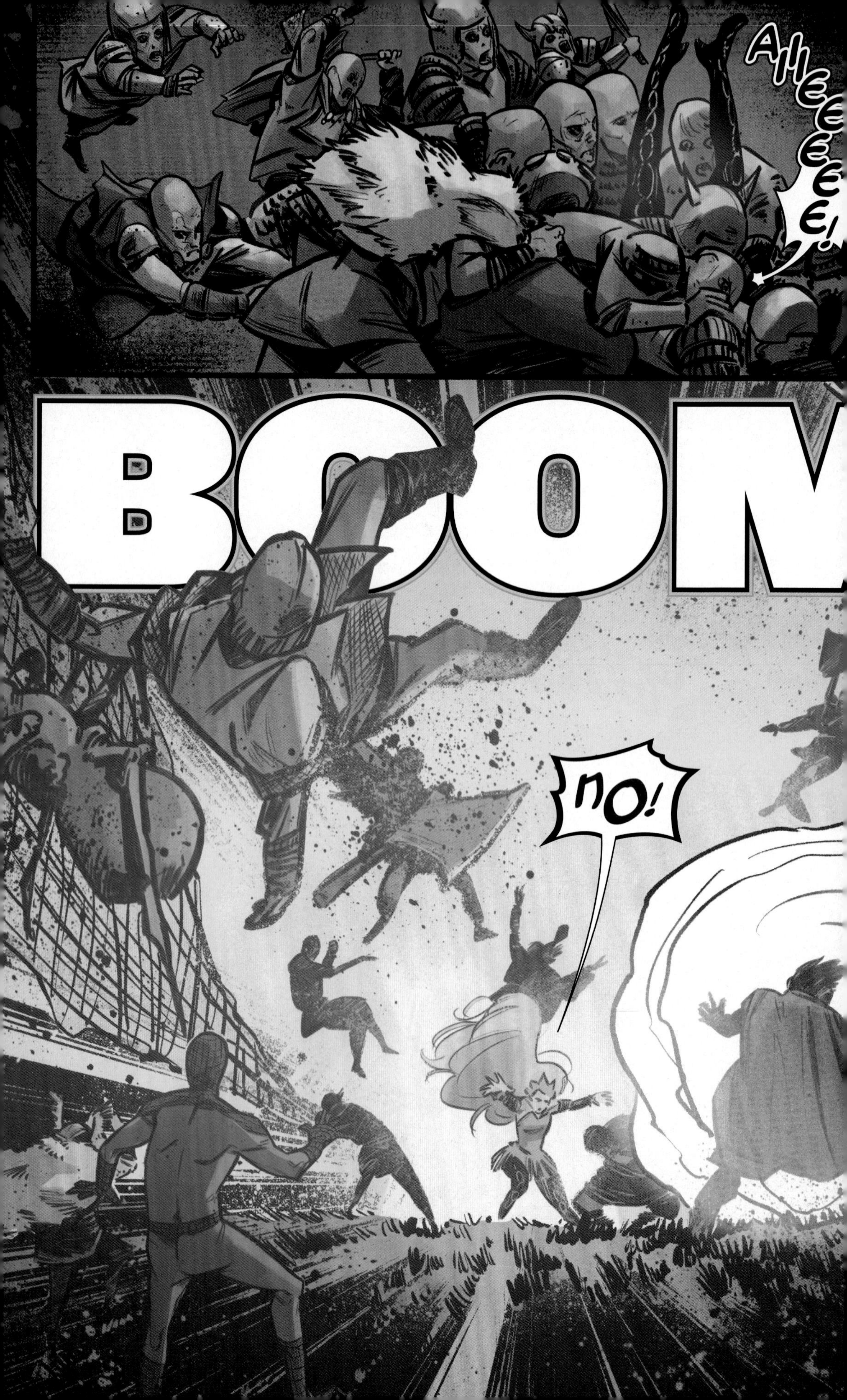
AIIEEEEEE!
BOOM
NO!

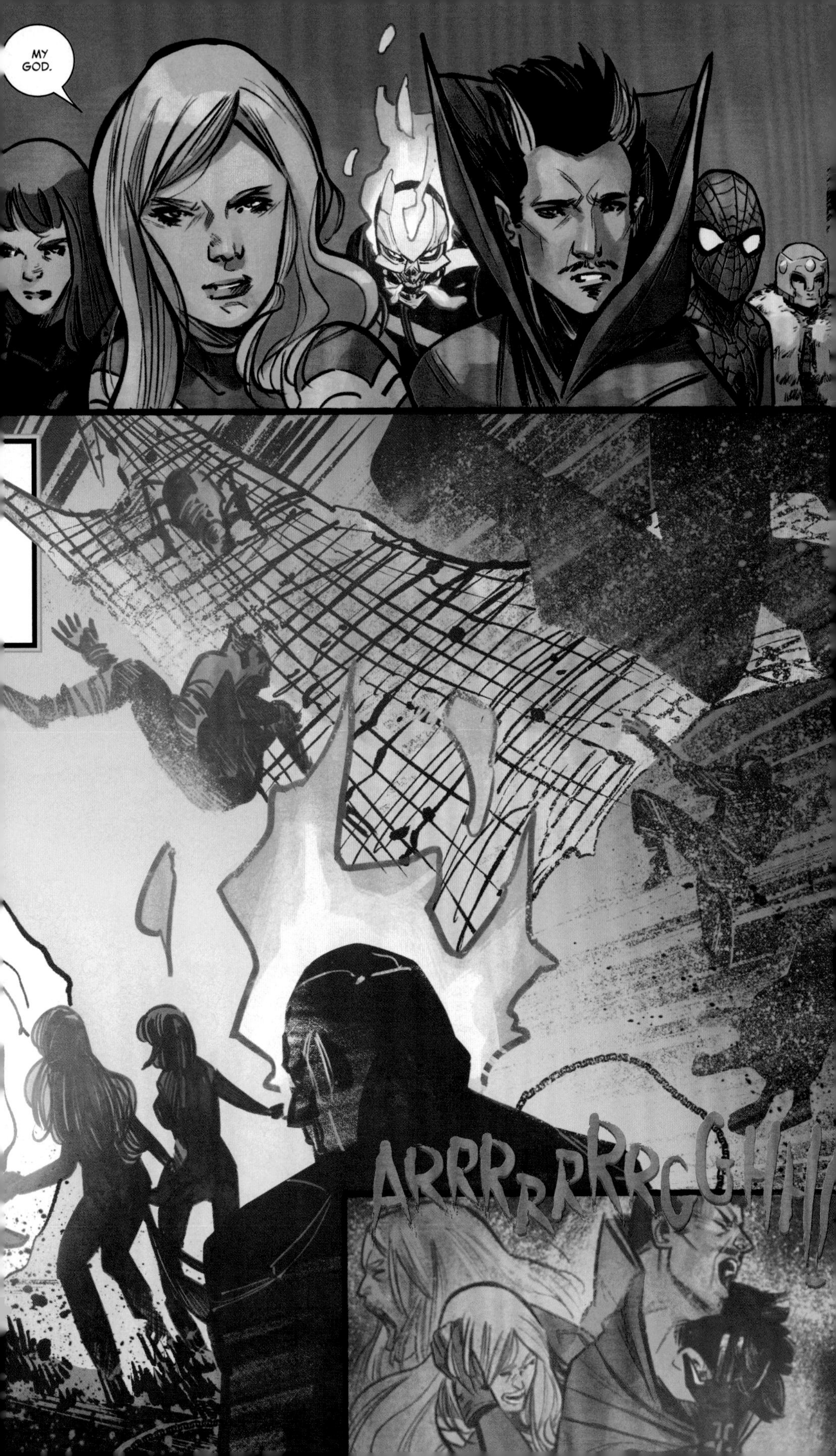
MY GOD.
ARRRRRRRGHH!!

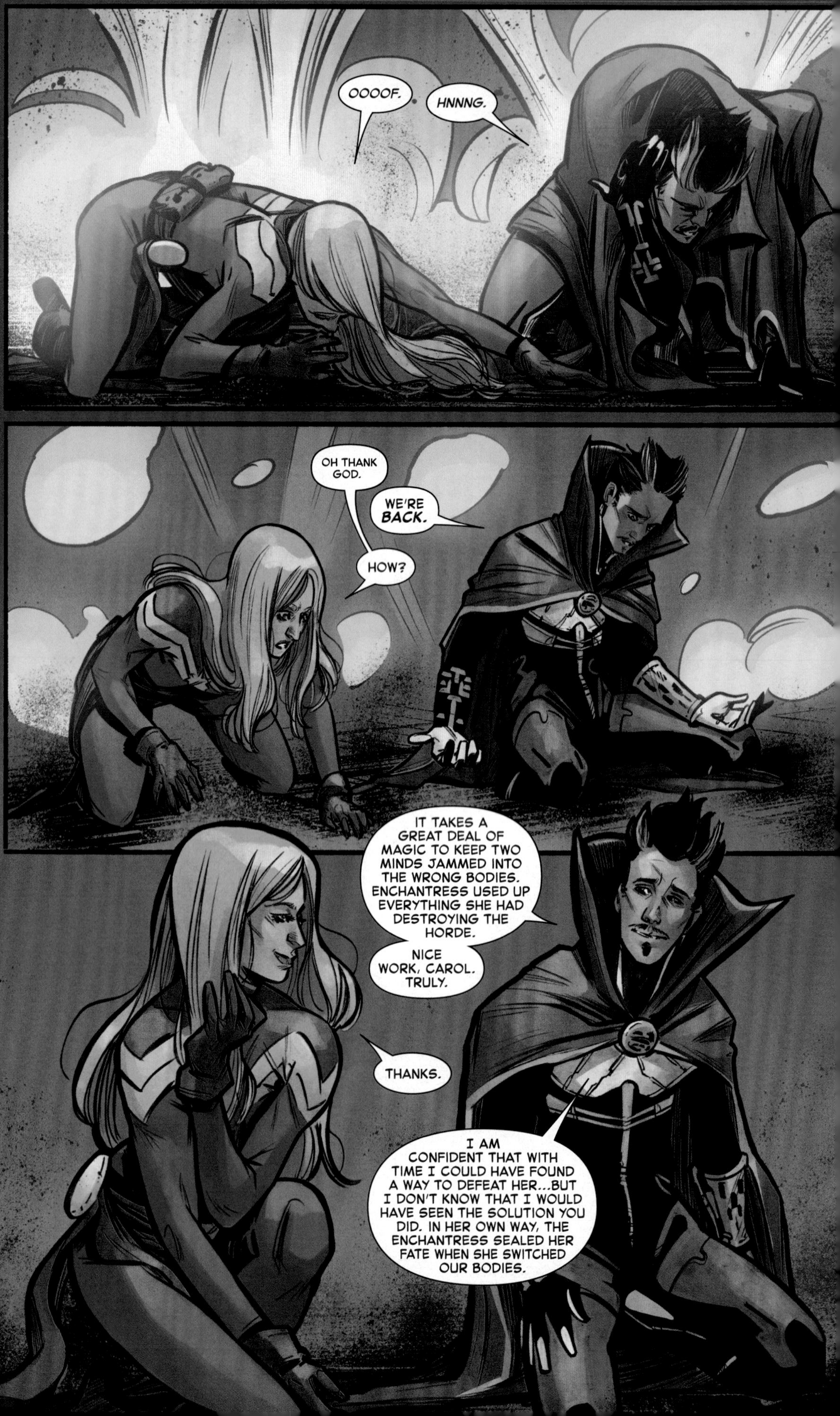
OOOOF.
HNNNG.
OH THANK GOD.
WE'RE BACK.
HOW?
IT TAKES A GREAT DEAL OF MAGIC TO KEEP TWO MINDS JAMMED INTO THE WRONG BODIES. ENCHANTRESS USED UP EVERYTHING SHE HAD DESTROYING THE HORDE.
NICE WORK, CAROL. TRULY.
THANKS.
I AM CONFIDENT THAT WITH TIME I COULD HAVE FOUND A WAY TO DEFEAT HER...BUT I DON'T KNOW THAT I WOULD HAVE SEEN THE SOLUTION YOU DID. IN HER OWN WAY, THE ENCHANTRESS SEALED HER FATE WHEN SHE SWITCHED OUR BODIES.

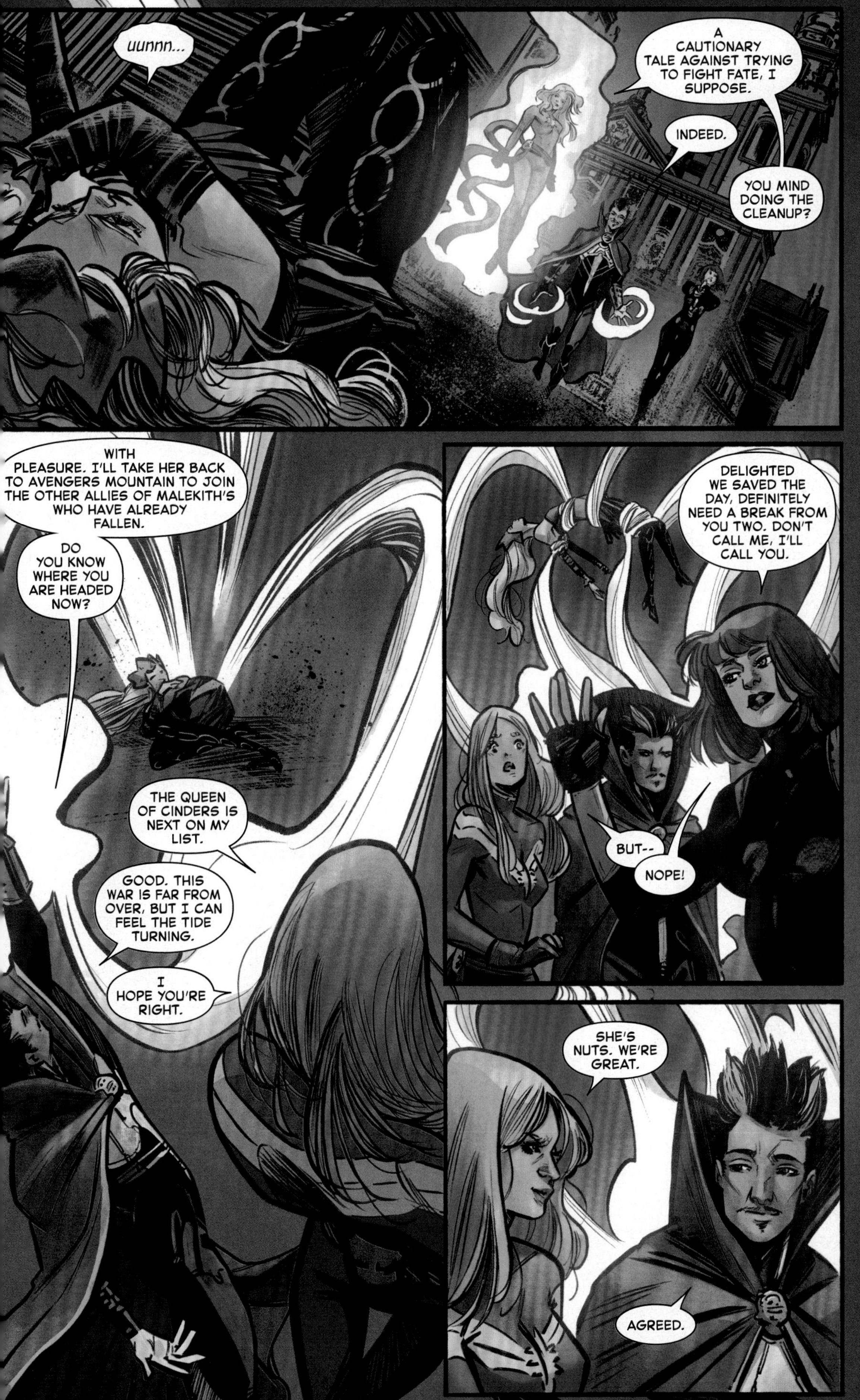
uunnn...
A CAUTIONARY TALE AGAINST TRYING TO FIGHT FATE, I SUPPOSE.
INDEED.
YOU MIND DOING THE CLEANUP?
WITH PLEASURE. I'LL TAKE HER BACK TO AVENGERS MOUNTAIN TO JOIN THE OTHER ALLIES OF MALEKITH'S WHO HAVE ALREADY FALLEN.
DO YOU KNOW WHERE YOU ARE HEADED NOW?
THE QUEEN OF CINDERS IS NEXT ON MY LIST.
GOOD. THIS WAR IS FAR FROM OVER, BUT I CAN FEEL THE TIDE TURNING.
I HOPE YOU'RE RIGHT.
DELIGHTED WE SAVED THE DAY, DEFINITELY NEED A BREAK FROM YOU TWO. DON'T CALL ME, I'LL CALL YOU.
BUT--
NOPE!
SHE'S NUTS. WE'RE GREAT.
AGREED.

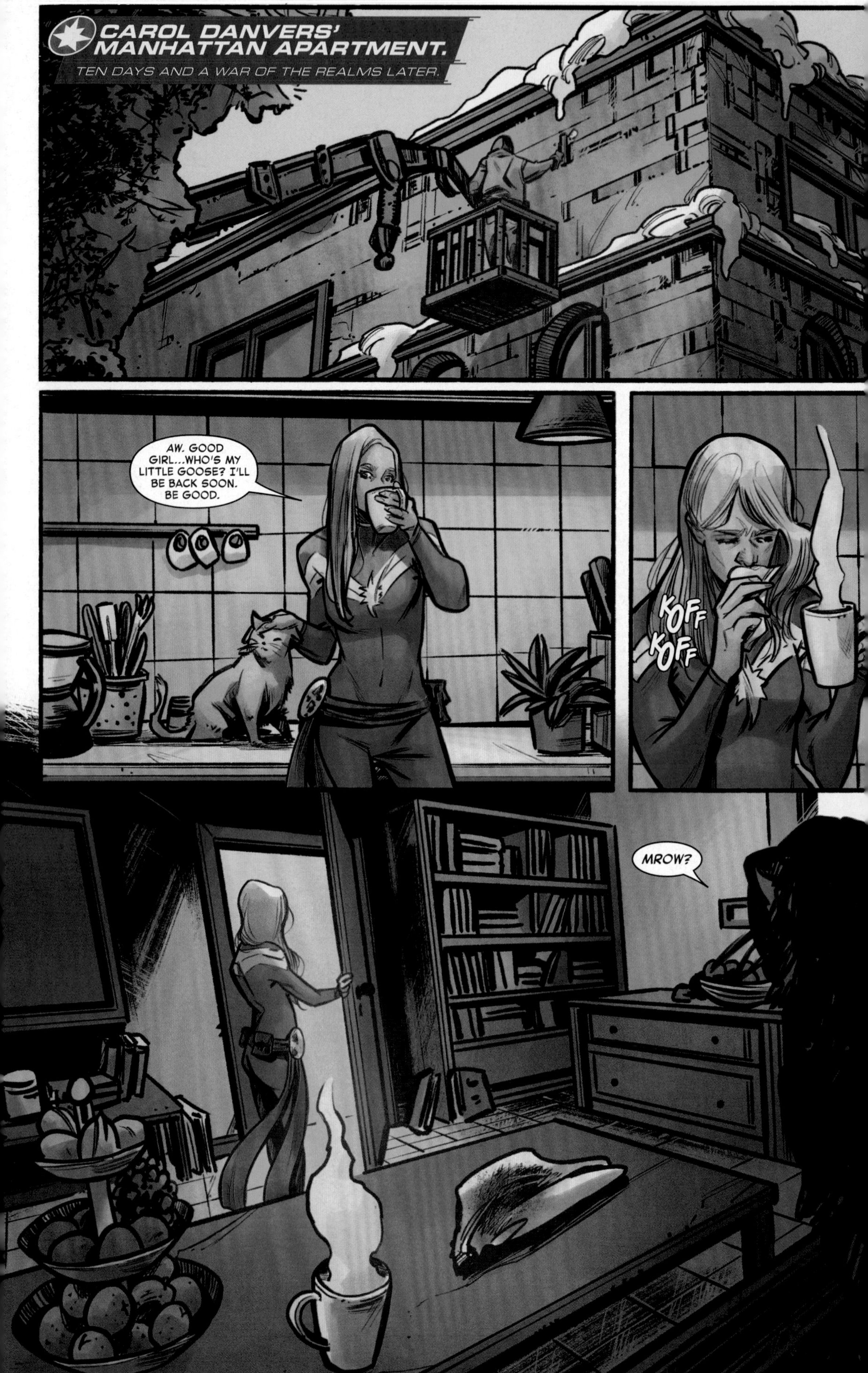
CAROL DANVERS' MANHATTAN APARTMENT.
TEN DAYS AND A WAR OF THE REALMS LATER.
AW. GOOD GIRL...WHO'S MY LITTLE GOOSE? I'LL BE BACK SOON. BE GOOD.
KOFF KOFF
MROW?

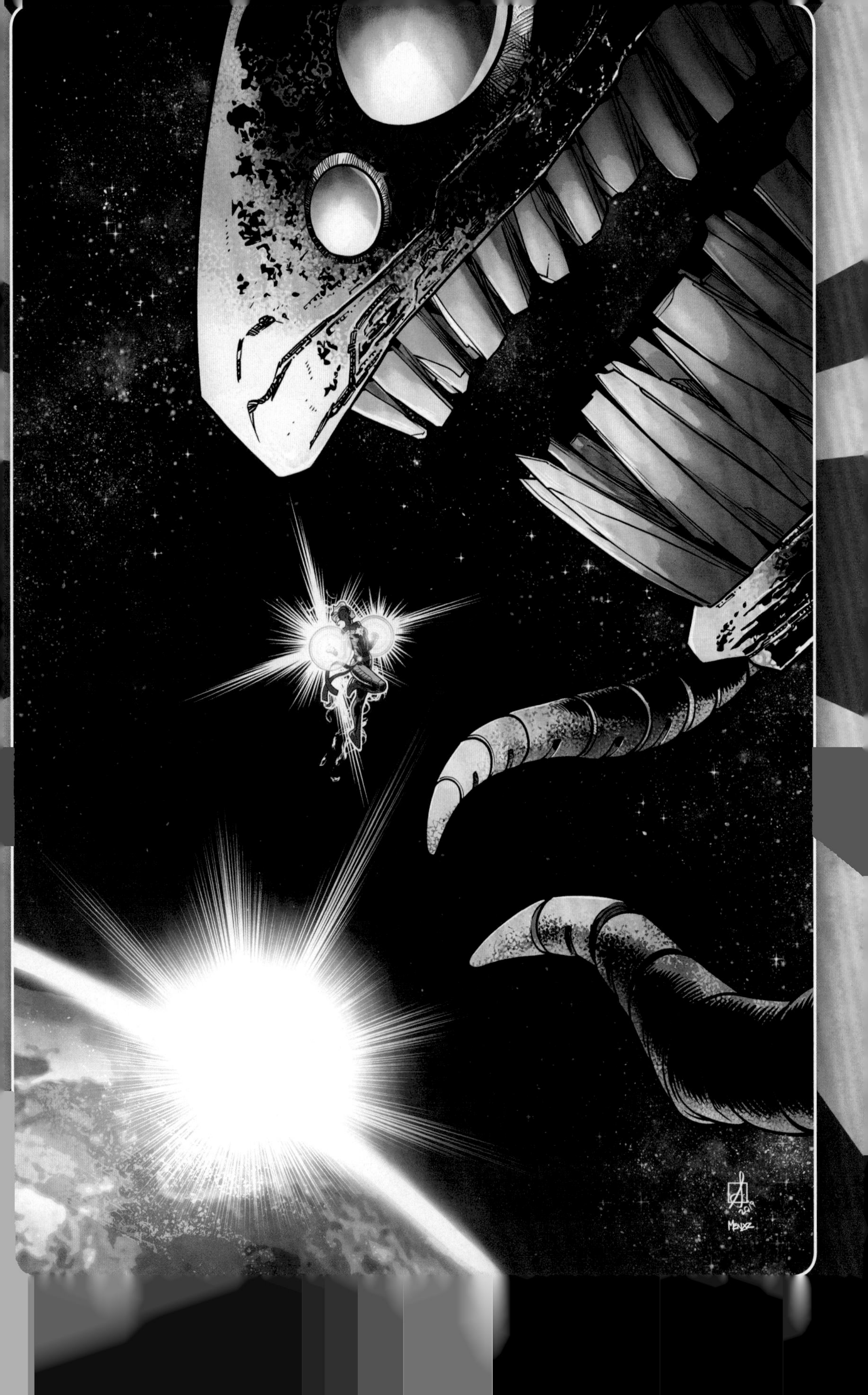

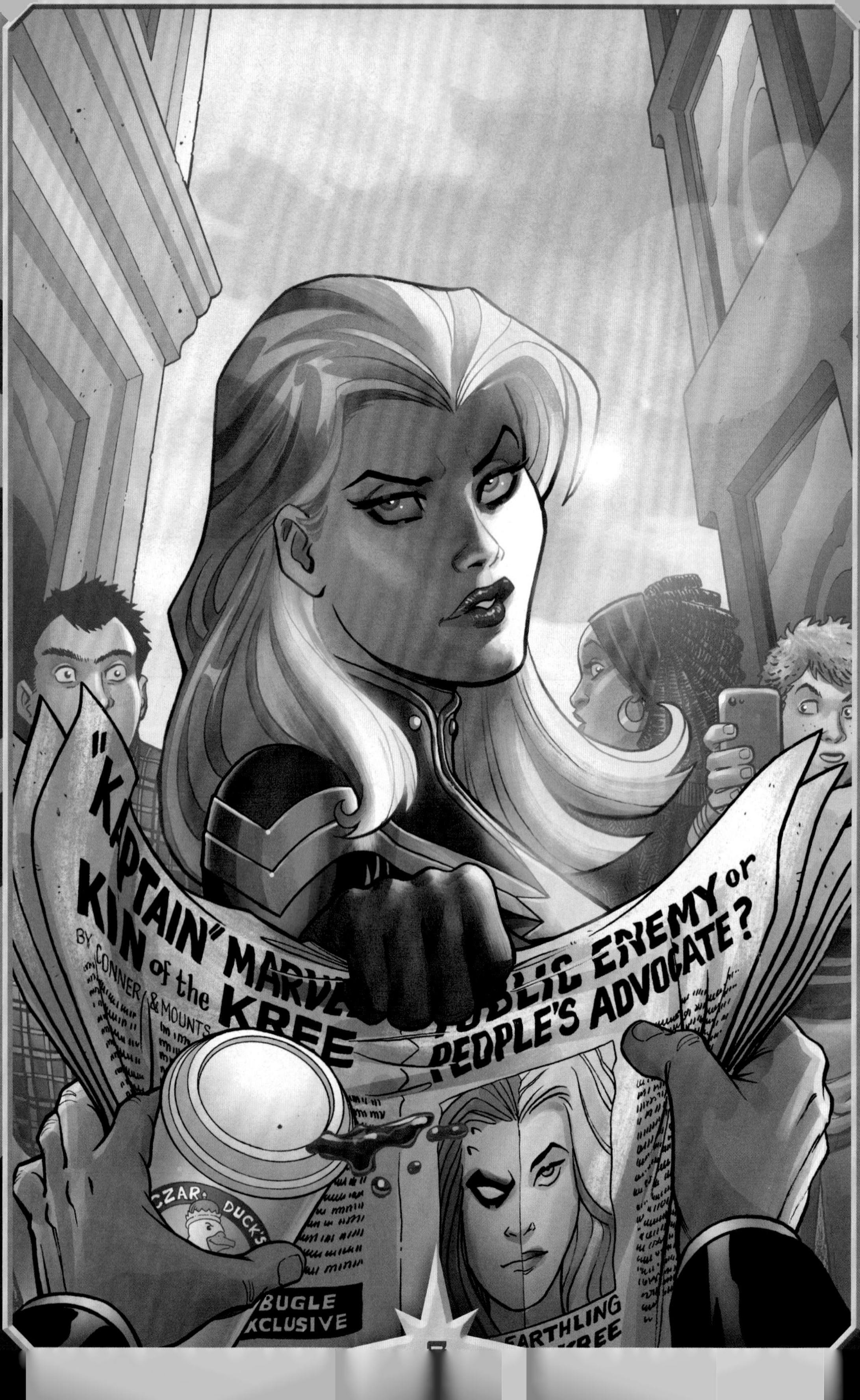

"KAPTAIN" MARVEL
KIN of the KREE
BY CONNER & MOUNTS
PUBLIC ENEMY or PEOPLE'S ADVOCATE?
CZAR DUCK'S
BUGLE EXCLUSIVE
EARTHLING
KREE

YOU THINK YOUR LIFE CAN'T IMPLODE TOO?

APPLY THE RIGHT PRESSURE TO JUST THE RIGHT PLACES, AND IT WILL BREAK APART FASTER THAN YOU'D BELIEVE.

NEW YORK TODAY

ENEMY AMONG US?

DEPARTMENT OF DEFENSE

DEPARTMENT OF THE AIR FORCE
WASHINGTON DC

OFFICE OF THE ASSISTANT SECRETARY

TO COLONEL DANVERS:

SIX DAYS. THAT'S ALL IT TOOK FOR ME. IT FELT EVEN FASTER.

HARPSWELL, MAINE.

CAROL'S FAMILY HOME.

IT FEELS INSANE TO BE YEARNING FOR "SIMPLER TIMES"...BACK WHEN I LIVED IN SPACE AND THE FATE OF MY ENTIRE PLANET DEPENDED ON ME.

AND I FIND I'M ANGRIER THAN I'VE BEEN IN A LONG TIME. I THINK IT'S BECAUSE THERE'S NOTHING TO *HIT* THIS TIME.

A DEFINITE PERK OF BEING A SUPER HERO IS THAT THINGS PRESENT THEMSELVES FOR HITTING ON A FAIRLY REGULAR BASIS.

I'D LIKE TO HIT *SO* MANY THINGS RIGHT NOW. I'D GIVE ANYTHING FOR ONE OF THOSE PLANET-EATING-LEVEL THREATS. HIT IT RIGHT IN ITS STUPID FACE. IF IT HAD ONE.

THE GOOD NEWS IS I STILL HAVEN'T HAD A DRINK. THE BAD NEWS IS...

...I *DID* BUY THIS BOTTLE.

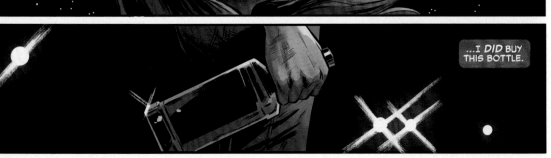

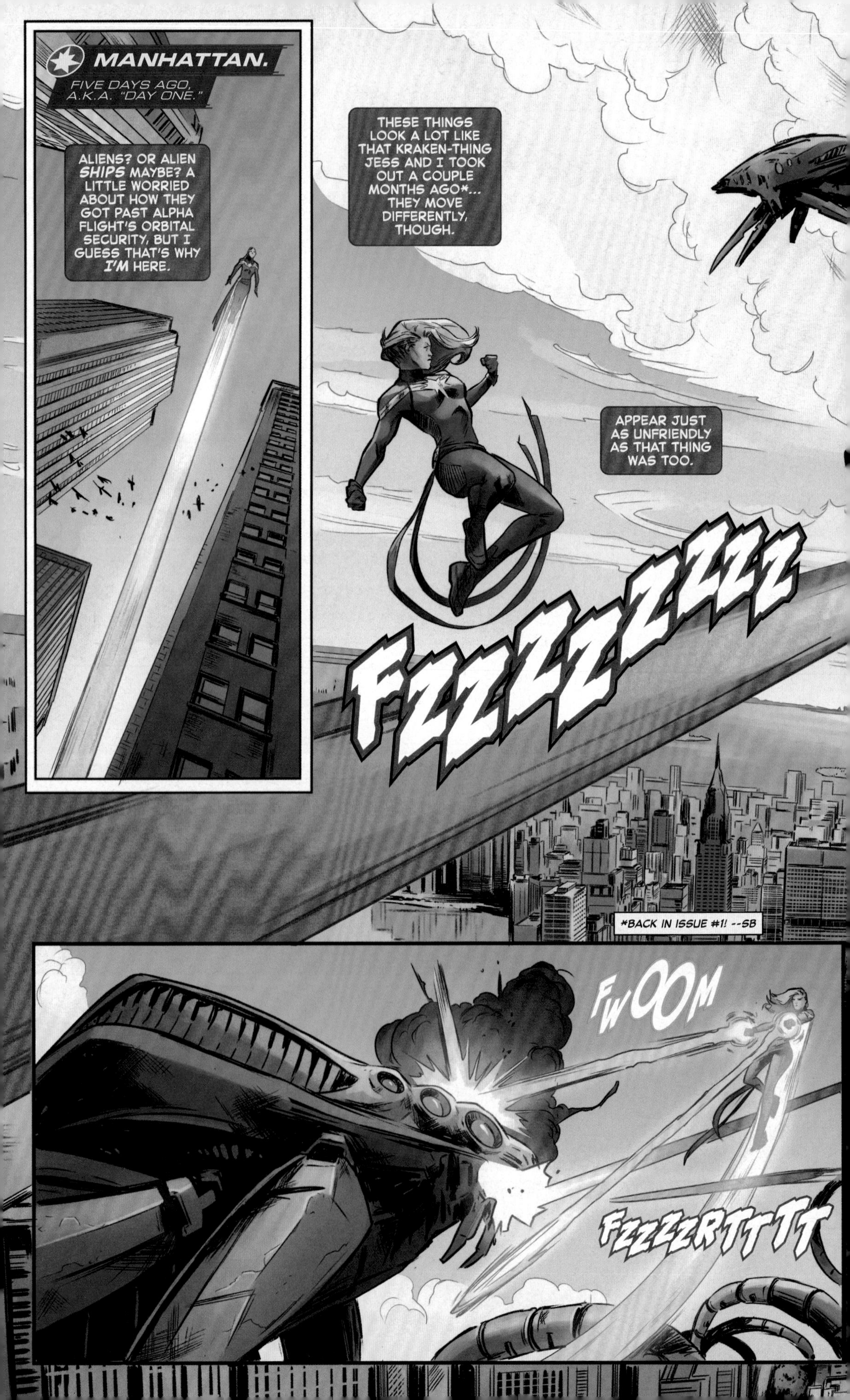
MANHATTAN.
FIVE DAYS AGO, A.K.A. "DAY ONE."
ALIENS? OR ALIEN SHIPS MAYBE? A LITTLE WORRIED ABOUT HOW THEY GOT PAST ALPHA FLIGHT'S ORBITAL SECURITY, BUT I GUESS THAT'S WHY I'M HERE.
THESE THINGS LOOK A LOT LIKE THAT KRAKEN-THING JESS AND I TOOK OUT A COUPLE MONTHS AGO*... THEY MOVE DIFFERENTLY, THOUGH.
APPEAR JUST AS UNFRIENDLY AS THAT THING WAS TOO.
FZZZZZZZZZ
*BACK IN ISSUE #1! --SB
FWOOM
FZZZZRTTTT

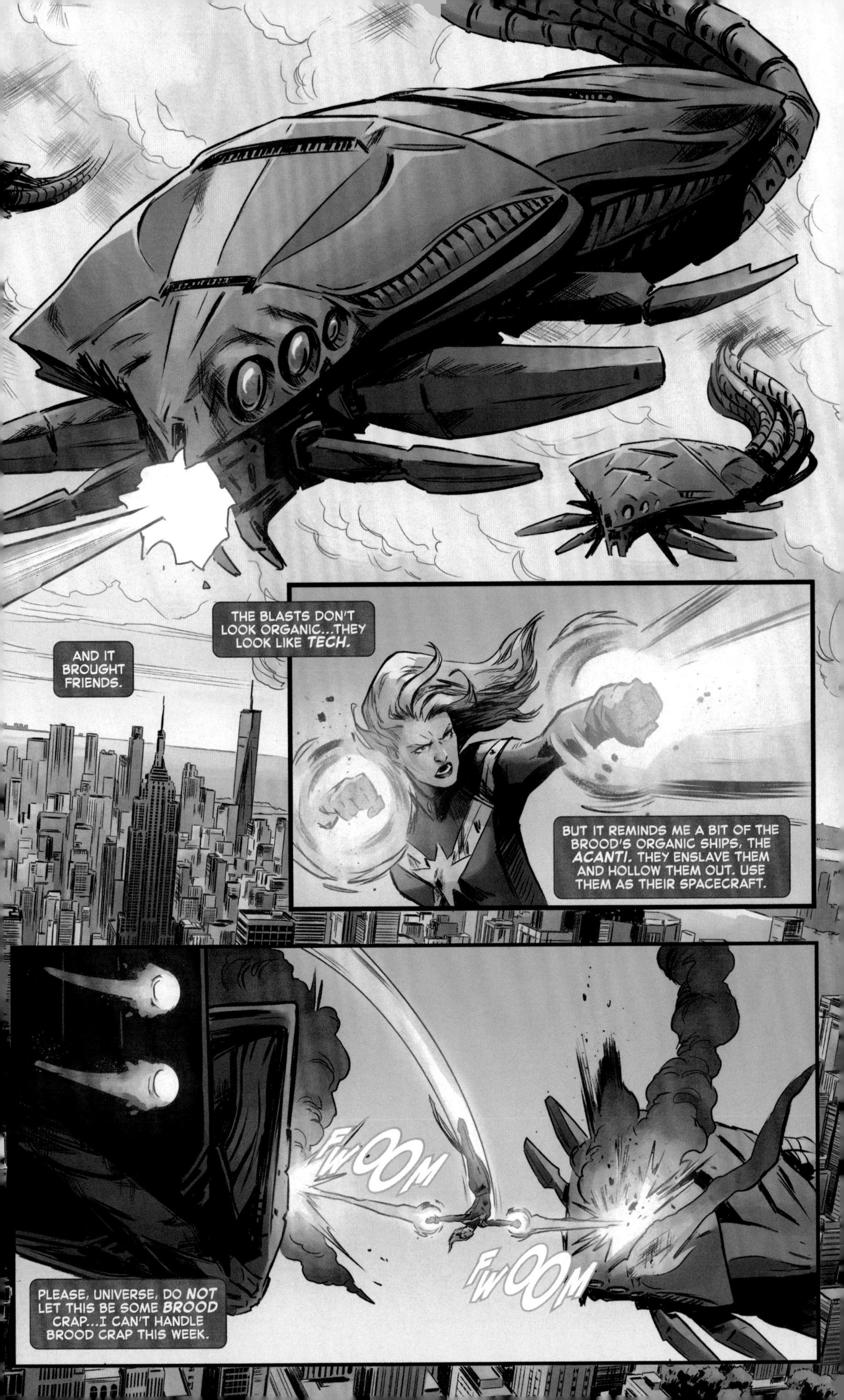
AND IT BROUGHT FRIENDS.
THE BLASTS DON'T LOOK ORGANIC...THEY LOOK LIKE TECH.
BUT IT REMINDS ME A BIT OF THE BROOD'S ORGANIC SHIPS, THE ACANTI. THEY ENSLAVE THEM AND HOLLOW THEM OUT. USE THEM AS THEIR SPACECRAFT.
FWOOM
FWOOM
PLEASE, UNIVERSE, DO NOT LET THIS BE SOME BROOD CRAP...I CAN'T HANDLE BROOD CRAP THIS WEEK.

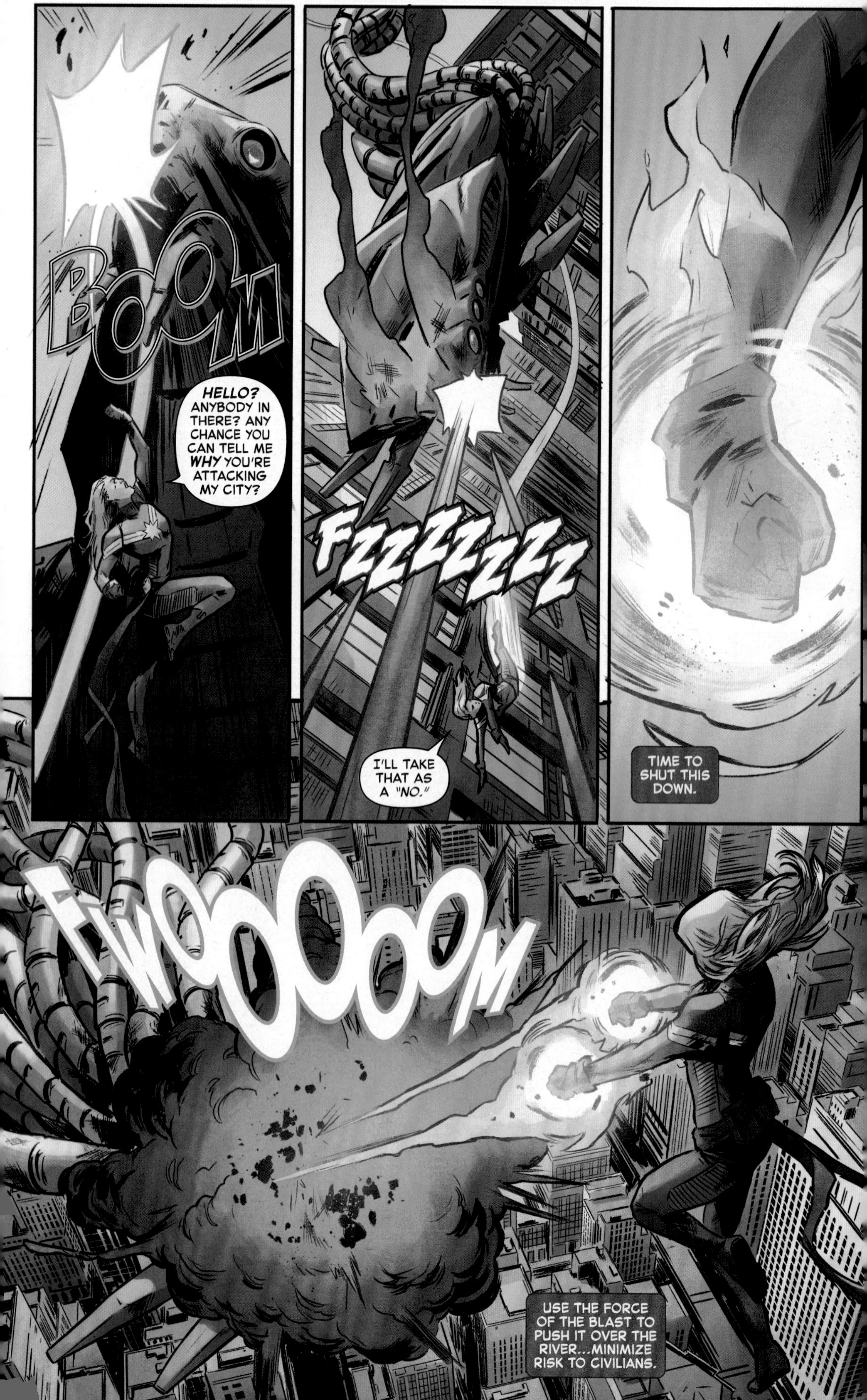
BOOM
HELLO? ANYBODY IN THERE? ANY CHANCE YOU CAN TELL ME WHY YOU'RE ATTACKING MY CITY?
FZZZZZZZZ
I'LL TAKE THAT AS A "NO."
TIME TO SHUT THIS DOWN.
FWOOOOOM
USE THE FORCE OF THE BLAST TO PUSH IT OVER THE RIVER...MINIMIZE RISK TO CIVILIANS.

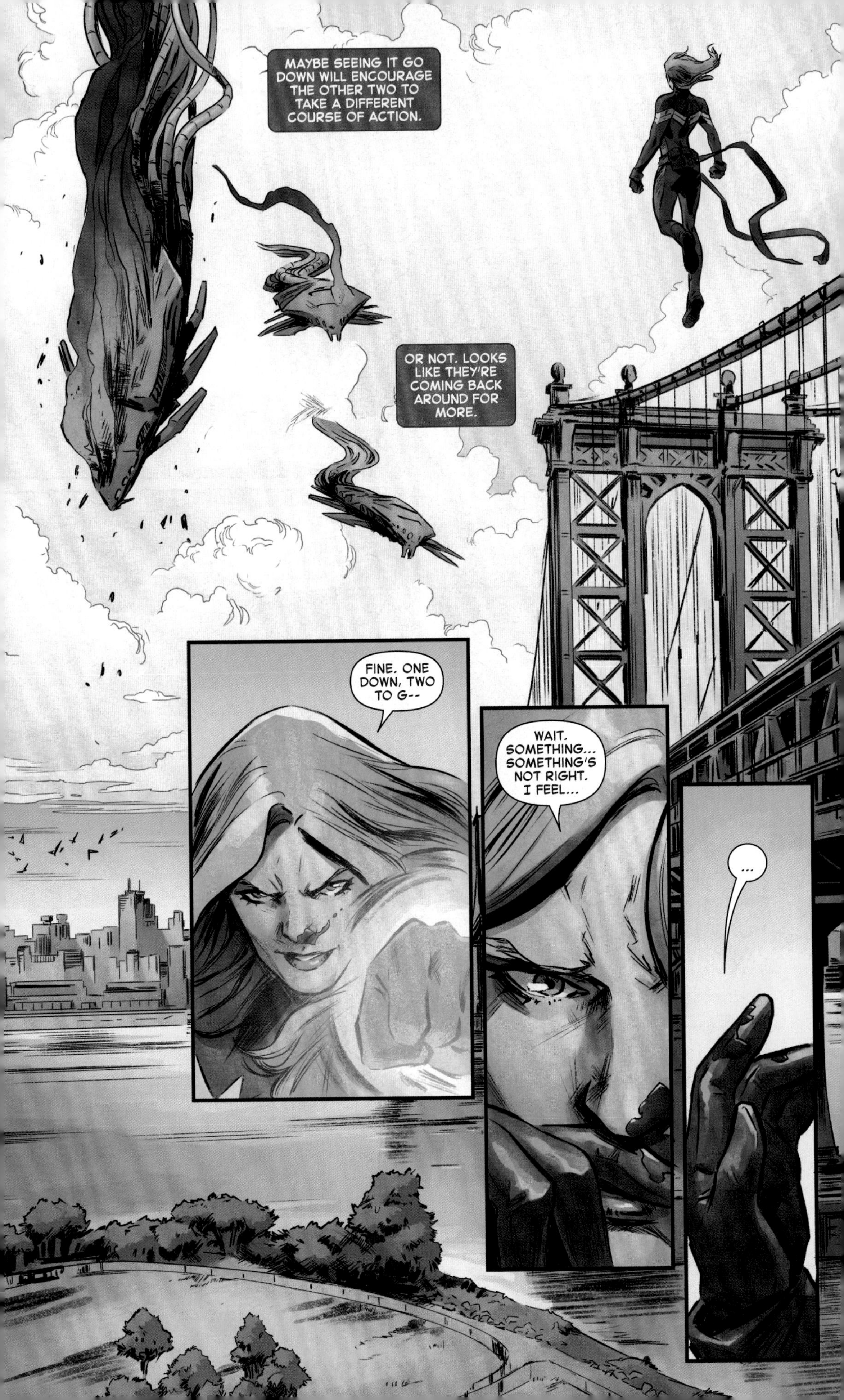
MAYBE SEEING IT GO DOWN WILL ENCOURAGE THE OTHER TWO TO TAKE A DIFFERENT COURSE OF ACTION.
OR NOT. LOOKS LIKE THEY'RE COMING BACK AROUND FOR MORE.
FINE. ONE DOWN, TWO TO G--
WAIT. SOMETHING... SOMETHING'S NOT RIGHT. I FEEL...
...

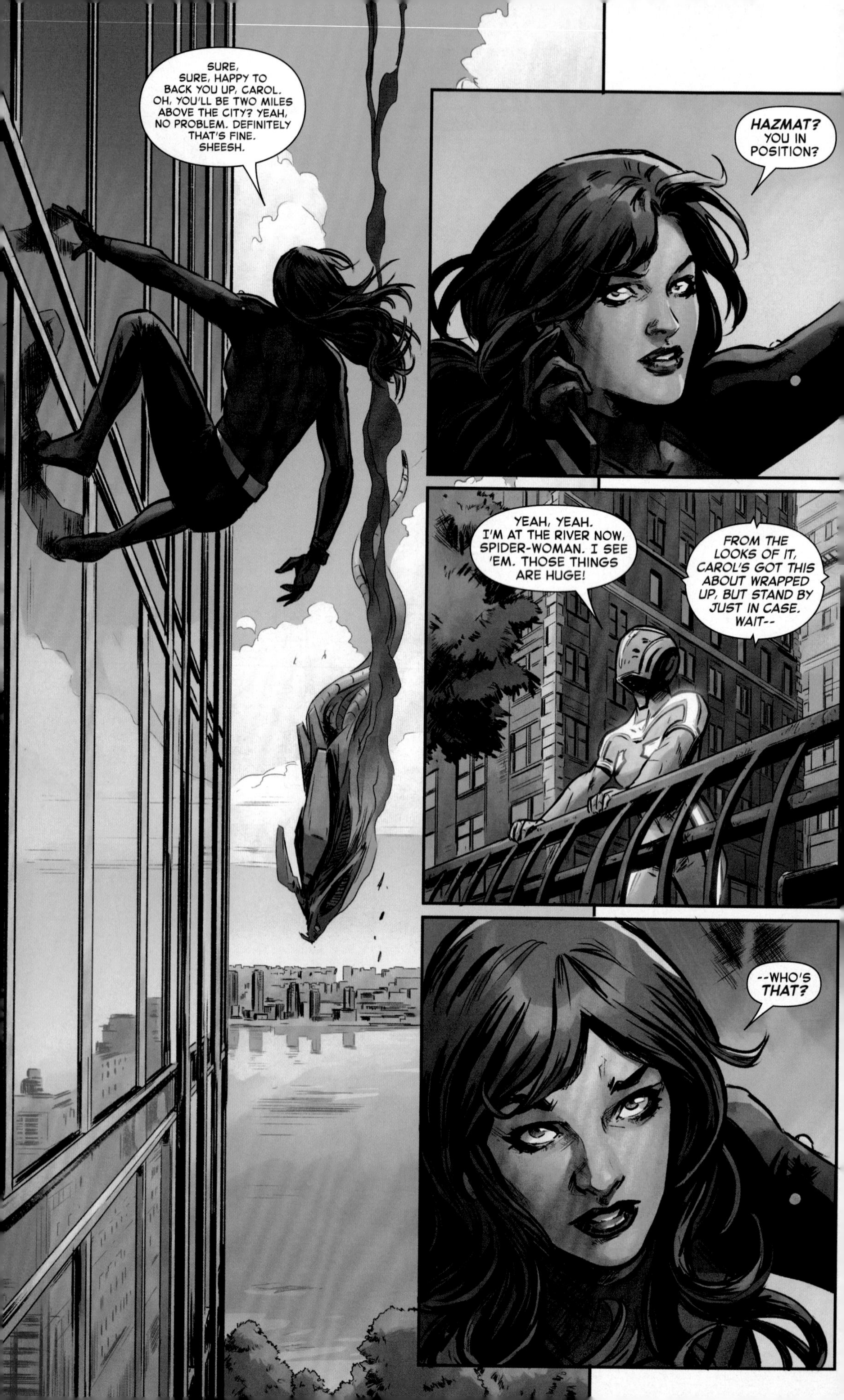
SURE, SURE, HAPPY TO BACK YOU UP, CAROL. OH, YOU'LL BE TWO MILES ABOVE THE CITY? YEAH, NO PROBLEM. DEFINITELY THAT'S FINE. SHEESH.
HAZMAT? YOU IN POSITION?
YEAH, YEAH. I'M AT THE RIVER NOW, SPIDER-WOMAN. I SEE 'EM. THOSE THINGS ARE HUGE!
FROM THE LOOKS OF IT, CAROL'S GOT THIS ABOUT WRAPPED UP, BUT STAND BY JUST IN CASE. WAIT--
--WHO'S THAT?

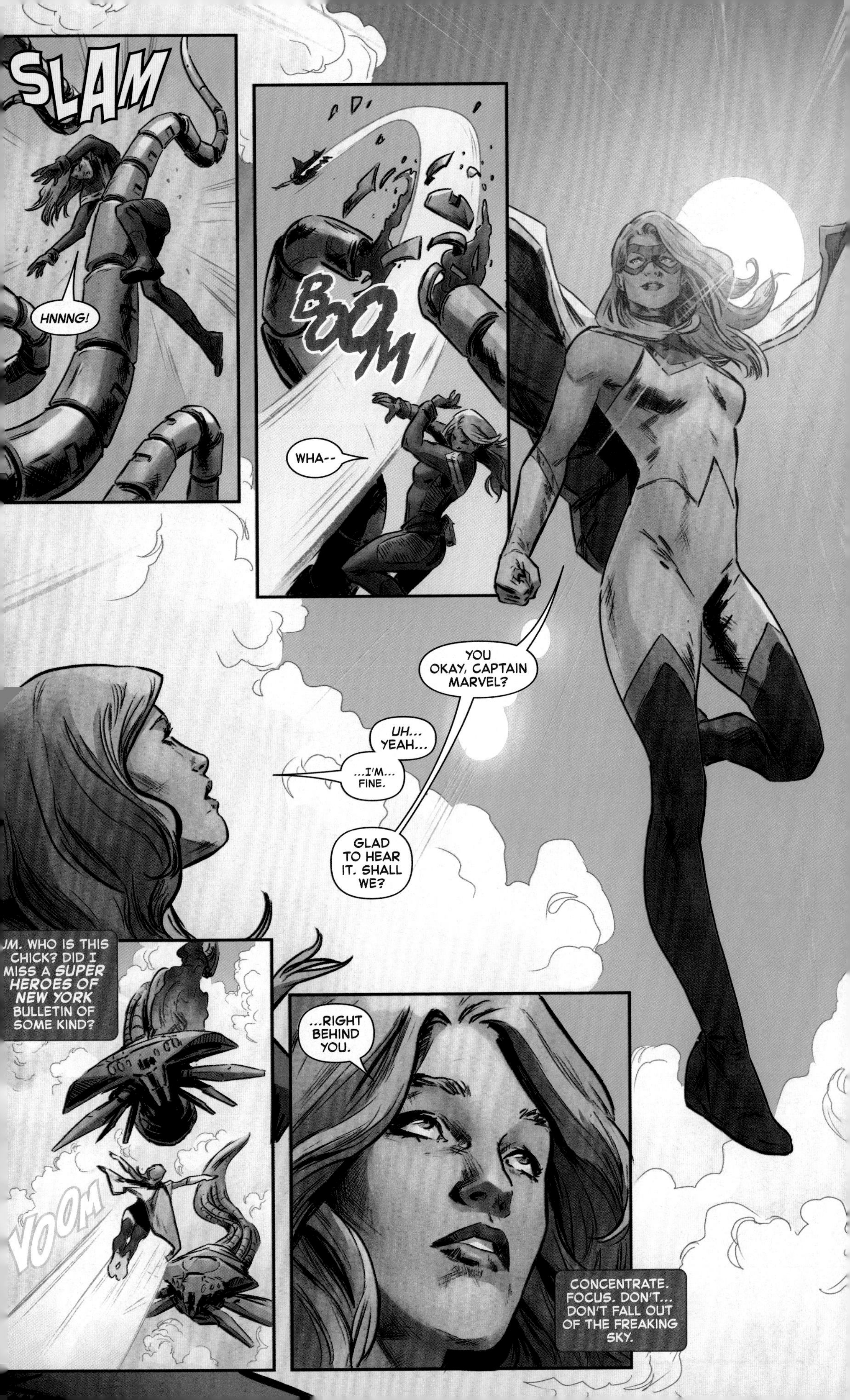
SLAM
HNNNG!
BOOM
WHA--
YOU OKAY, CAPTAIN MARVEL?
UH... YEAH...
...I'M... FINE.
GLAD TO HEAR IT. SHALL WE?
UM. WHO IS THIS CHICK? DID I MISS A SUPER HEROES OF NEW YORK BULLETIN OF SOME KIND?
VOOM
...RIGHT BEHIND YOU.
CONCENTRATE. FOCUS. DON'T... DON'T FALL OUT OF THE FREAKING SKY.

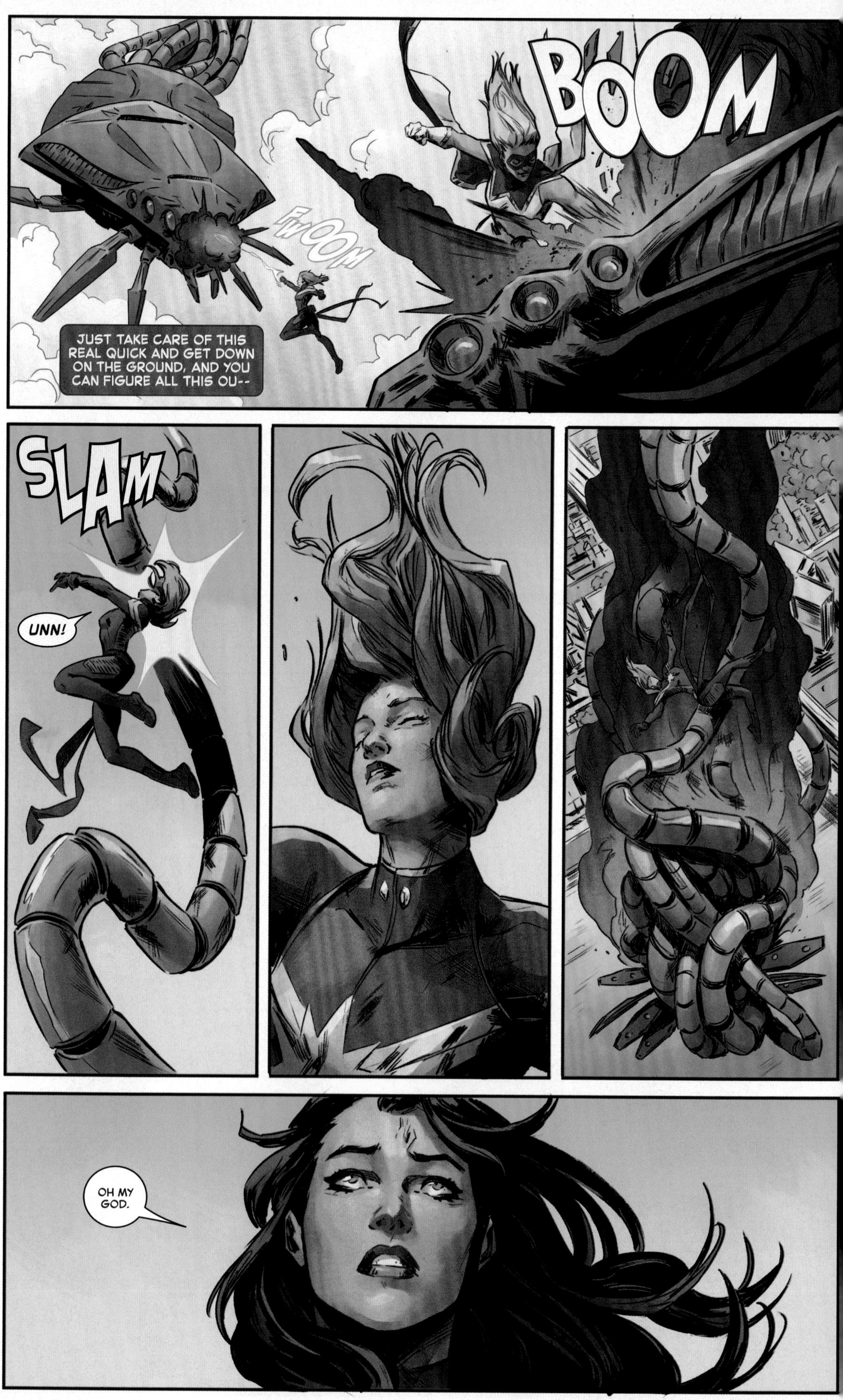
BOOM
FWOOM
JUST TAKE CARE OF THIS REAL QUICK AND GET DOWN ON THE GROUND, AND YOU CAN FIGURE ALL THIS OU--
SLAM
UNN!
OH MY GOD.

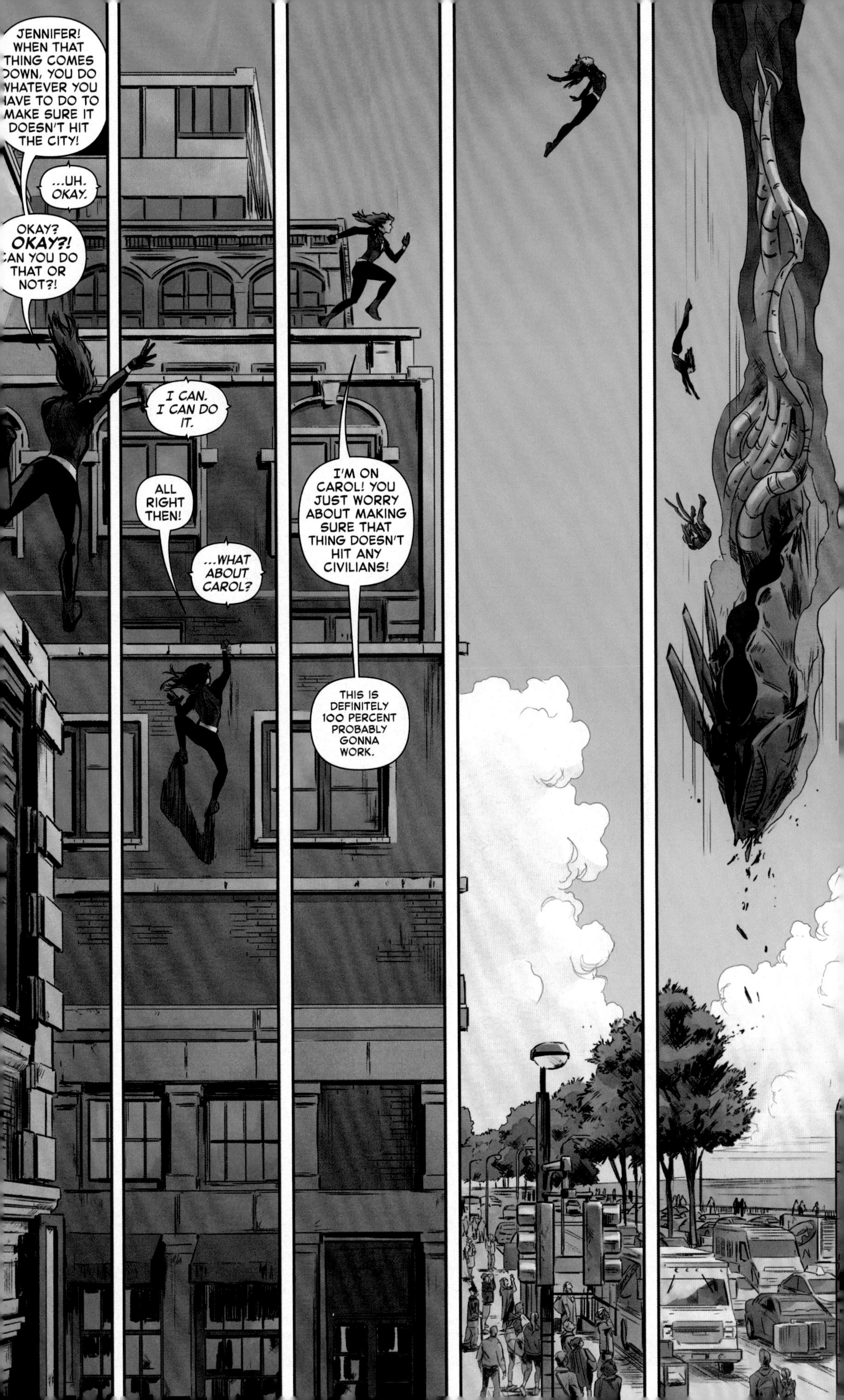
JENNIFER! WHEN THAT THING COMES DOWN, YOU DO WHATEVER YOU HAVE TO DO TO MAKE SURE IT DOESN'T HIT THE CITY!
...UH. OKAY.
OKAY? OKAY?! CAN YOU DO THAT OR NOT?!
I CAN. I CAN DO IT.
ALL RIGHT THEN!
...WHAT ABOUT CAROL?
I'M ON CAROL! YOU JUST WORRY ABOUT MAKING SURE THAT THING DOESN'T HIT ANY CIVILIANS!
THIS IS DEFINITELY 100 PERCENT PROBABLY GONNA WORK.

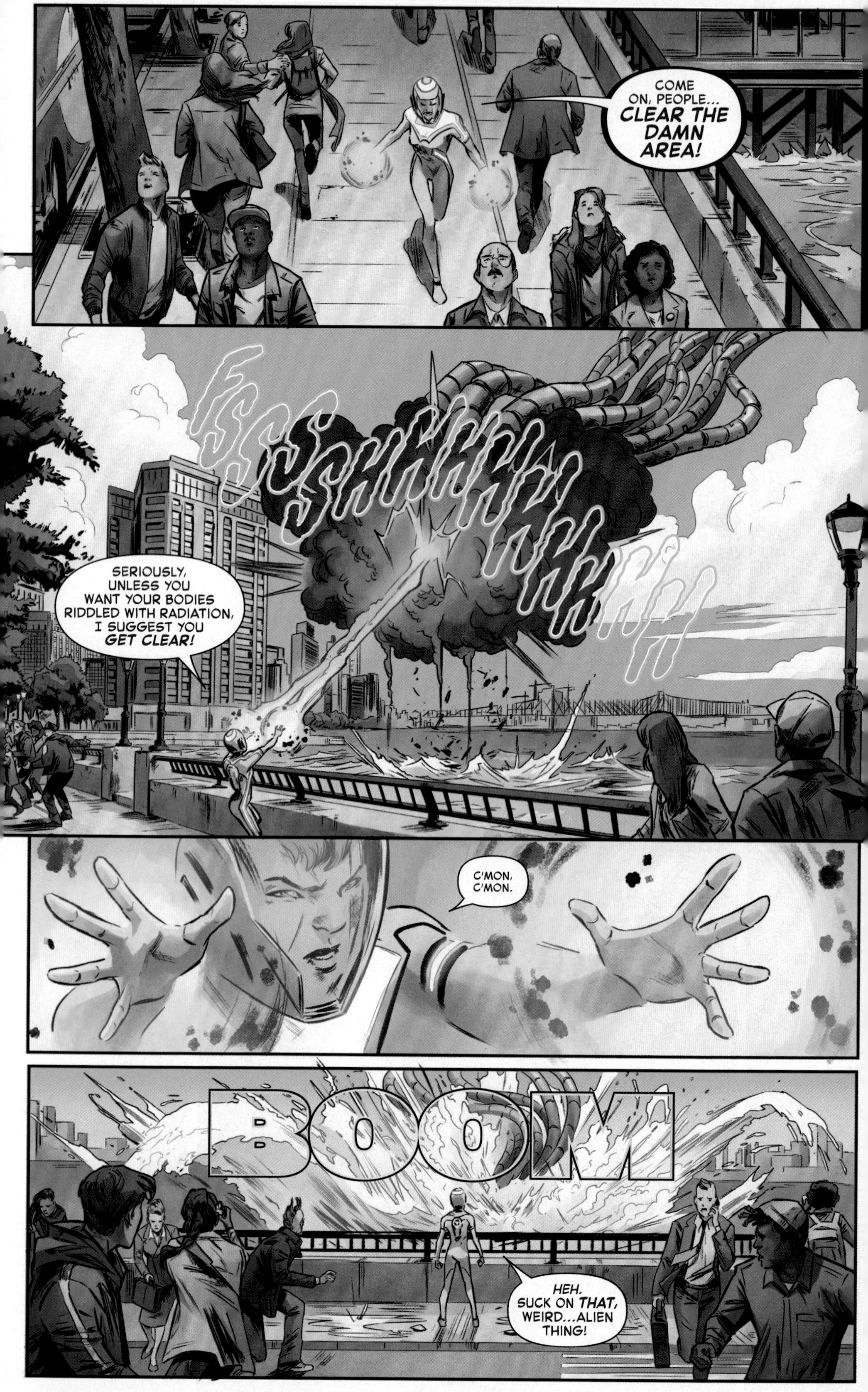
COME ON, PEOPLE... CLEAR THE DAMN AREA!
FSSSSHHHHHHHHH
SERIOUSLY, UNLESS YOU WANT YOUR BODIES RIDDLED WITH RADIATION, I SUGGEST YOU GET CLEAR!
C'MON, C'MON.
BOOM
HEH. SUCK ON THAT, WEIRD...ALIEN THING!

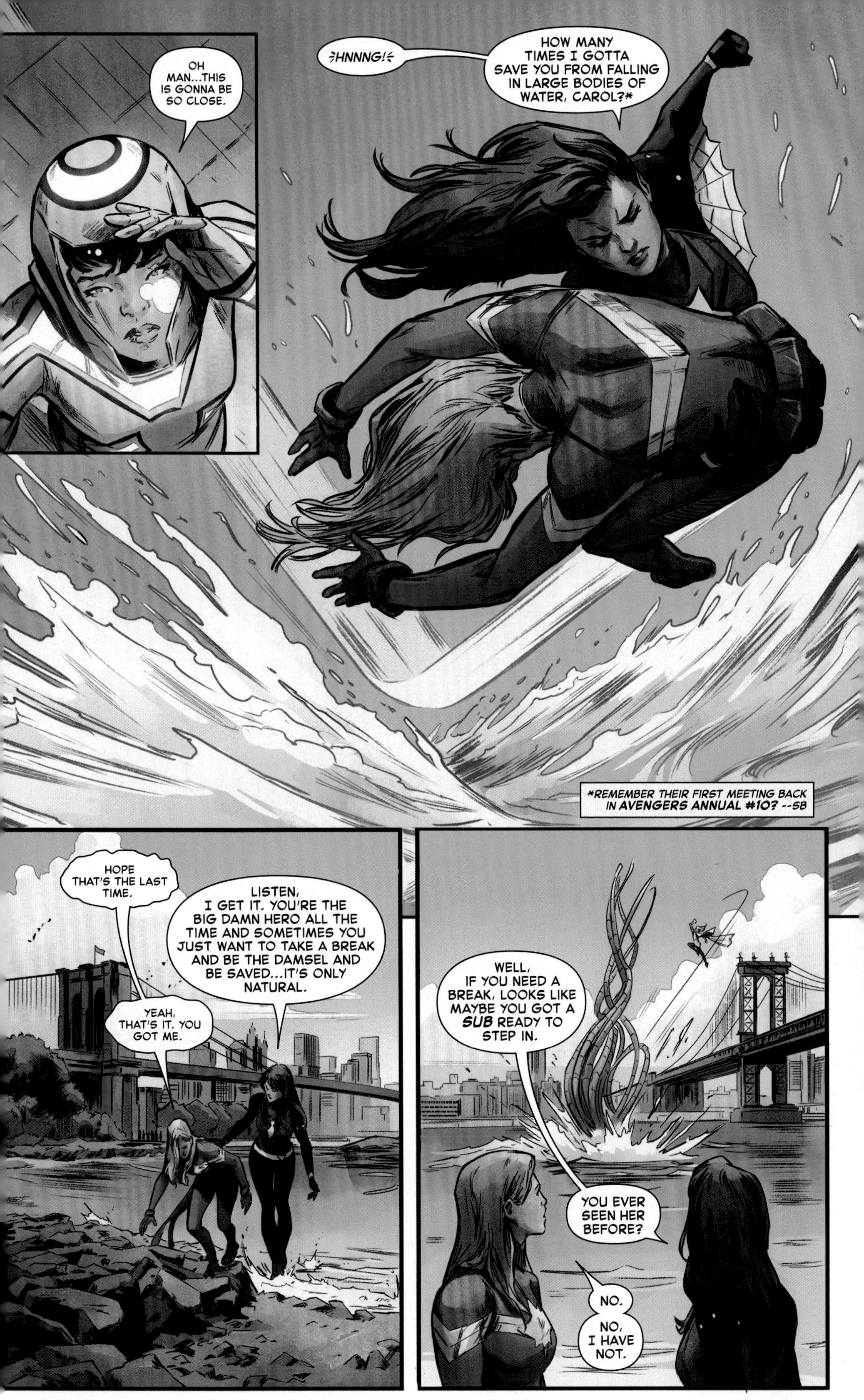
OH MAN...THIS IS GONNA BE SO CLOSE.
HNNNG!
HOW MANY TIMES I GOTTA SAVE YOU FROM FALLING IN LARGE BODIES OF WATER, CAROL?*
*REMEMBER THEIR FIRST MEETING BACK IN AVENGERS ANNUAL #10? --SB
HOPE THAT'S THE LAST TIME.
LISTEN, I GET IT. YOU'RE THE BIG DAMN HERO ALL THE TIME AND SOMETIMES YOU JUST WANT TO TAKE A BREAK AND BE THE DAMSEL AND BE SAVED...IT'S ONLY NATURAL.
YEAH, THAT'S IT. YOU GOT ME.
WELL, IF YOU NEED A BREAK, LOOKS LIKE MAYBE YOU GOT A SUB READY TO STEP IN.
YOU EVER SEEN HER BEFORE?
NO.
NO, I HAVE NOT.

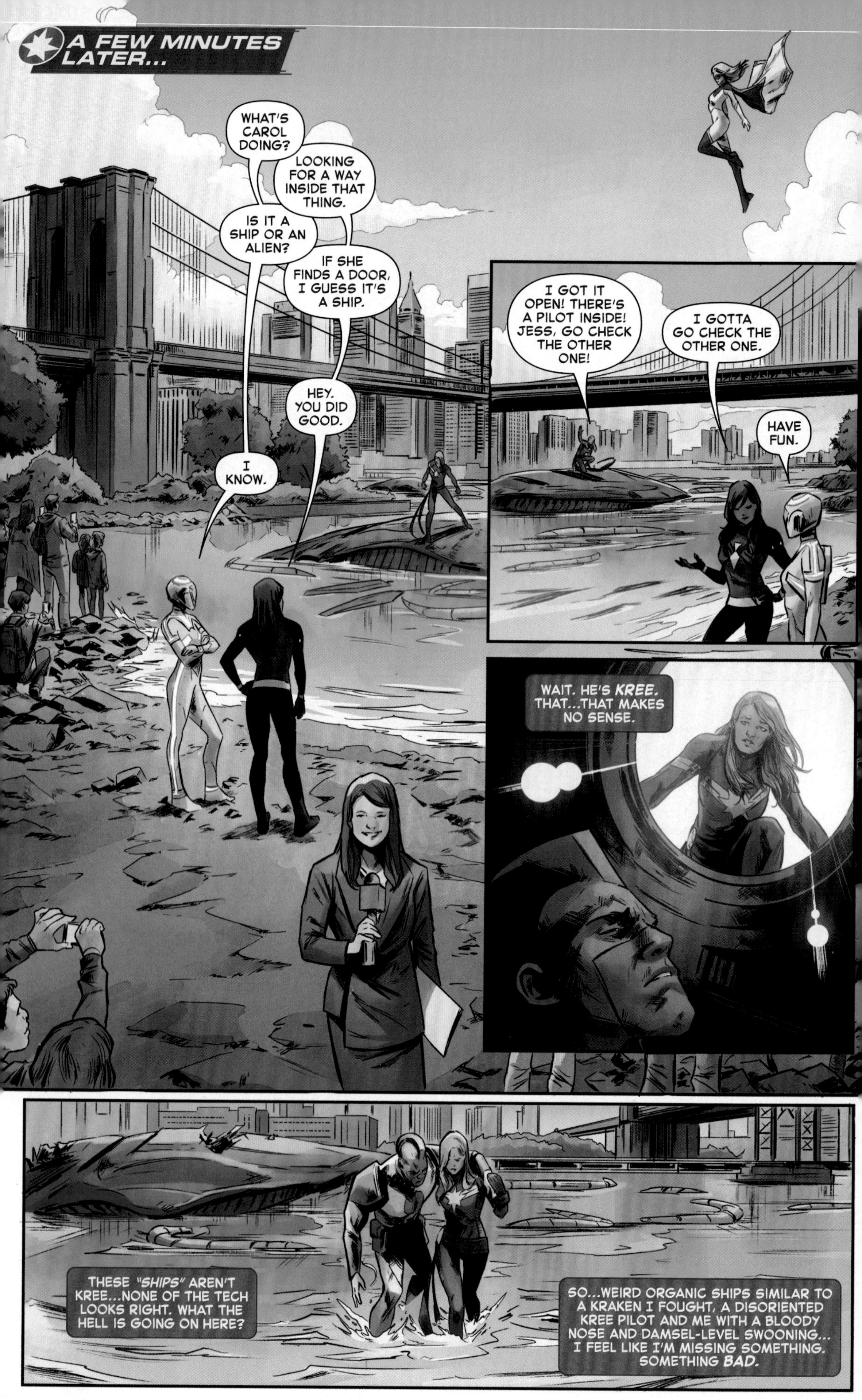

A FEW MINUTES LATER...
WHAT'S CAROL DOING?
LOOKING FOR A WAY INSIDE THAT THING.
IS IT A SHIP OR AN ALIEN?
IF SHE FINDS A DOOR, I GUESS IT'S A SHIP.
HEY. YOU DID GOOD.
I KNOW.
I GOT IT OPEN! THERE'S A PILOT INSIDE! JESS, GO CHECK THE OTHER ONE!
I GOTTA GO CHECK THE OTHER ONE.
HAVE FUN.
WAIT. HE'S KREE. THAT...THAT MAKES NO SENSE.
THESE "SHIPS" AREN'T KREE...NONE OF THE TECH LOOKS RIGHT. WHAT THE HELL IS GOING ON HERE?
SO...WEIRD ORGANIC SHIPS SIMILAR TO A KRAKEN I FOUGHT, A DISORIENTED KREE PILOT AND ME WITH A BLOODY NOSE AND DAMSEL-LEVEL SWOONING... I FEEL LIKE I'M MISSING SOMETHING. SOMETHING BAD.

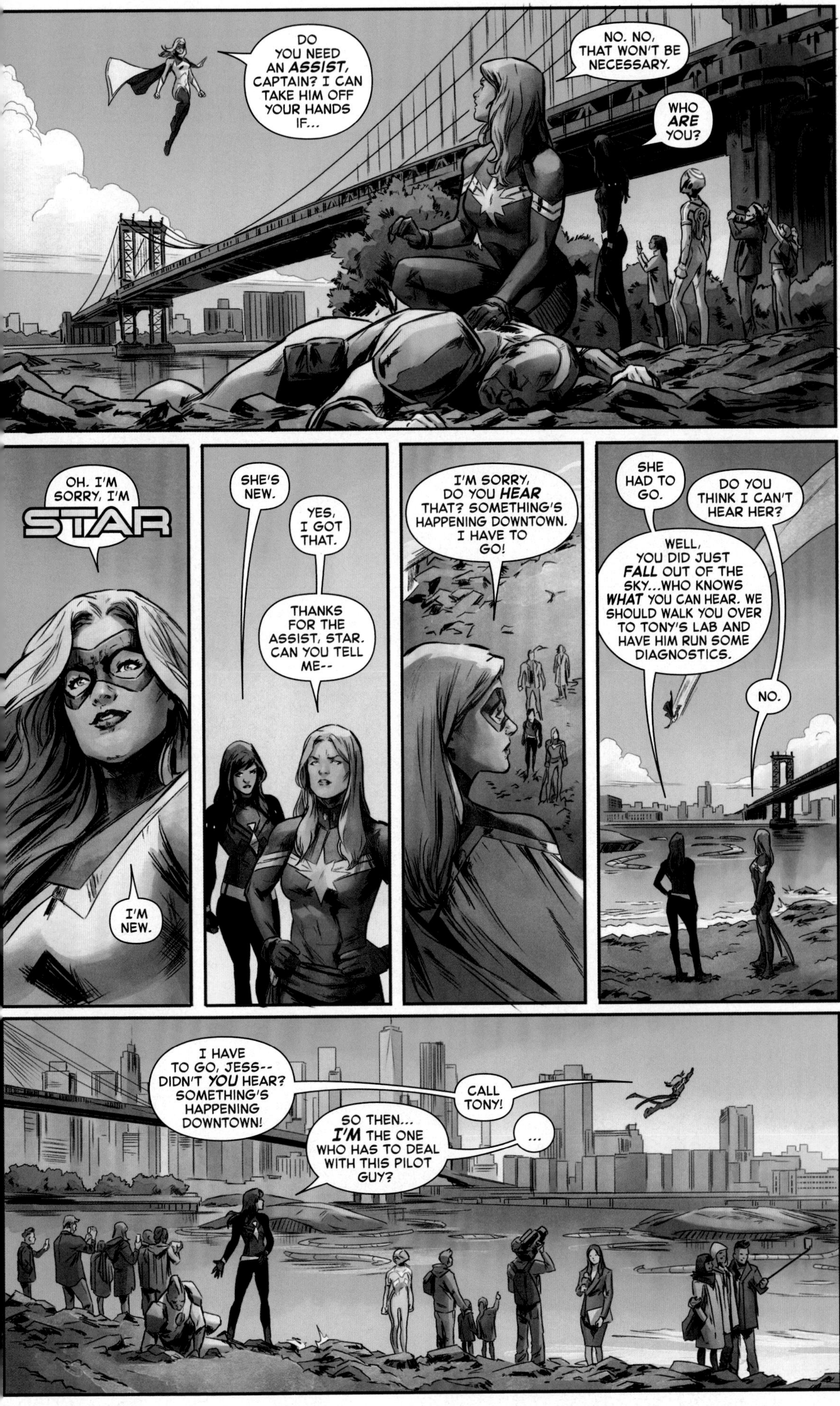
DO YOU NEED AN ASSIST, CAPTAIN? I CAN TAKE HIM OFF YOUR HANDS IF...
NO. NO, THAT WON'T BE NECESSARY.
WHO ARE YOU?
OH. I'M SORRY, I'M
STAR
I'M NEW.
SHE'S NEW.
YES, I GOT THAT.
THANKS FOR THE ASSIST, STAR. CAN YOU TELL ME--
I'M SORRY, DO YOU HEAR THAT? SOMETHING'S HAPPENING DOWNTOWN. I HAVE TO GO!
SHE HAD TO GO.
DO YOU THINK I CAN'T HEAR HER?
WELL, YOU DID JUST FALL OUT OF THE SKY...WHO KNOWS WHAT YOU CAN HEAR. WE SHOULD WALK YOU OVER TO TONY'S LAB AND HAVE HIM RUN SOME DIAGNOSTICS.
NO.
I HAVE TO GO, JESS-- DIDN'T YOU HEAR? SOMETHING'S HAPPENING DOWNTOWN!
CALL TONY!
SO THEN... I'M THE ONE WHO HAS TO DEAL WITH THIS PILOT GUY?
...

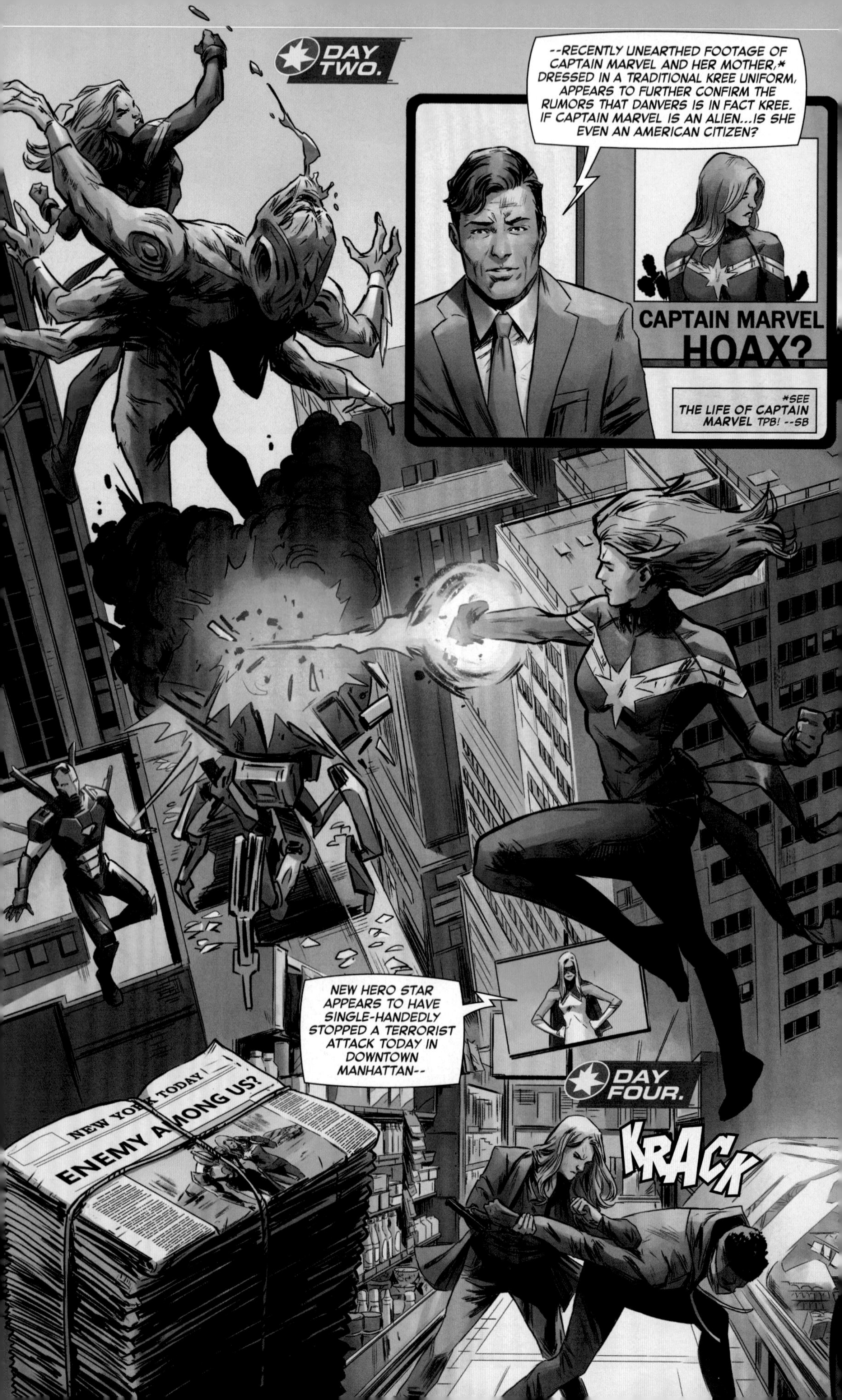

DAY TWO.
--RECENTLY UNEARTHED FOOTAGE OF CAPTAIN MARVEL AND HER MOTHER,* DRESSED IN A TRADITIONAL KREE UNIFORM, APPEARS TO FURTHER CONFIRM THE RUMORS THAT DANVERS IS IN FACT KREE. IF CAPTAIN MARVEL IS AN ALIEN...IS SHE EVEN AN AMERICAN CITIZEN?
CAPTAIN MARVEL HOAX?
*SEE THE LIFE OF CAPTAIN MARVEL TPB! --SB
NEW HERO STAR APPEARS TO HAVE SINGLE-HANDEDLY STOPPED A TERRORIST ATTACK TODAY IN DOWNTOWN MANHATTAN--
NEW YORK TODAY
ENEMY AMONG US?
DAY FOUR.
KRACK

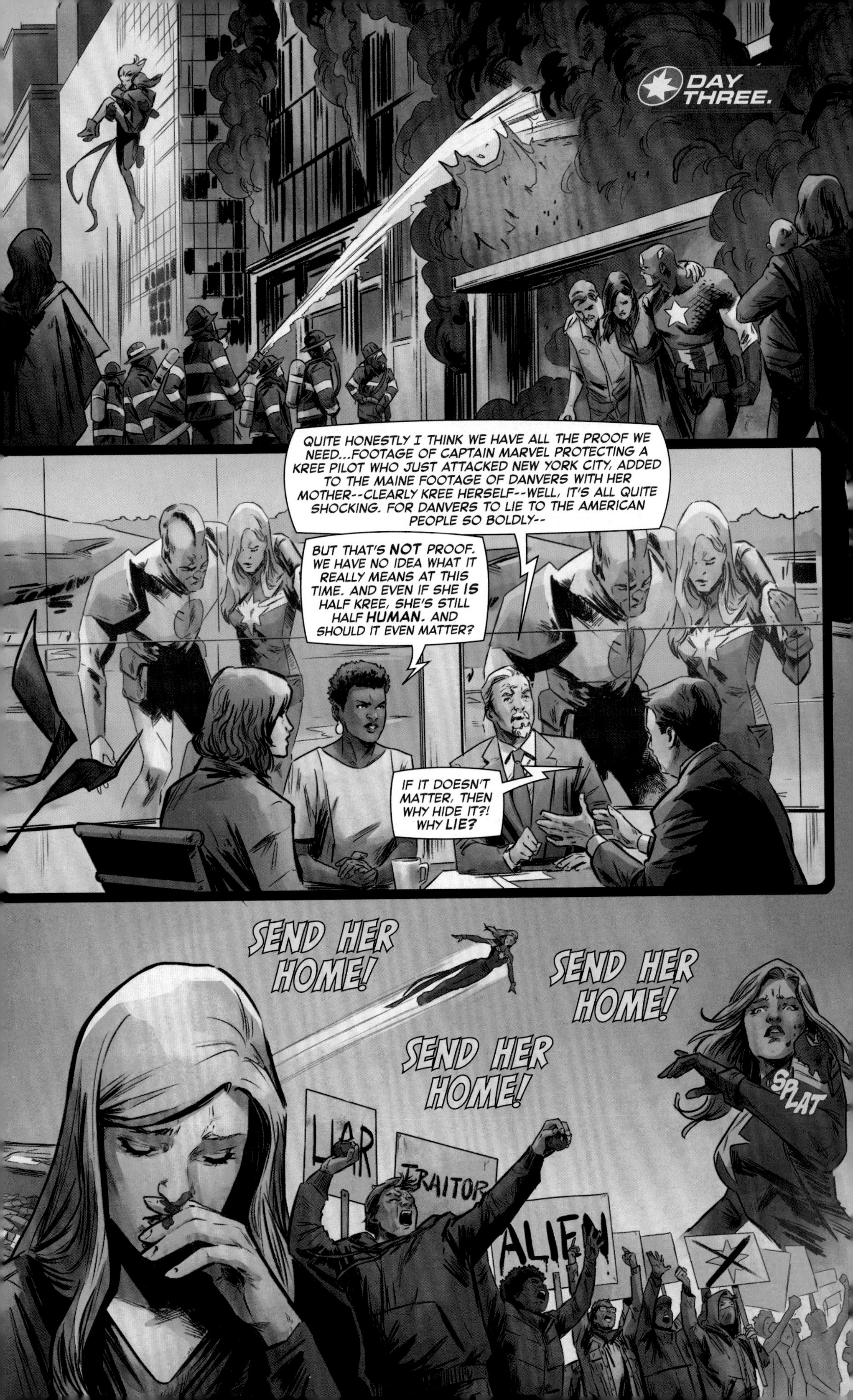
DAY THREE.
QUITE HONESTLY I THINK WE HAVE ALL THE PROOF WE NEED...FOOTAGE OF CAPTAIN MARVEL PROTECTING A KREE PILOT WHO JUST ATTACKED NEW YORK CITY, ADDED TO THE MAINE FOOTAGE OF DANVERS WITH HER MOTHER--CLEARLY KREE HERSELF--WELL, IT'S ALL QUITE SHOCKING. FOR DANVERS TO LIE TO THE AMERICAN PEOPLE SO BOLDLY--
BUT THAT'S **NOT** PROOF. WE HAVE NO IDEA WHAT IT REALLY MEANS AT THIS TIME. AND EVEN IF SHE **IS** HALF KREE, SHE'S STILL HALF **HUMAN.** AND SHOULD IT EVEN MATTER?
IF IT DOESN'T MATTER, THEN WHY HIDE IT?! WHY **LIE?**
SEND HER HOME!
SEND HER HOME!
SEND HER HOME!
SPLAT
LIAR
TRAITOR
ALIEN

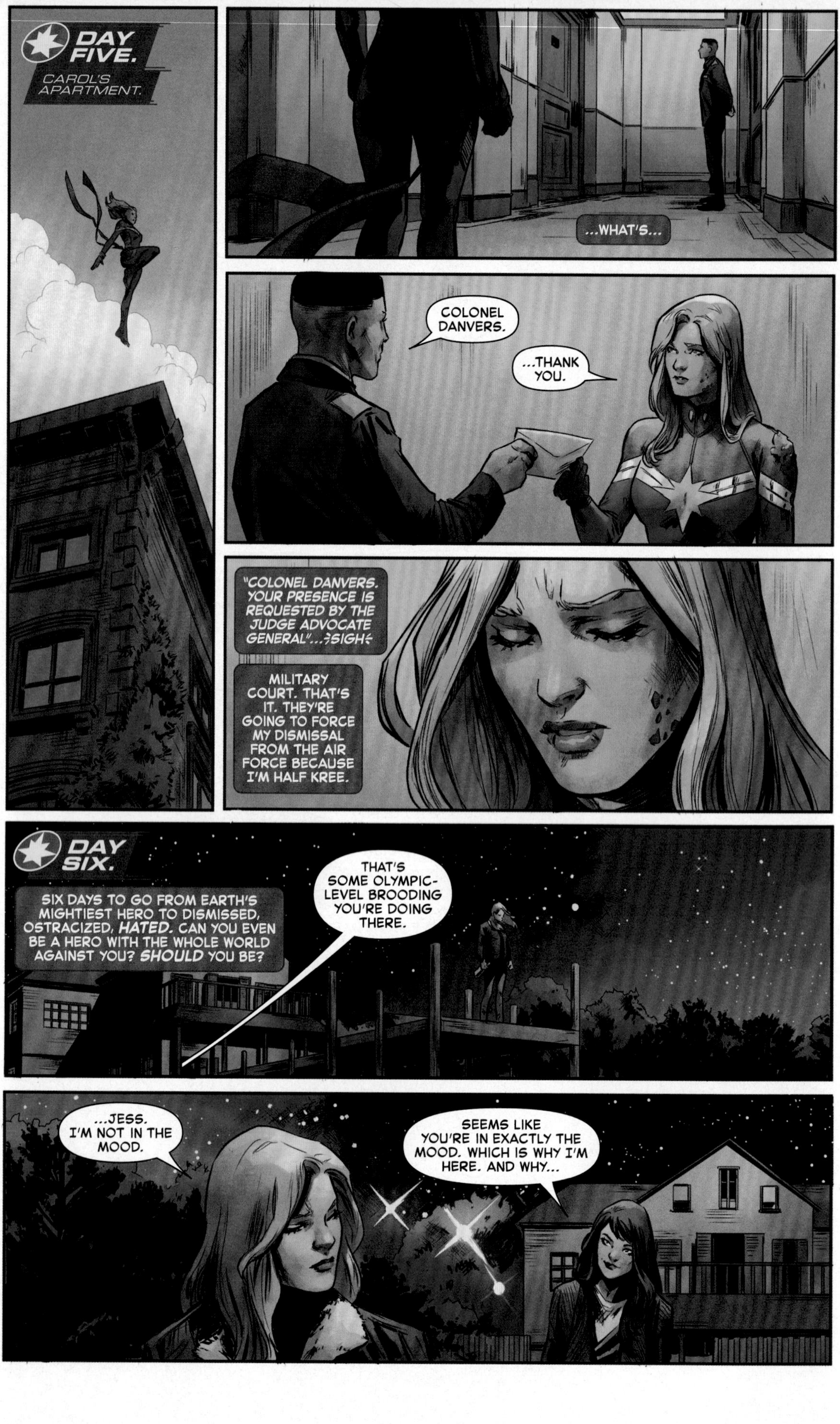
DAY FIVE.
CAROL'S APARTMENT.
...WHAT'S...
COLONEL DANVERS.
...THANK YOU.
"COLONEL DANVERS. YOUR PRESENCE IS REQUESTED BY THE JUDGE ADVOCATE GENERAL"...⸮SIGH⸮
MILITARY COURT. THAT'S IT. THEY'RE GOING TO FORCE MY DISMISSAL FROM THE AIR FORCE BECAUSE I'M HALF KREE.
DAY SIX.
SIX DAYS TO GO FROM EARTH'S MIGHTIEST HERO TO DISMISSED, OSTRACIZED, HATED. CAN YOU EVEN BE A HERO WITH THE WHOLE WORLD AGAINST YOU? SHOULD YOU BE?
THAT'S SOME OLYMPIC-LEVEL BROODING YOU'RE DOING THERE.
...JESS. I'M NOT IN THE MOOD.
SEEMS LIKE YOU'RE IN EXACTLY THE MOOD. WHICH IS WHY I'M HERE. AND WHY...

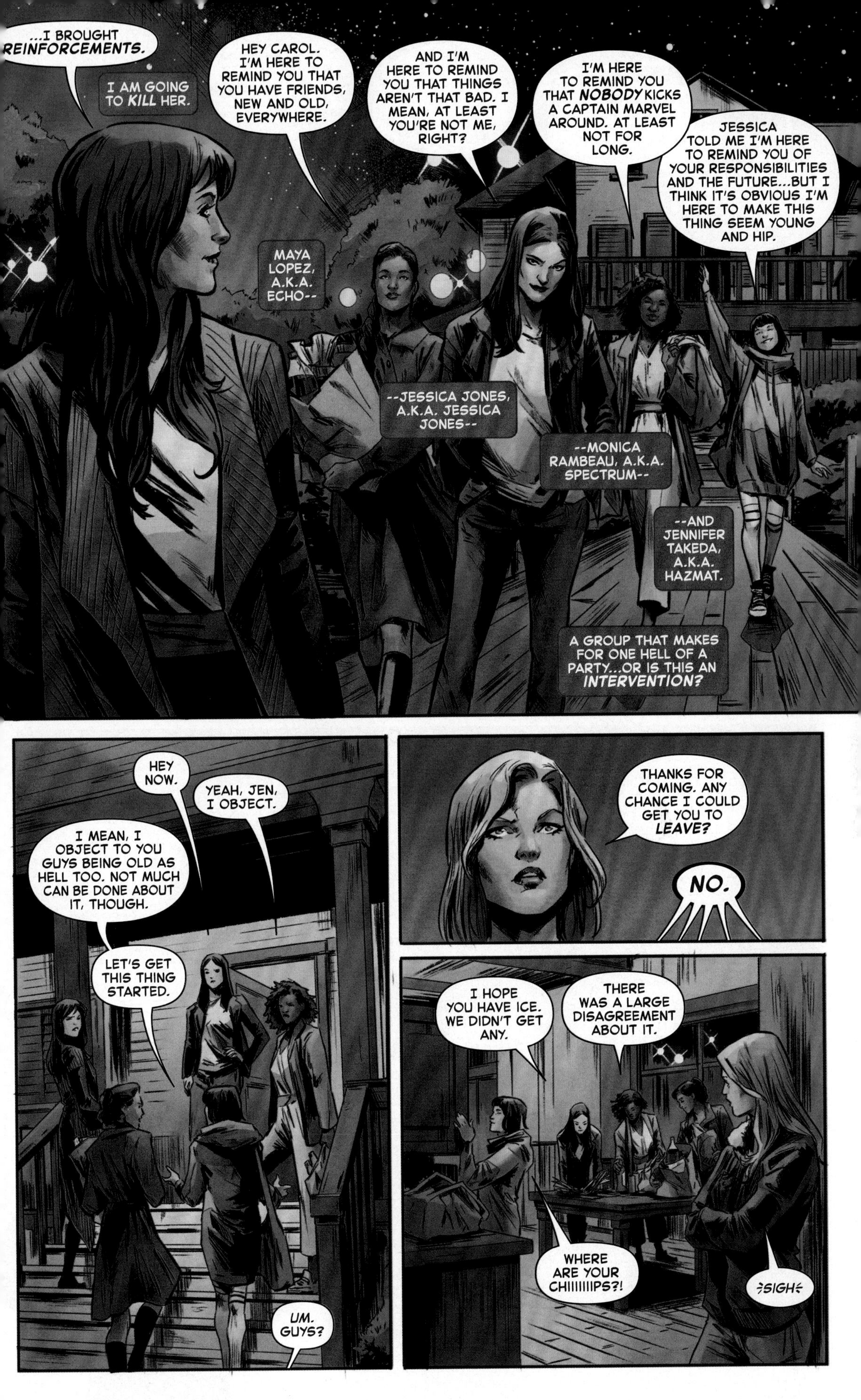
...I BROUGHT REINFORCEMENTS.
I AM GOING TO KILL HER.
HEY CAROL. I'M HERE TO REMIND YOU THAT YOU HAVE FRIENDS, NEW AND OLD, EVERYWHERE.
AND I'M HERE TO REMIND YOU THAT THINGS AREN'T THAT BAD. I MEAN, AT LEAST YOU'RE NOT ME, RIGHT?
I'M HERE TO REMIND YOU THAT NOBODY KICKS A CAPTAIN MARVEL AROUND. AT LEAST NOT FOR LONG.
JESSICA TOLD ME I'M HERE TO REMIND YOU OF YOUR RESPONSIBILITIES AND THE FUTURE...BUT I THINK IT'S OBVIOUS I'M HERE TO MAKE THIS THING SEEM YOUNG AND HIP.
MAYA LOPEZ, A.K.A. ECHO--
--JESSICA JONES, A.K.A. JESSICA JONES--
--MONICA RAMBEAU, A.K.A. SPECTRUM--
--AND JENNIFER TAKEDA, A.K.A. HAZMAT.
A GROUP THAT MAKES FOR ONE HELL OF A PARTY...OR IS THIS AN INTERVENTION?
HEY NOW.
YEAH, JEN, I OBJECT.
I MEAN, I OBJECT TO YOU GUYS BEING OLD AS HELL TOO. NOT MUCH CAN BE DONE ABOUT IT, THOUGH.
LET'S GET THIS THING STARTED.
UM. GUYS?
THANKS FOR COMING. ANY CHANCE I COULD GET YOU TO LEAVE?
NO.
I HOPE YOU HAVE ICE. WE DIDN'T GET ANY.
THERE WAS A LARGE DISAGREEMENT ABOUT IT.
WHERE ARE YOUR CHIIIIIIPS?!
SIGH

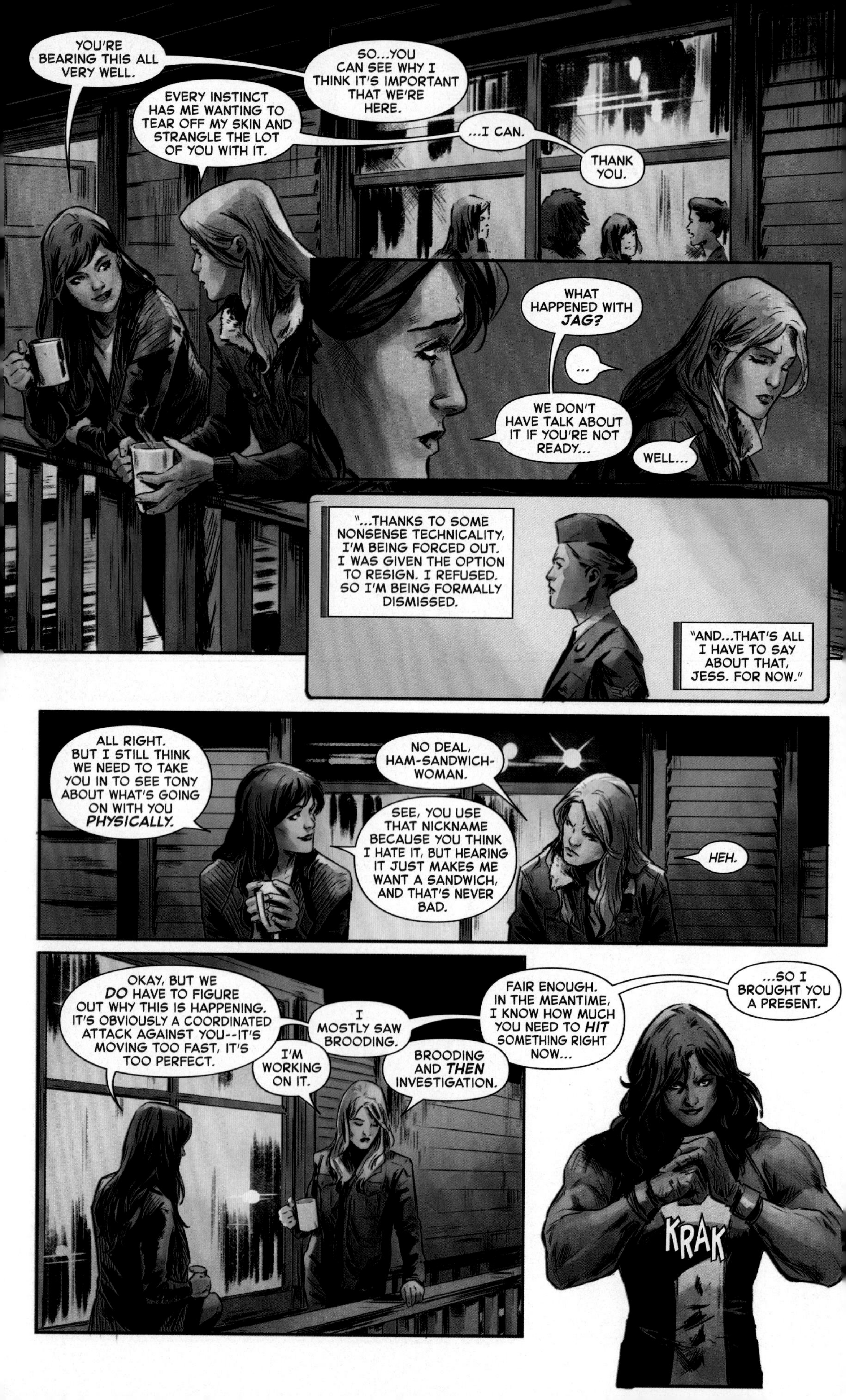
YOU'RE BEARING THIS ALL VERY WELL.
SO...YOU CAN SEE WHY I THINK IT'S IMPORTANT THAT WE'RE HERE.
EVERY INSTINCT HAS ME WANTING TO TEAR OFF MY SKIN AND STRANGLE THE LOT OF YOU WITH IT.
...I CAN.
THANK YOU.
WHAT HAPPENED WITH JAG?
...
WE DON'T HAVE TALK ABOUT IT IF YOU'RE NOT READY...
WELL...
"...THANKS TO SOME NONSENSE TECHNICALITY, I'M BEING FORCED OUT. I WAS GIVEN THE OPTION TO RESIGN. I REFUSED. SO I'M BEING FORMALLY DISMISSED.
"AND...THAT'S ALL I HAVE TO SAY ABOUT THAT, JESS. FOR NOW."
ALL RIGHT. BUT I STILL THINK WE NEED TO TAKE YOU IN TO SEE TONY ABOUT WHAT'S GOING ON WITH YOU PHYSICALLY.
NO DEAL, HAM-SANDWICH-WOMAN.
SEE, YOU USE THAT NICKNAME BECAUSE YOU THINK I HATE IT, BUT HEARING IT JUST MAKES ME WANT A SANDWICH, AND THAT'S NEVER BAD.
HEH.
OKAY, BUT WE DO HAVE TO FIGURE OUT WHY THIS IS HAPPENING. IT'S OBVIOUSLY A COORDINATED ATTACK AGAINST YOU--IT'S MOVING TOO FAST, IT'S TOO PERFECT.
I'M WORKING ON IT.
I MOSTLY SAW BROODING.
BROODING AND THEN INVESTIGATION.
FAIR ENOUGH. IN THE MEANTIME, I KNOW HOW MUCH YOU NEED TO HIT SOMETHING RIGHT NOW...
...SO I BROUGHT YOU A PRESENT.
KRAK

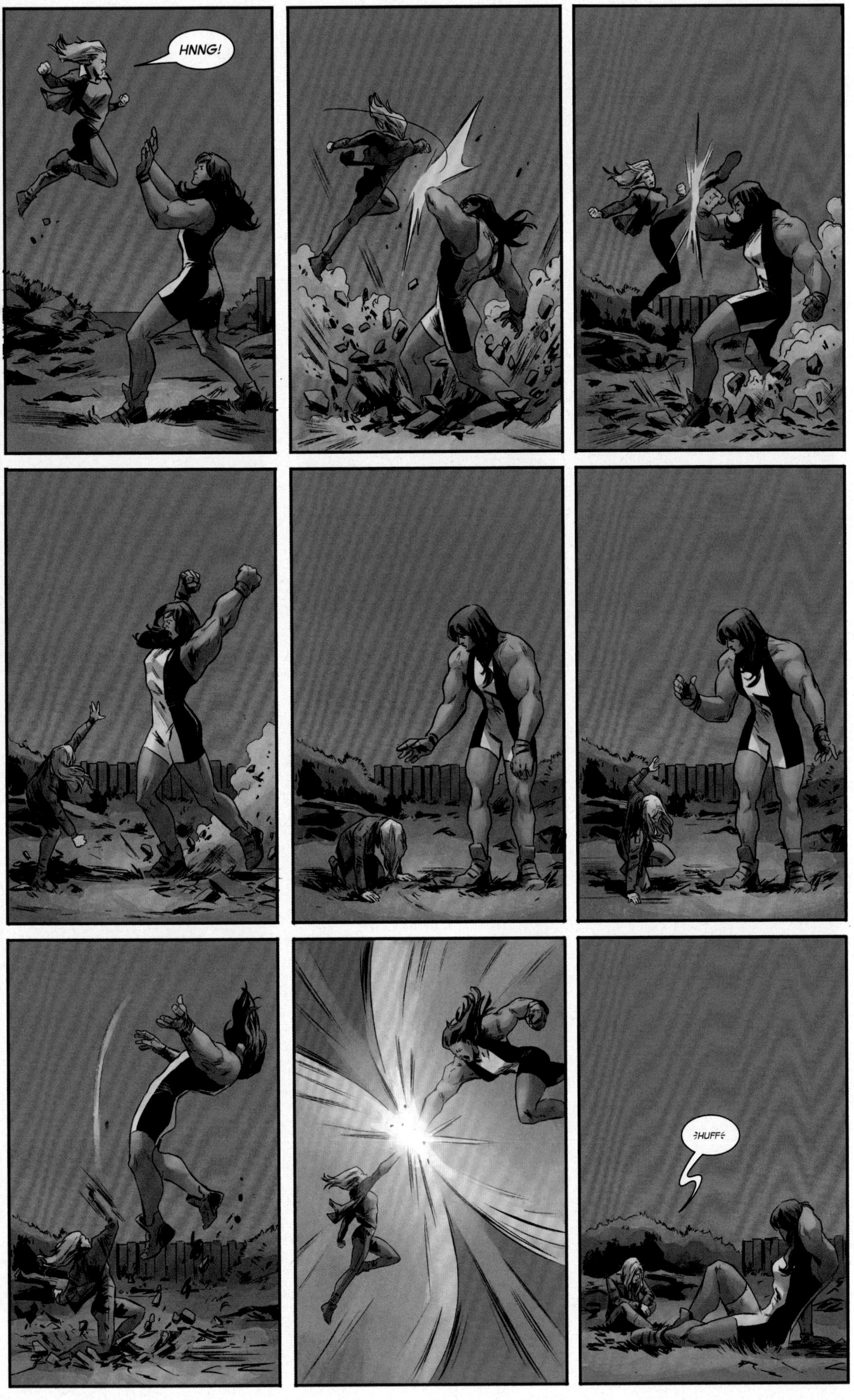
HNNG!
HUFF

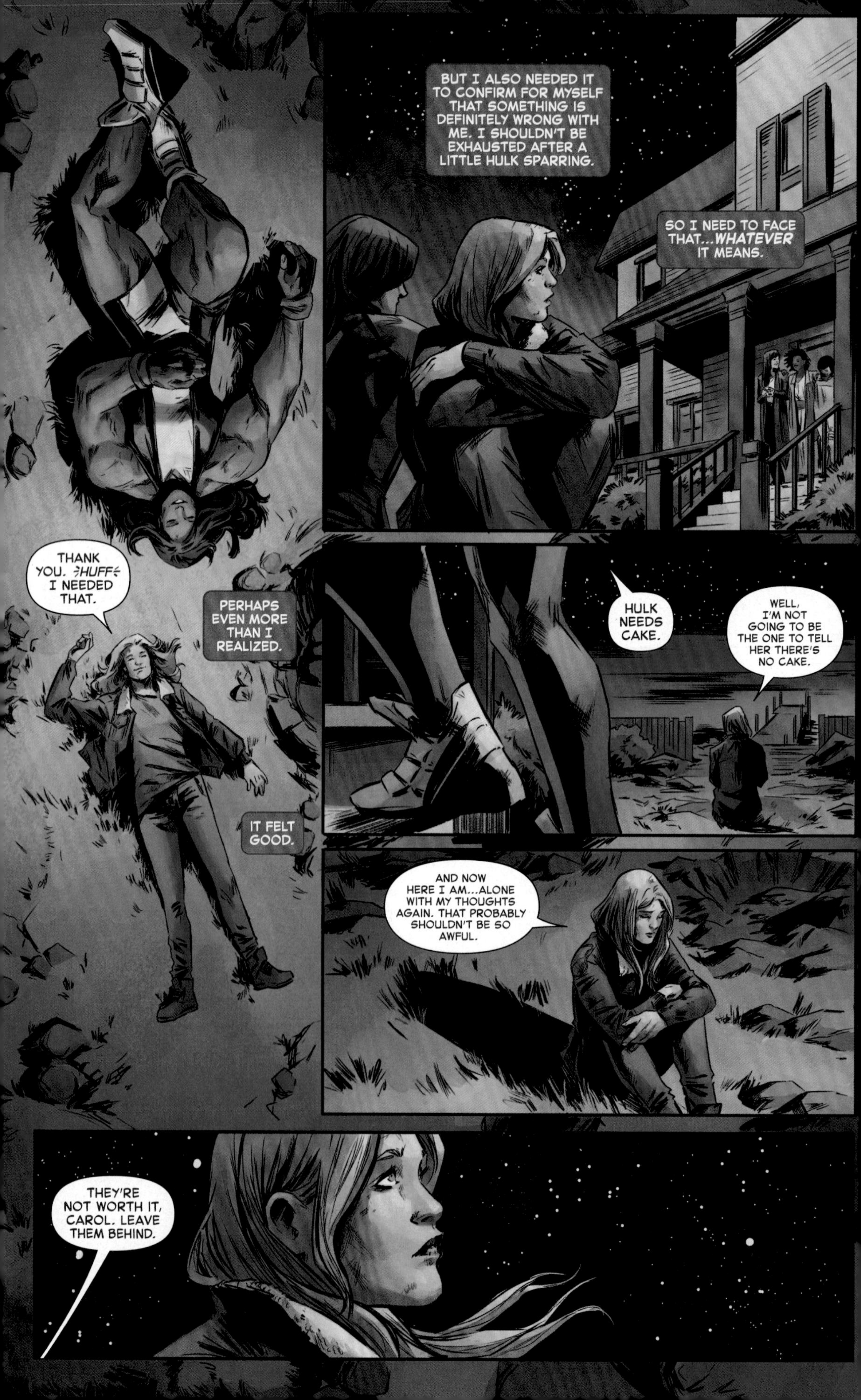
BUT I ALSO NEEDED IT TO CONFIRM FOR MYSELF THAT SOMETHING IS DEFINITELY WRONG WITH ME. I SHOULDN'T BE EXHAUSTED AFTER A LITTLE HULK SPARRING.
SO I NEED TO FACE THAT...*WHATEVER* IT MEANS.
THANK YOU. *HUFF* I NEEDED THAT.
PERHAPS EVEN MORE THAN I REALIZED.
IT FELT GOOD.
HULK NEEDS CAKE.
WELL, I'M NOT GOING TO BE THE ONE TO TELL HER THERE'S NO CAKE.
AND NOW HERE I AM...ALONE WITH MY THOUGHTS AGAIN. THAT PROBABLY SHOULDN'T BE SO AWFUL.
THEY'RE NOT WORTH IT, CAROL. LEAVE THEM BEHIND.

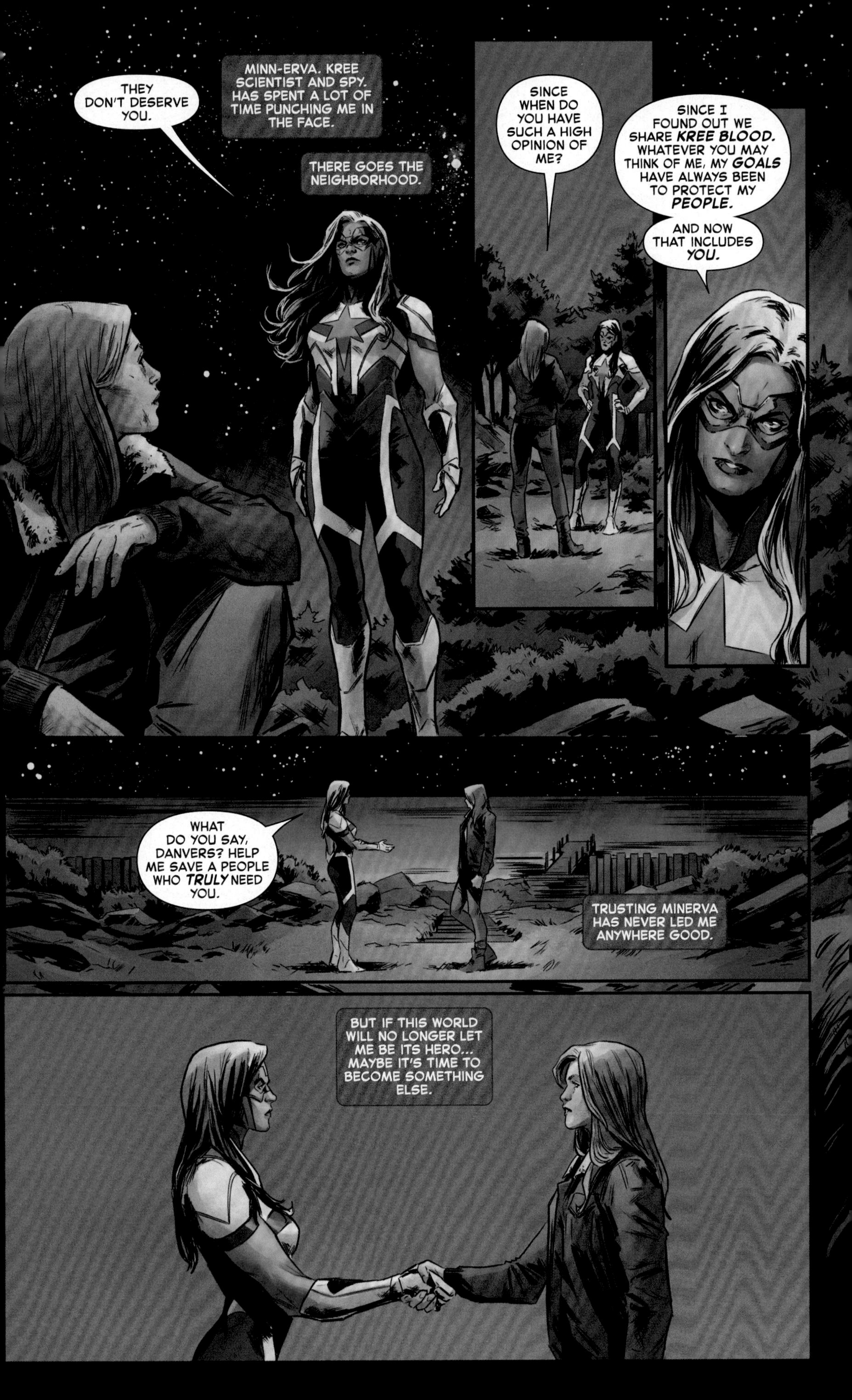
THEY DON'T DESERVE YOU.
MINN-ERVA. KREE SCIENTIST AND SPY. HAS SPENT A LOT OF TIME PUNCHING ME IN THE FACE.
THERE GOES THE NEIGHBORHOOD.
SINCE WHEN DO YOU HAVE SUCH A HIGH OPINION OF ME?
SINCE I FOUND OUT WE SHARE KREE BLOOD. WHATEVER YOU MAY THINK OF ME, MY GOALS HAVE ALWAYS BEEN TO PROTECT MY PEOPLE.
AND NOW THAT INCLUDES YOU.
WHAT DO YOU SAY, DANVERS? HELP ME SAVE A PEOPLE WHO TRULY NEED YOU.
TRUSTING MINERVA HAS NEVER LED ME ANYWHERE GOOD.
BUT IF THIS WORLD WILL NO LONGER LET ME BE ITS HERO... MAYBE IT'S TIME TO BECOME SOMETHING ELSE.

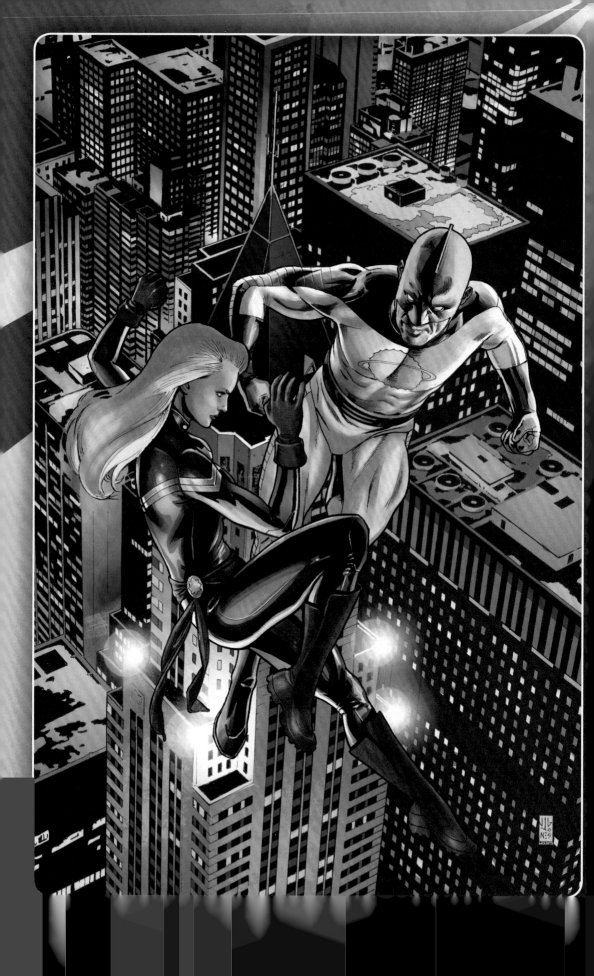

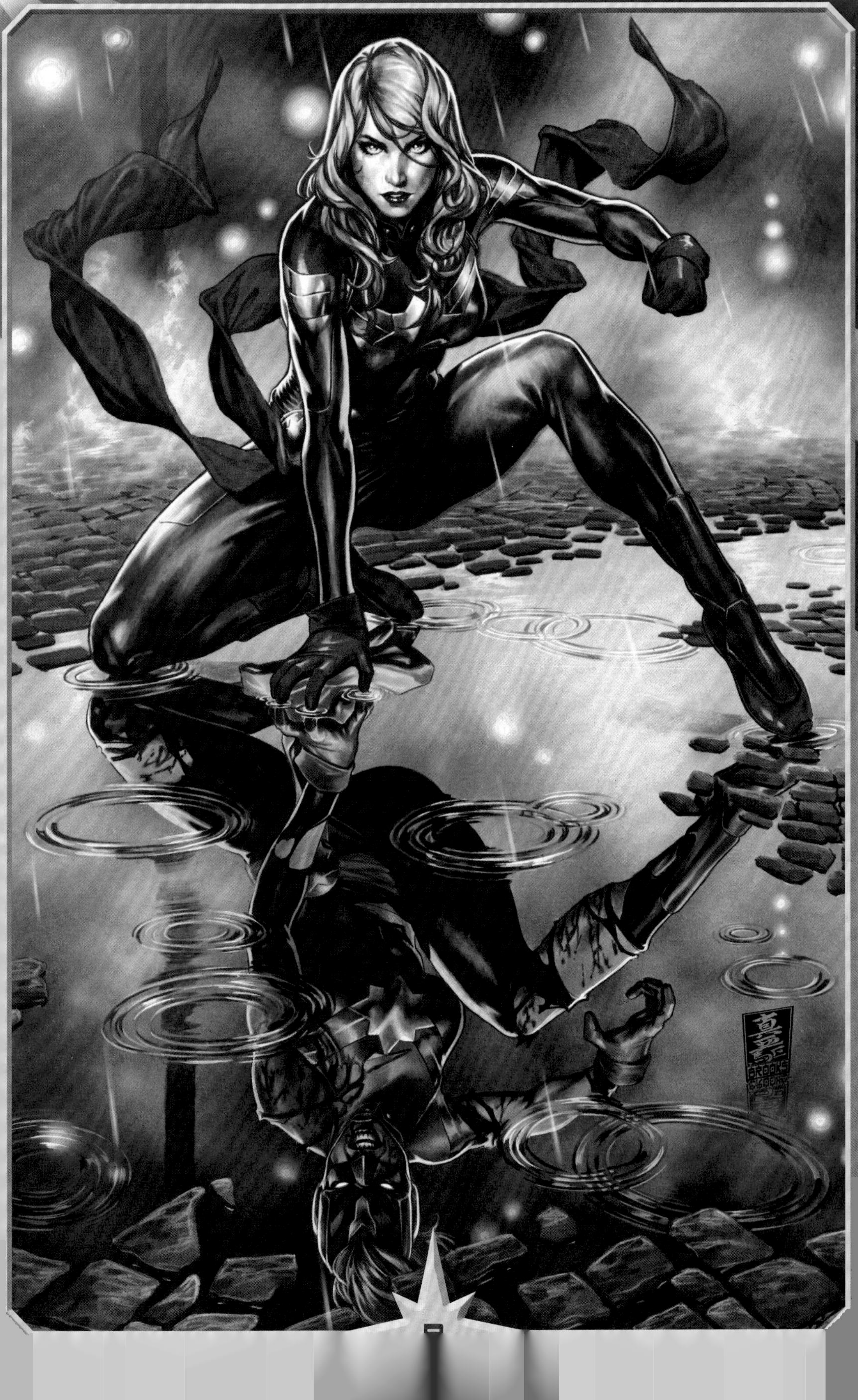

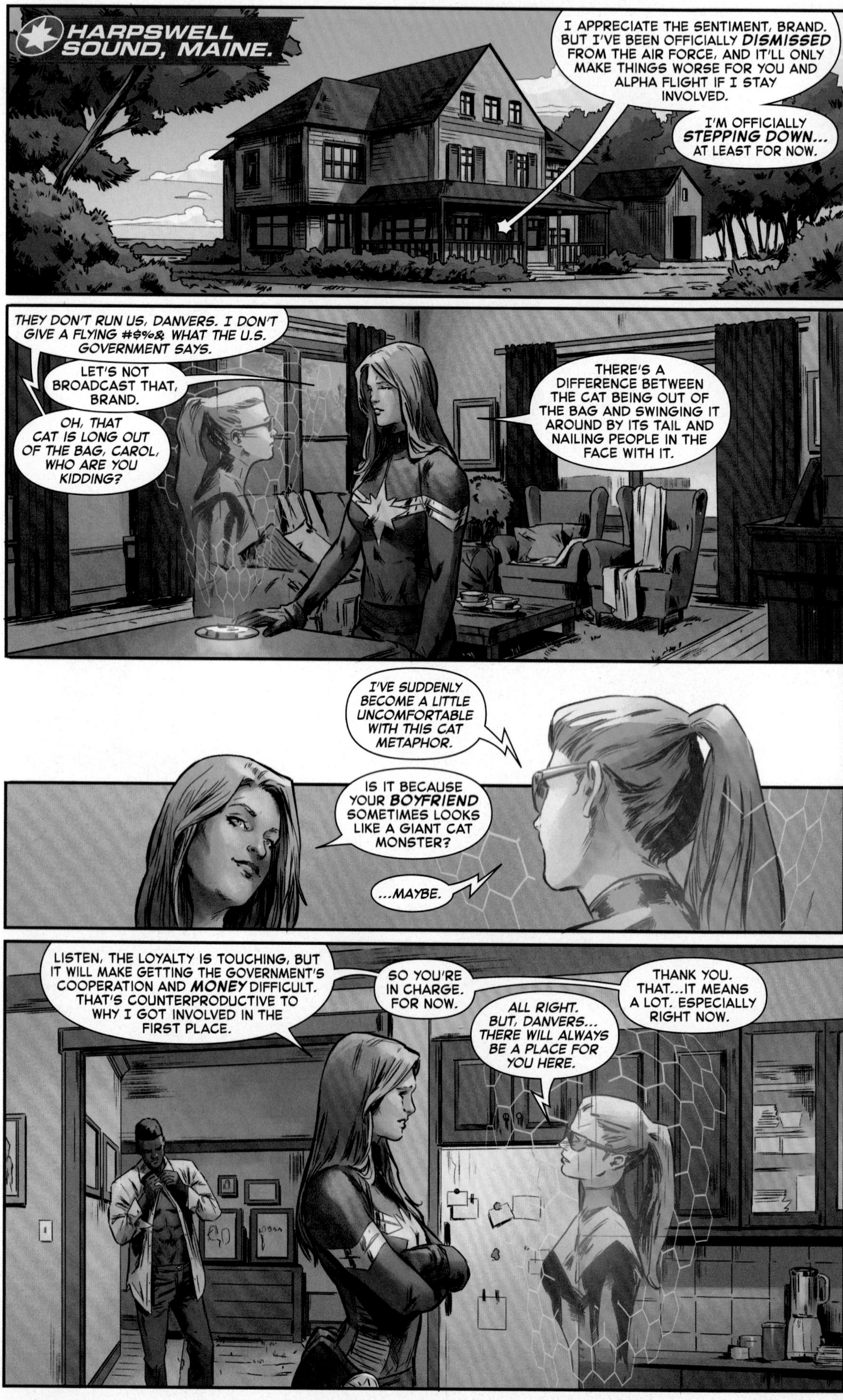
HARPSWELL SOUND, MAINE.
I APPRECIATE THE SENTIMENT, BRAND. BUT I'VE BEEN OFFICIALLY DISMISSED FROM THE AIR FORCE, AND IT'LL ONLY MAKE THINGS WORSE FOR YOU AND ALPHA FLIGHT IF I STAY INVOLVED.
I'M OFFICIALLY STEPPING DOWN... AT LEAST FOR NOW.
THEY DON'T RUN US, DANVERS. I DON'T GIVE A FLYING #$%& WHAT THE U.S. GOVERNMENT SAYS.
LET'S NOT BROADCAST THAT, BRAND.
OH, THAT CAT IS LONG OUT OF THE BAG, CAROL, WHO ARE YOU KIDDING?
THERE'S A DIFFERENCE BETWEEN THE CAT BEING OUT OF THE BAG AND SWINGING IT AROUND BY ITS TAIL AND NAILING PEOPLE IN THE FACE WITH IT.
I'VE SUDDENLY BECOME A LITTLE UNCOMFORTABLE WITH THIS CAT METAPHOR.
IS IT BECAUSE YOUR BOYFRIEND SOMETIMES LOOKS LIKE A GIANT CAT MONSTER?
...MAYBE.
LISTEN, THE LOYALTY IS TOUCHING, BUT IT WILL MAKE GETTING THE GOVERNMENT'S COOPERATION AND MONEY DIFFICULT. THAT'S COUNTERPRODUCTIVE TO WHY I GOT INVOLVED IN THE FIRST PLACE.
SO YOU'RE IN CHARGE. FOR NOW.
ALL RIGHT. BUT, DANVERS... THERE WILL ALWAYS BE A PLACE FOR YOU HERE.
THANK YOU. THAT...IT MEANS A LOT. ESPECIALLY RIGHT NOW.

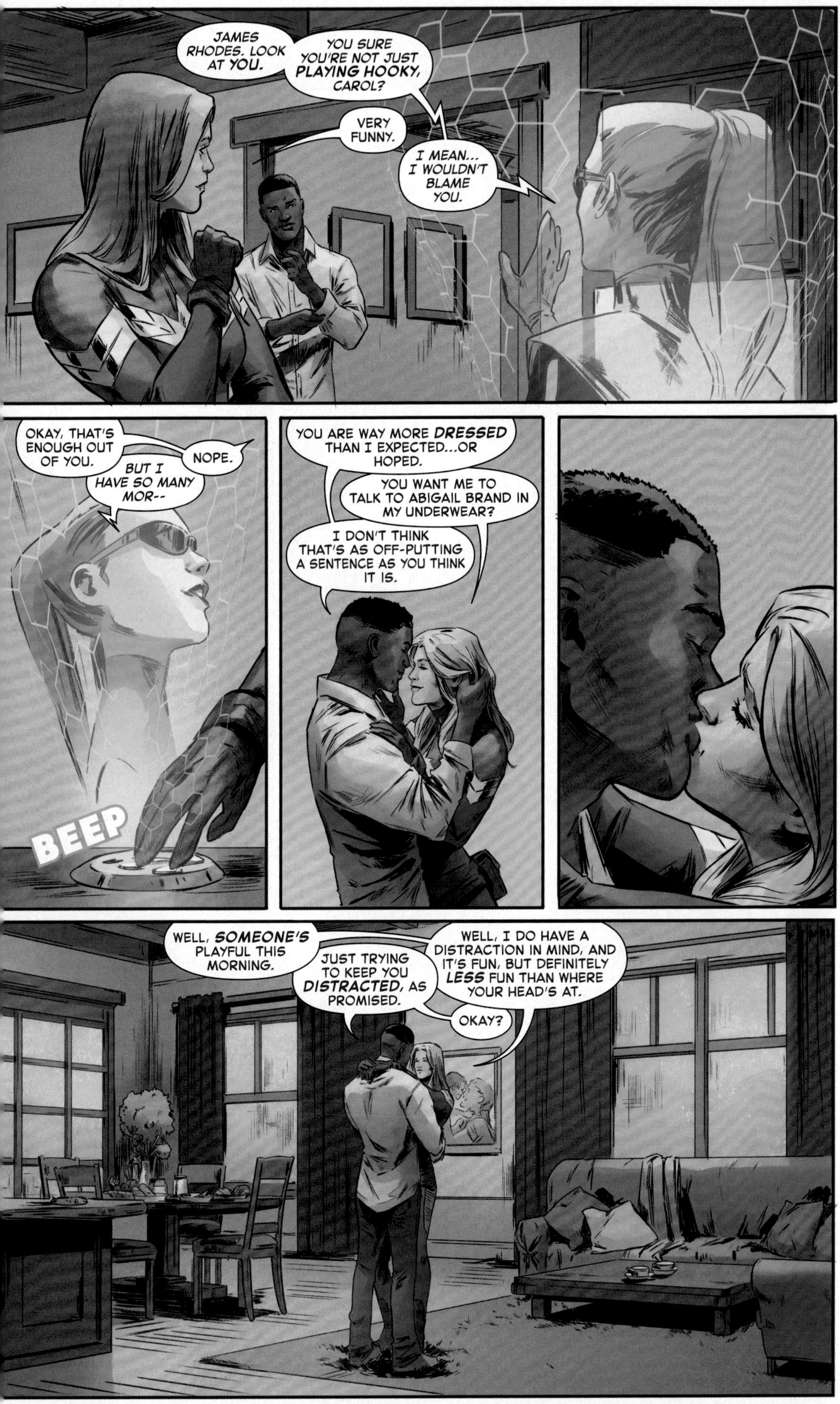
JAMES RHODES. LOOK AT YOU.
YOU SURE YOU'RE NOT JUST PLAYING HOOKY, CAROL?
VERY FUNNY.
I MEAN... I WOULDN'T BLAME YOU.
OKAY, THAT'S ENOUGH OUT OF YOU.
NOPE.
BUT I HAVE SO MANY MOR--
BEEP
YOU ARE WAY MORE DRESSED THAN I EXPECTED...OR HOPED.
YOU WANT ME TO TALK TO ABIGAIL BRAND IN MY UNDERWEAR?
I DON'T THINK THAT'S AS OFF-PUTTING A SENTENCE AS YOU THINK IT IS.
WELL, SOMEONE'S PLAYFUL THIS MORNING.
JUST TRYING TO KEEP YOU DISTRACTED, AS PROMISED.
WELL, I DO HAVE A DISTRACTION IN MIND, AND IT'S FUN, BUT DEFINITELY LESS FUN THAN WHERE YOUR HEAD'S AT.
OKAY?

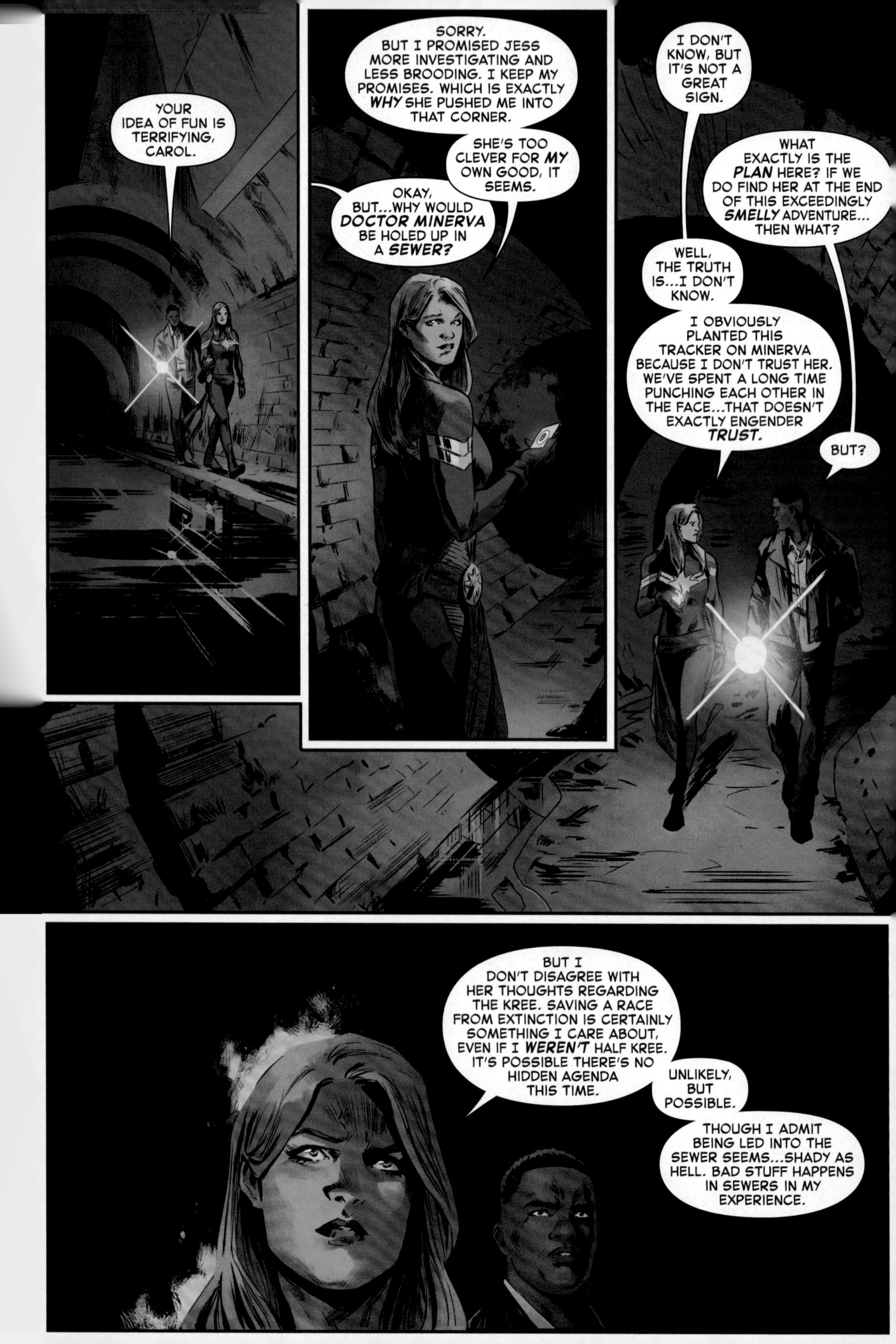

YOUR IDEA OF FUN IS TERRIFYING, CAROL.
SORRY. BUT I PROMISED JESS MORE INVESTIGATING AND LESS BROODING. I KEEP MY PROMISES. WHICH IS EXACTLY WHY SHE PUSHED ME INTO THAT CORNER.
SHE'S TOO CLEVER FOR MY OWN GOOD, IT SEEMS.
OKAY, BUT...WHY WOULD DOCTOR MINERVA BE HOLED UP IN A SEWER?
I DON'T KNOW, BUT IT'S NOT A GREAT SIGN.
WHAT EXACTLY IS THE PLAN HERE? IF WE DO FIND HER AT THE END OF THIS EXCEEDINGLY SMELLY ADVENTURE... THEN WHAT?
WELL, THE TRUTH IS...I DON'T KNOW.
I OBVIOUSLY PLANTED THIS TRACKER ON MINERVA BECAUSE I DON'T TRUST HER. WE'VE SPENT A LONG TIME PUNCHING EACH OTHER IN THE FACE...THAT DOESN'T EXACTLY ENGENDER TRUST.
BUT?
BUT I DON'T DISAGREE WITH HER THOUGHTS REGARDING THE KREE. SAVING A RACE FROM EXTINCTION IS CERTAINLY SOMETHING I CARE ABOUT, EVEN IF I WEREN'T HALF KREE. IT'S POSSIBLE THERE'S NO HIDDEN AGENDA THIS TIME.
UNLIKELY, BUT POSSIBLE.
THOUGH I ADMIT BEING LED INTO THE SEWER SEEMS...SHADY AS HELL. BAD STUFF HAPPENS IN SEWERS IN MY EXPERIENCE.

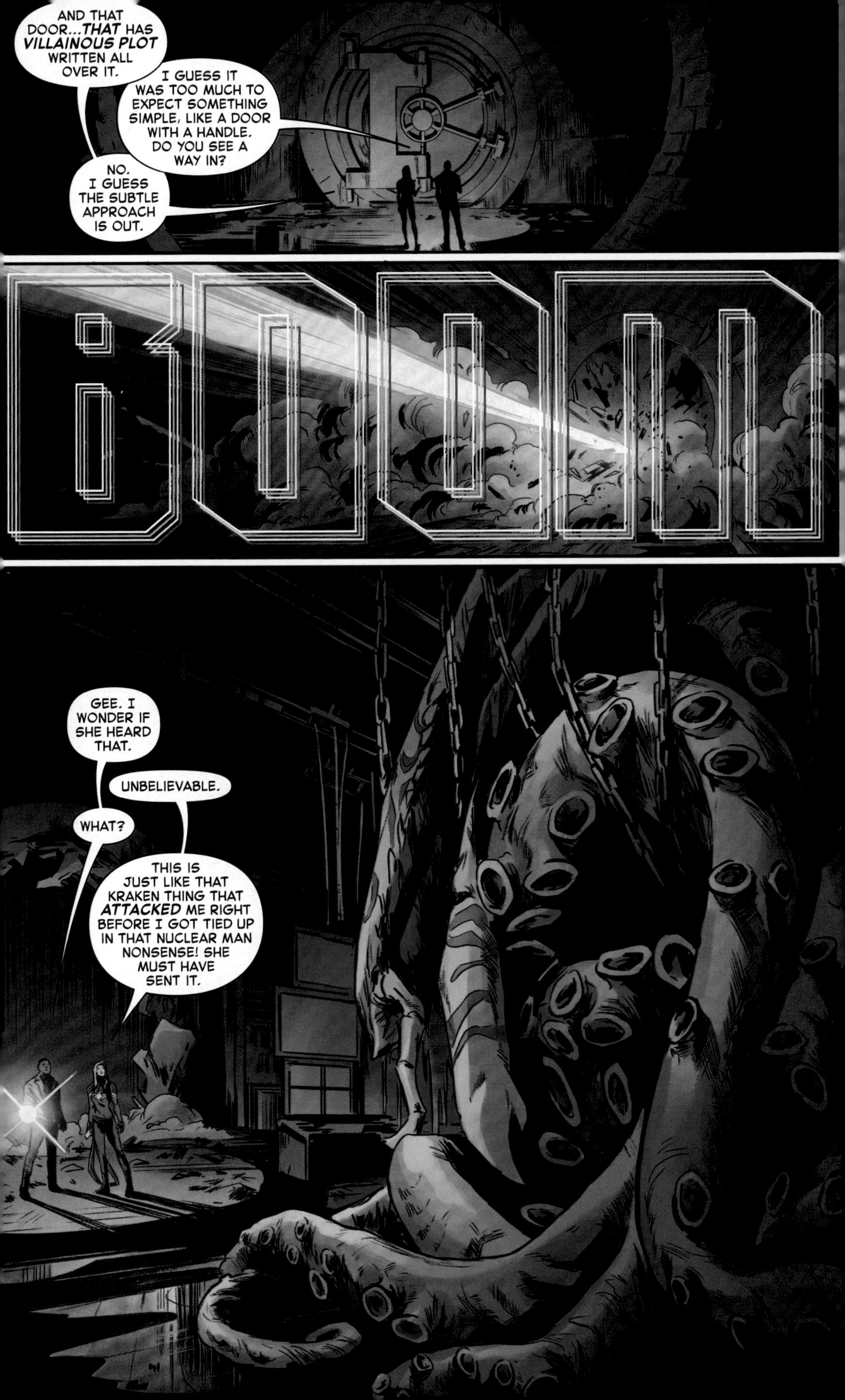
AND THAT DOOR...*THAT* HAS *VILLAINOUS PLOT* WRITTEN ALL OVER IT.
I GUESS IT WAS TOO MUCH TO EXPECT SOMETHING SIMPLE, LIKE A DOOR WITH A HANDLE. DO YOU SEE A WAY IN?
NO. I GUESS THE SUBTLE APPROACH IS OUT.
BOOM
GEE. I WONDER IF SHE HEARD THAT.
UNBELIEVABLE.
WHAT?
THIS IS JUST LIKE THAT KRAKEN THING THAT *ATTACKED* ME RIGHT BEFORE I GOT TIED UP IN THAT NUCLEAR MAN NONSENSE! SHE MUST HAVE SENT IT.

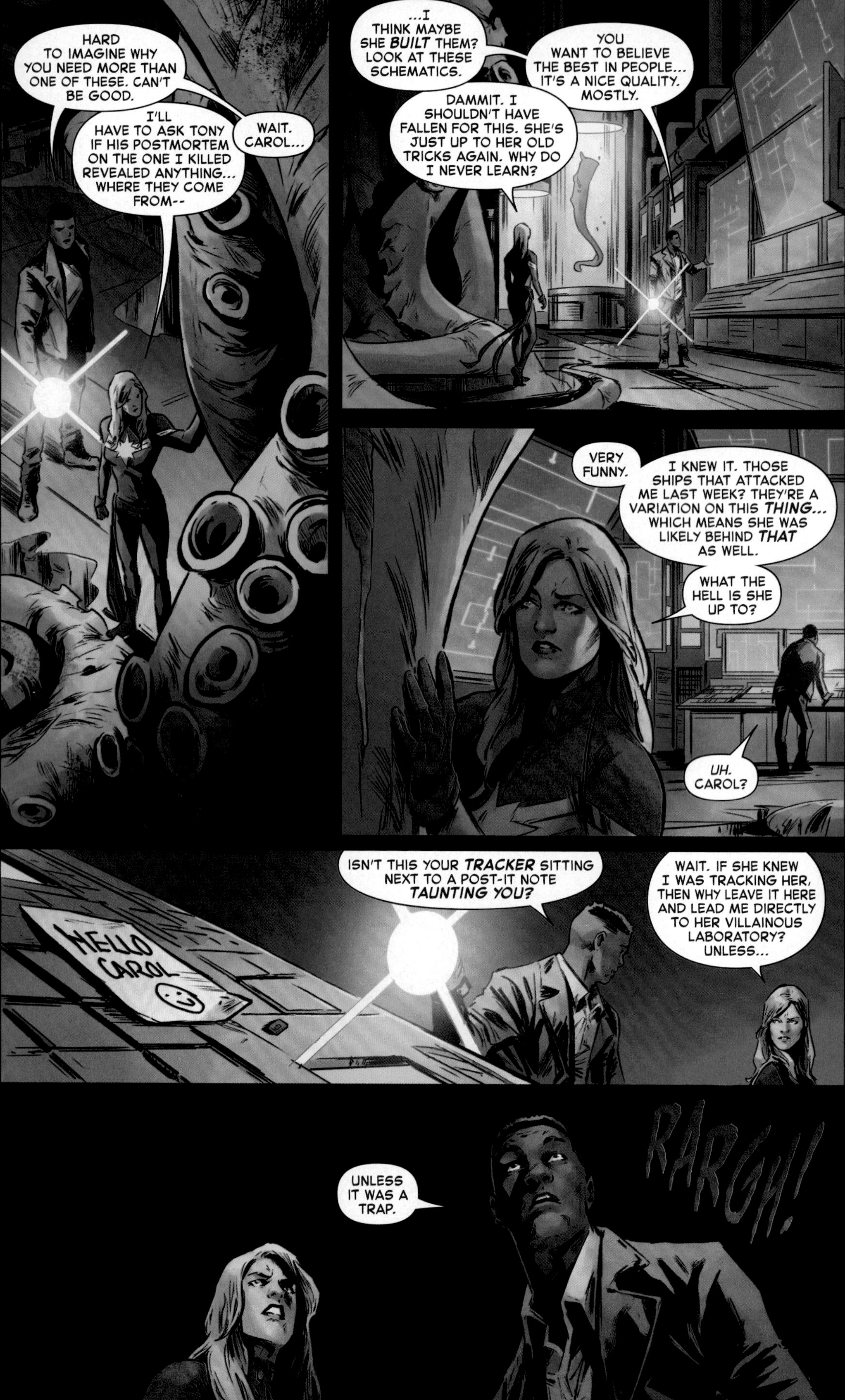
HARD TO IMAGINE WHY YOU NEED MORE THAN ONE OF THESE. CAN'T BE GOOD.
I'LL HAVE TO ASK TONY IF HIS POSTMORTEM ON THE ONE I KILLED REVEALED ANYTHING... WHERE THEY COME FROM--
WAIT. CAROL...
...I THINK MAYBE SHE BUILT THEM? LOOK AT THESE SCHEMATICS.
YOU WANT TO BELIEVE THE BEST IN PEOPLE... IT'S A NICE QUALITY. MOSTLY.
DAMMIT. I SHOULDN'T HAVE FALLEN FOR THIS. SHE'S JUST UP TO HER OLD TRICKS AGAIN. WHY DO I NEVER LEARN?
VERY FUNNY.
I KNEW IT. THOSE SHIPS THAT ATTACKED ME LAST WEEK? THEY'RE A VARIATION ON THIS THING... WHICH MEANS SHE WAS LIKELY BEHIND THAT AS WELL.
WHAT THE HELL IS SHE UP TO?
UH. CAROL?
ISN'T THIS YOUR TRACKER SITTING NEXT TO A POST-IT NOTE TAUNTING YOU?
HELLO CAROL
WAIT. IF SHE KNEW I WAS TRACKING HER, THEN WHY LEAVE IT HERE AND LEAD ME DIRECTLY TO HER VILLAINOUS LABORATORY? UNLESS...
UNLESS IT WAS A TRAP.
RARGH!

CAROL DOESN'T KNOW YOU FILMED THIS?

NO.

YOU KNOW SHE'S GOING TO KILL YOU.

I'M AWARE.

STARK UNLIMITED.

TONY STARK,
A.K.A. IRON MAN.

SO LET'S MAKE MY DEATH WORTH IT AND FIGURE OUT WHAT'S *WRONG* WITH HER.

JESSICA DREW,
A.K.A. SPIDER-WOMAN.

WELL, THERE DEFINITELY *IS* SOMETHING WRONG. THIS DATA IS ALL OVER THE PLACE. HER PUNCH IMPACT IS REDUCED, HER HEART RATE IS ALL OFF...

I *KNOW* SOMETHING'S WRONG WITH HER. BUT *WHAT* IS IT THAT'S WRONG?

I MEAN, I HAVE NO IDEA, JESS. I HAVE TO GET HER IN THE LAB...DO A COMPLETE BODY SCAN, A FULL BATTERY OF TESTS.

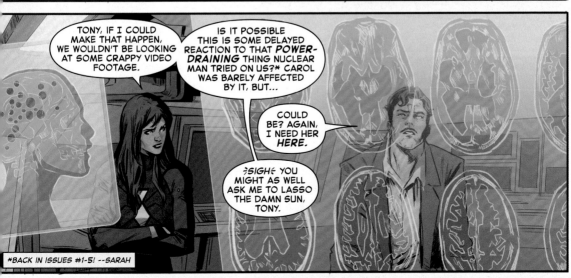

TONY, IF I COULD MAKE THAT HAPPEN, WE WOULDN'T BE LOOKING AT SOME CRAPPY VIDEO FOOTAGE.

IS IT POSSIBLE THIS IS SOME DELAYED REACTION TO THAT *POWER-DRAINING* THING NUCLEAR MAN TRIED ON US?* CAROL WAS BARELY AFFECTED BY IT, BUT...

COULD BE? AGAIN, I NEED HER *HERE.*

≶SIGH≷ YOU MIGHT AS WELL ASK ME TO LASSO THE DAMN SUN, TONY.

*BACK IN ISSUES #1-5! --SARAH

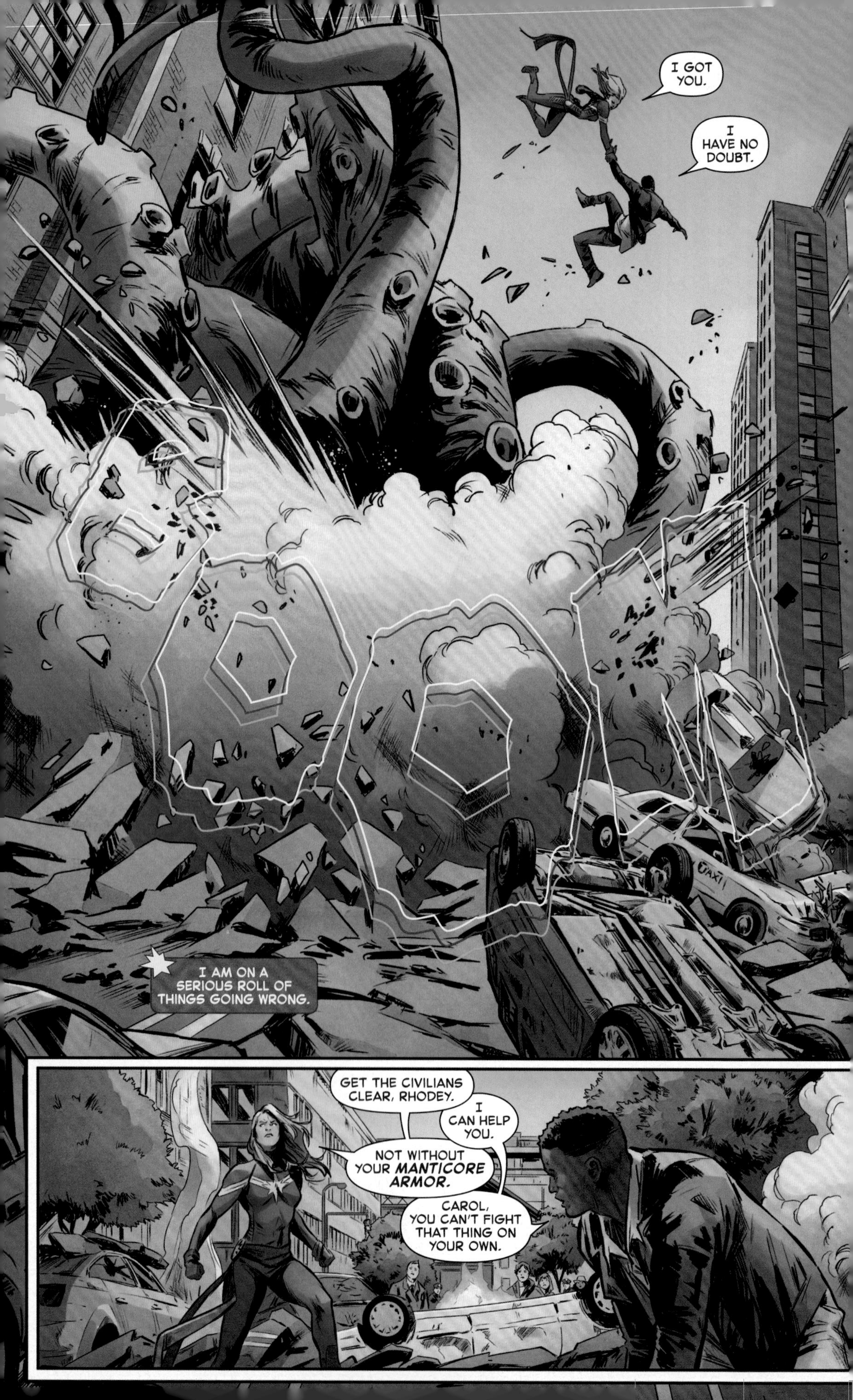
I GOT YOU.
I HAVE NO DOUBT.
DOOM
I AM ON A SERIOUS ROLL OF THINGS GOING WRONG.
GET THE CIVILIANS CLEAR, RHODEY.
I CAN HELP YOU.
NOT WITHOUT YOUR *MANTICORE ARMOR.*
CAROL, YOU CAN'T FIGHT THAT THING ON YOUR OWN.

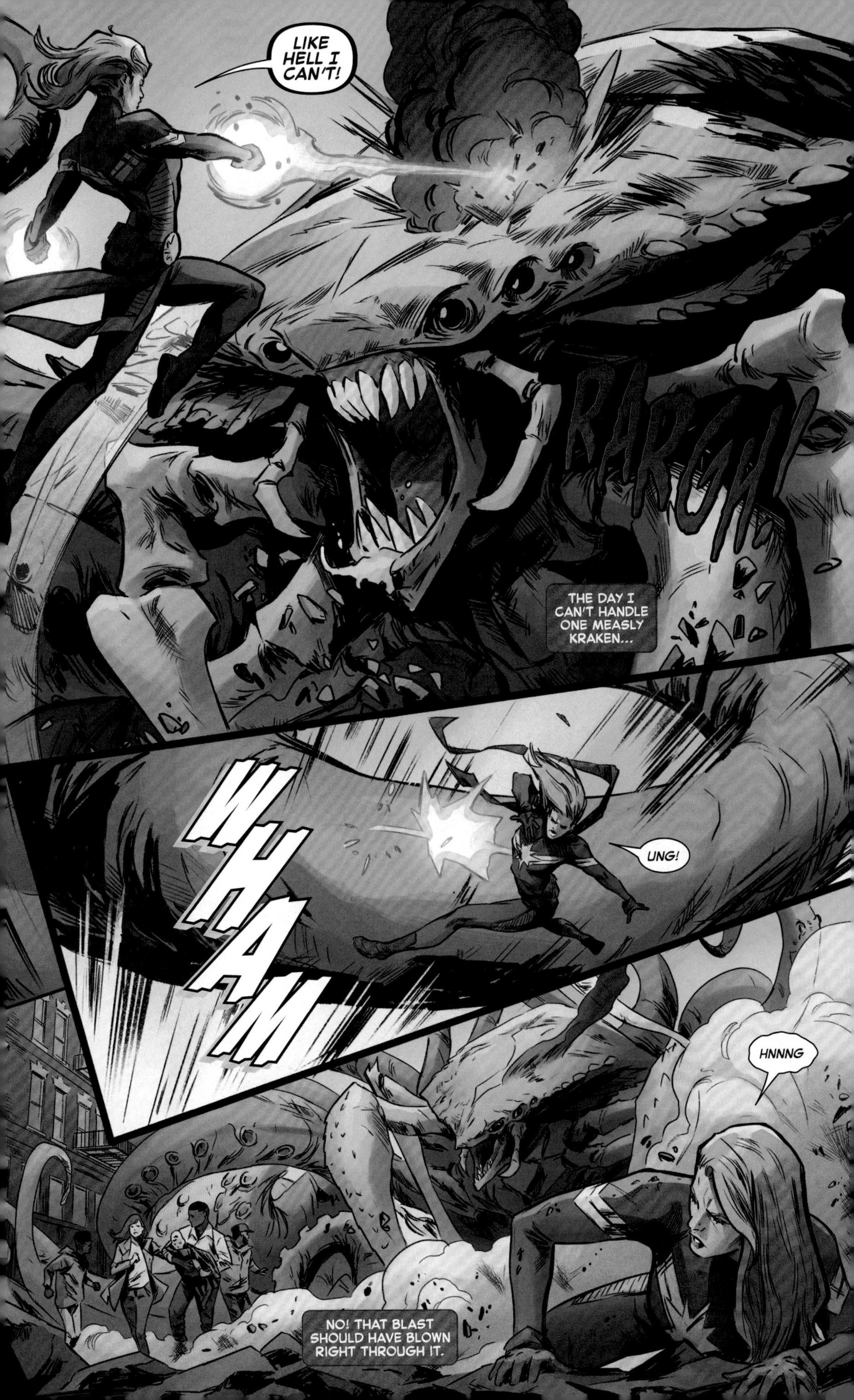
LIKE HELL I CAN'T!
RARGH!
THE DAY I CAN'T HANDLE ONE MEASLY KRAKEN...
WHAM
UNG!
HNNNG
NO! THAT BLAST SHOULD HAVE BLOWN RIGHT THROUGH IT.

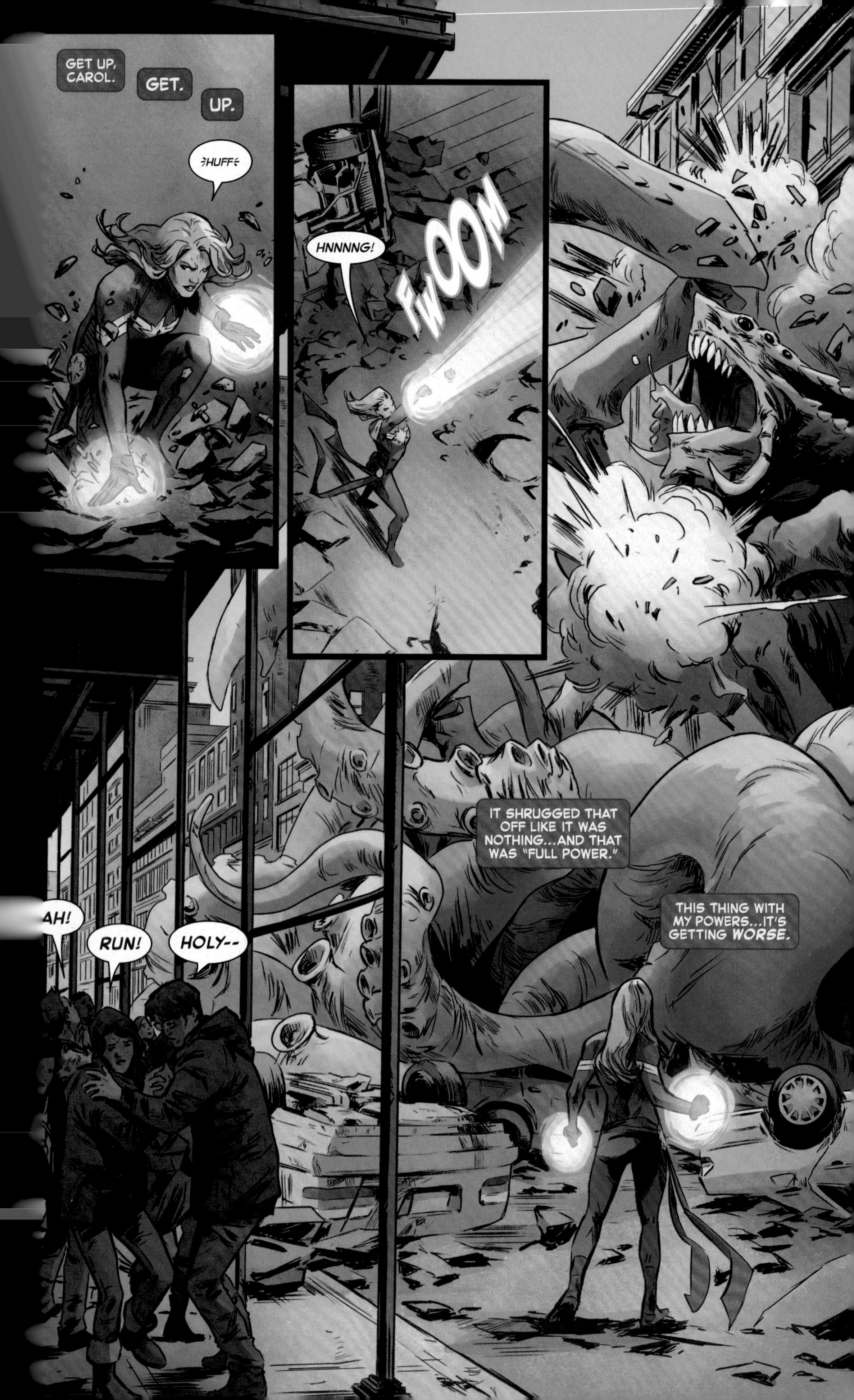
GET UP, CAROL.
GET.
UP.
HUFF
HNNNNG!
FWOOM
IT SHRUGGED THAT OFF LIKE IT WAS NOTHING...AND THAT WAS "FULL POWER."
THIS THING WITH MY POWERS...IT'S GETTING *WORSE.*
AH!
RUN!
HOLY--

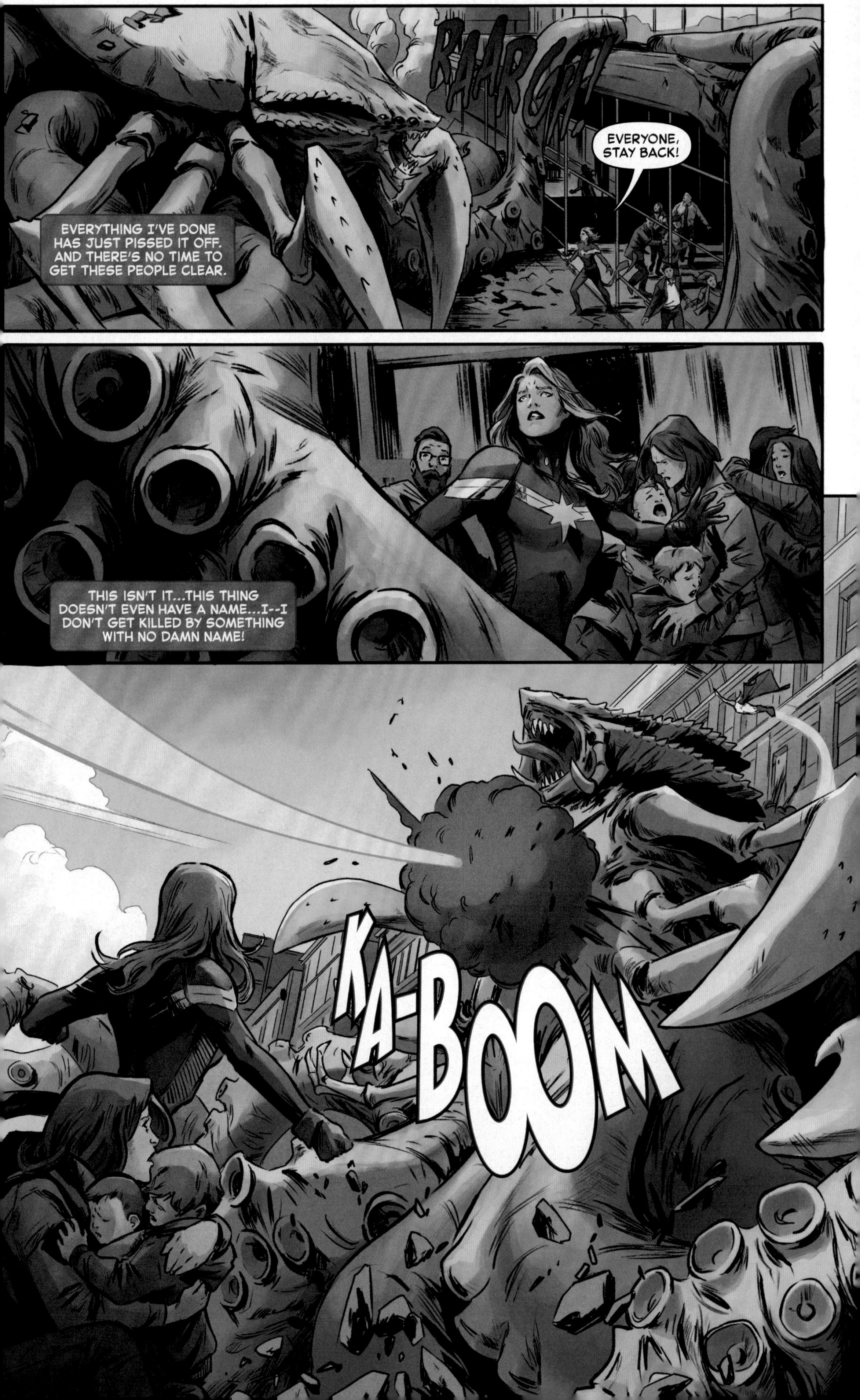
RAARGH!
EVERYONE, STAY BACK!
EVERYTHING I'VE DONE HAS JUST PISSED IT OFF. AND THERE'S NO TIME TO GET THESE PEOPLE CLEAR.
THIS ISN'T IT...THIS THING DOESN'T EVEN HAVE A NAME...I--I DON'T GET KILLED BY SOMETHING WITH NO DAMN NAME!
KA-BOOM

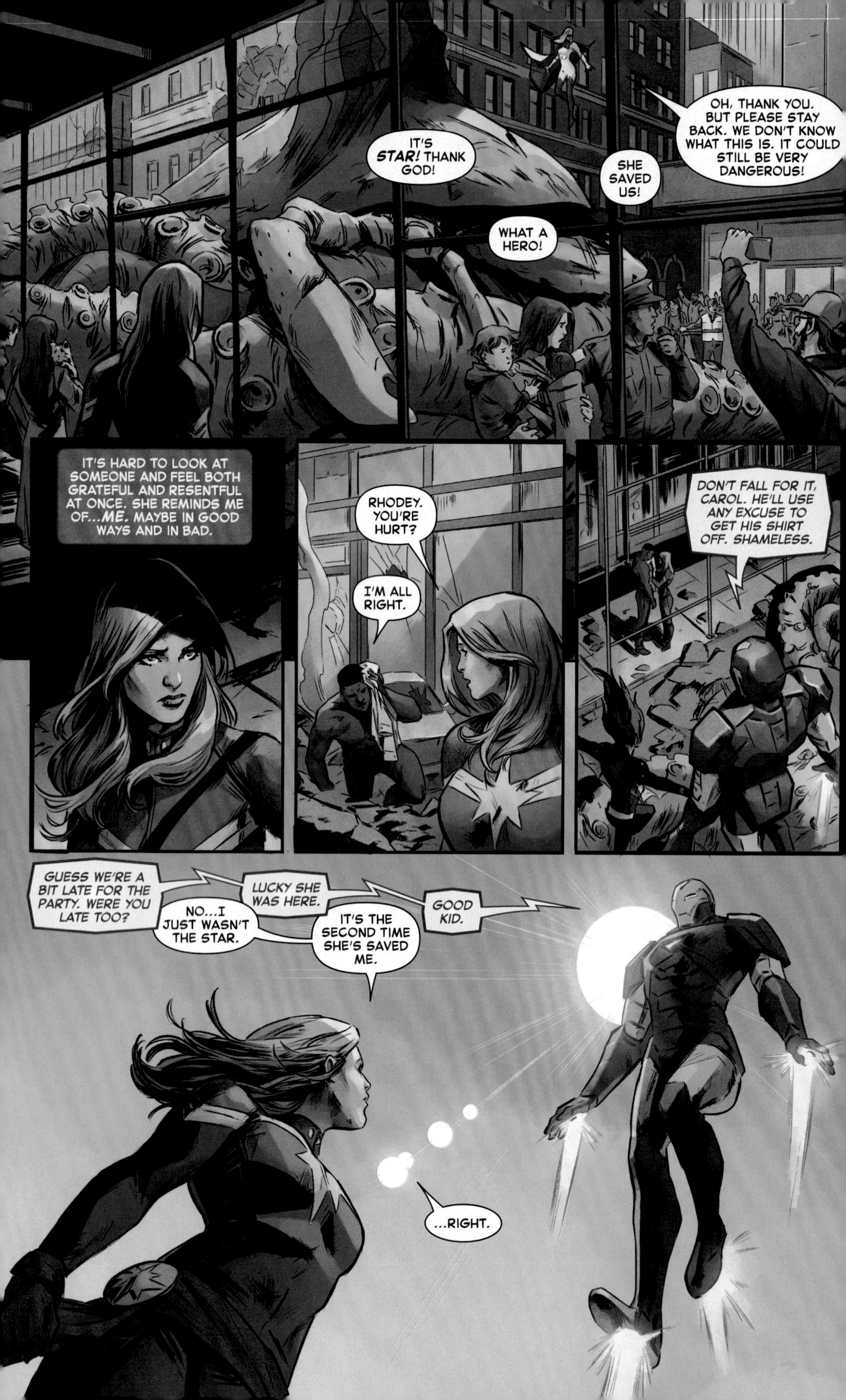
IT'S STAR! THANK GOD!
SHE SAVED US!
OH, THANK YOU. BUT PLEASE STAY BACK. WE DON'T KNOW WHAT THIS IS. IT COULD STILL BE VERY DANGEROUS!
WHAT A HERO!
IT'S HARD TO LOOK AT SOMEONE AND FEEL BOTH GRATEFUL AND RESENTFUL AT ONCE. SHE REMINDS ME OF...ME. MAYBE IN GOOD WAYS AND IN BAD.
RHODEY. YOU'RE HURT?
I'M ALL RIGHT.
DON'T FALL FOR IT, CAROL. HE'LL USE ANY EXCUSE TO GET HIS SHIRT OFF. SHAMELESS.
GUESS WE'RE A BIT LATE FOR THE PARTY. WERE YOU LATE TOO?
NO...I JUST WASN'T THE STAR.
LUCKY SHE WAS HERE.
IT'S THE SECOND TIME SHE'S SAVED ME.
GOOD KID.
...RIGHT.

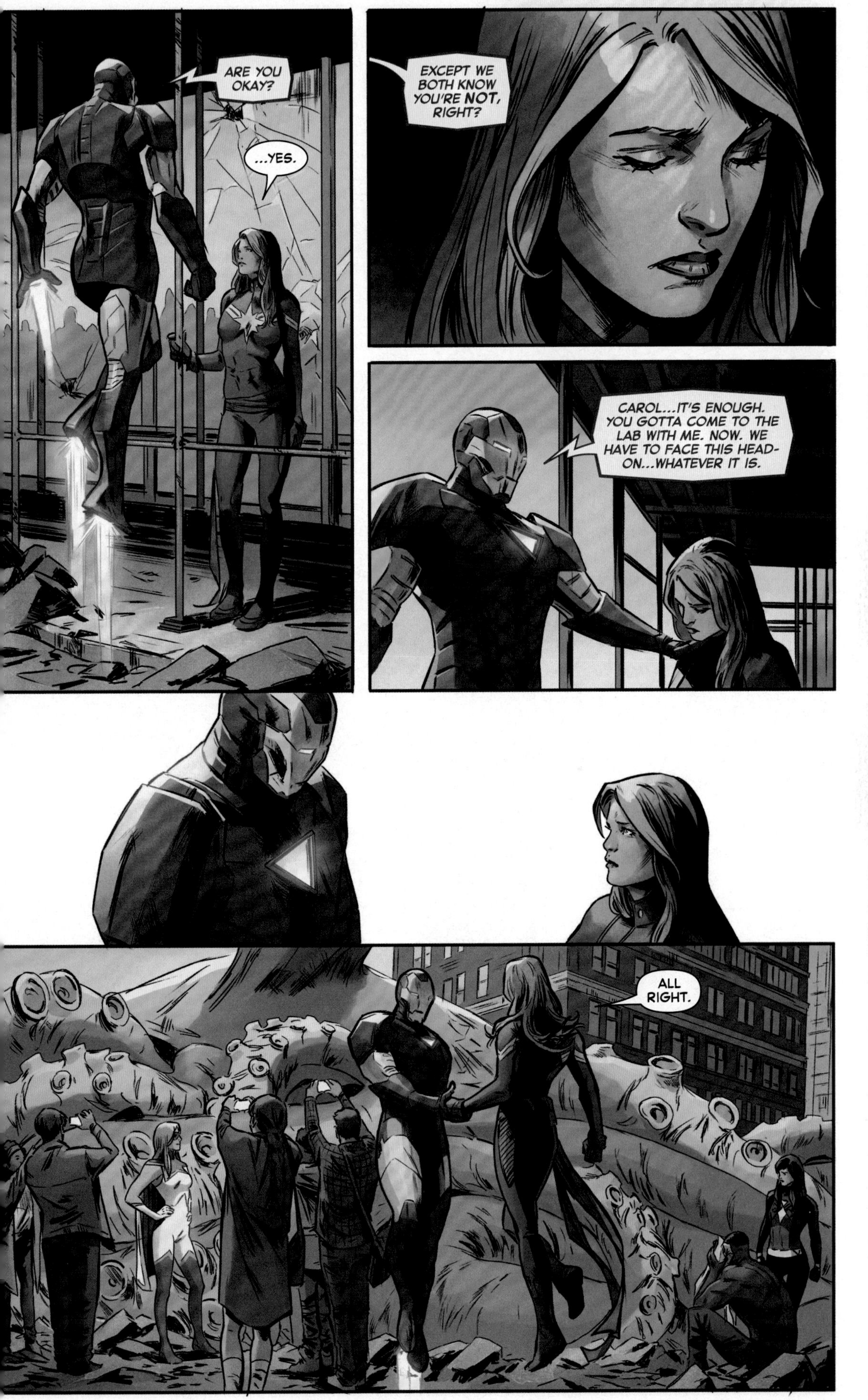

ARE YOU OKAY?
...YES.
EXCEPT WE BOTH KNOW YOU'RE **NOT**, RIGHT?
CAROL...IT'S ENOUGH. YOU GOTTA COME TO THE LAB WITH ME. NOW. WE HAVE TO FACE THIS HEAD-ON...WHATEVER IT IS.
ALL RIGHT.

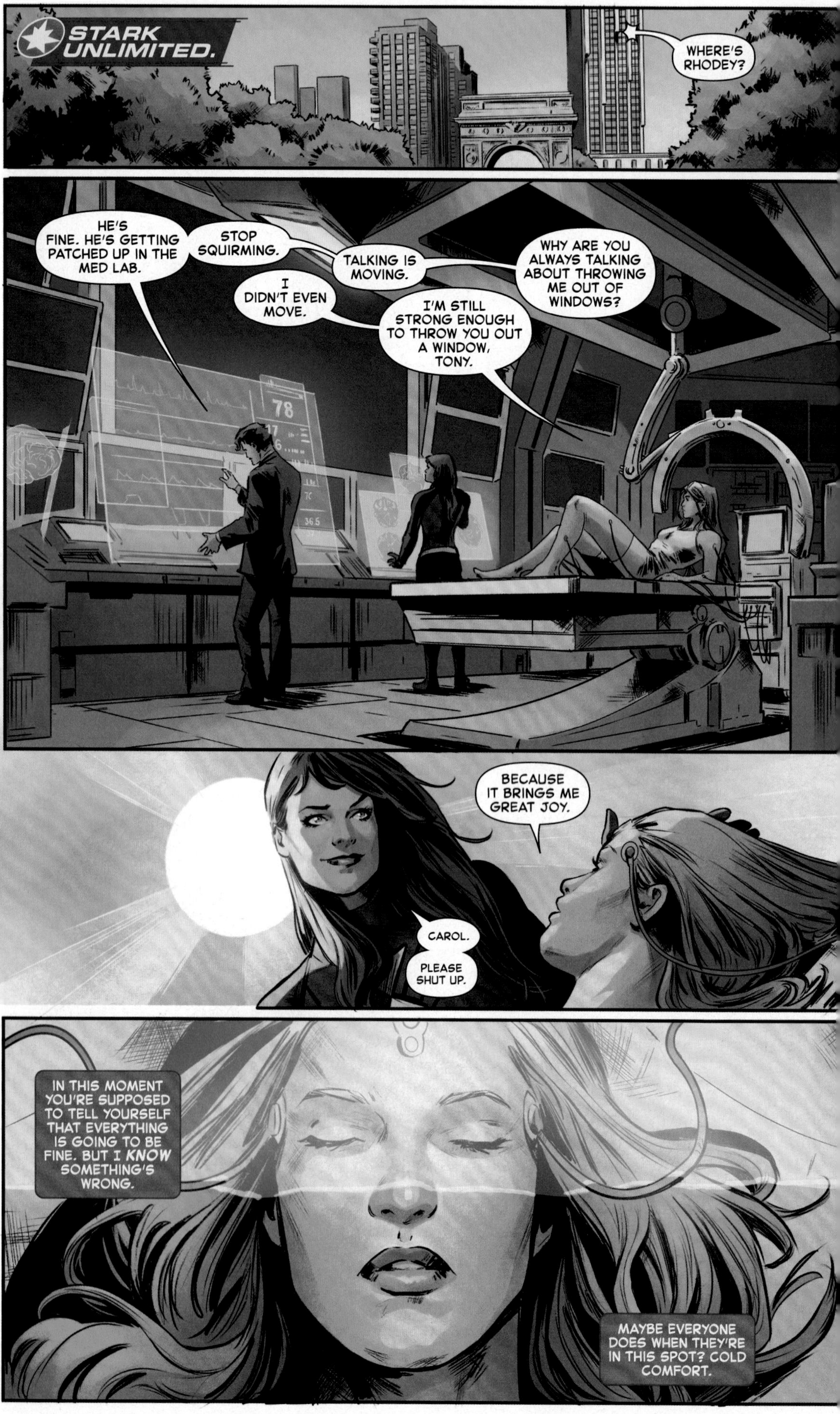
STARK UNLIMITED.
WHERE'S RHODEY?
HE'S FINE. HE'S GETTING PATCHED UP IN THE MED LAB.
STOP SQUIRMING.
TALKING IS MOVING.
WHY ARE YOU ALWAYS TALKING ABOUT THROWING ME OUT OF WINDOWS?
I DIDN'T EVEN MOVE.
I'M STILL STRONG ENOUGH TO THROW YOU OUT A WINDOW, TONY.
BECAUSE IT BRINGS ME GREAT JOY.
CAROL.
PLEASE SHUT UP.
IN THIS MOMENT YOU'RE SUPPOSED TO TELL YOURSELF THAT EVERYTHING IS GOING TO BE FINE. BUT I KNOW SOMETHING'S WRONG.
MAYBE EVERYONE DOES WHEN THEY'RE IN THIS SPOT? COLD COMFORT.

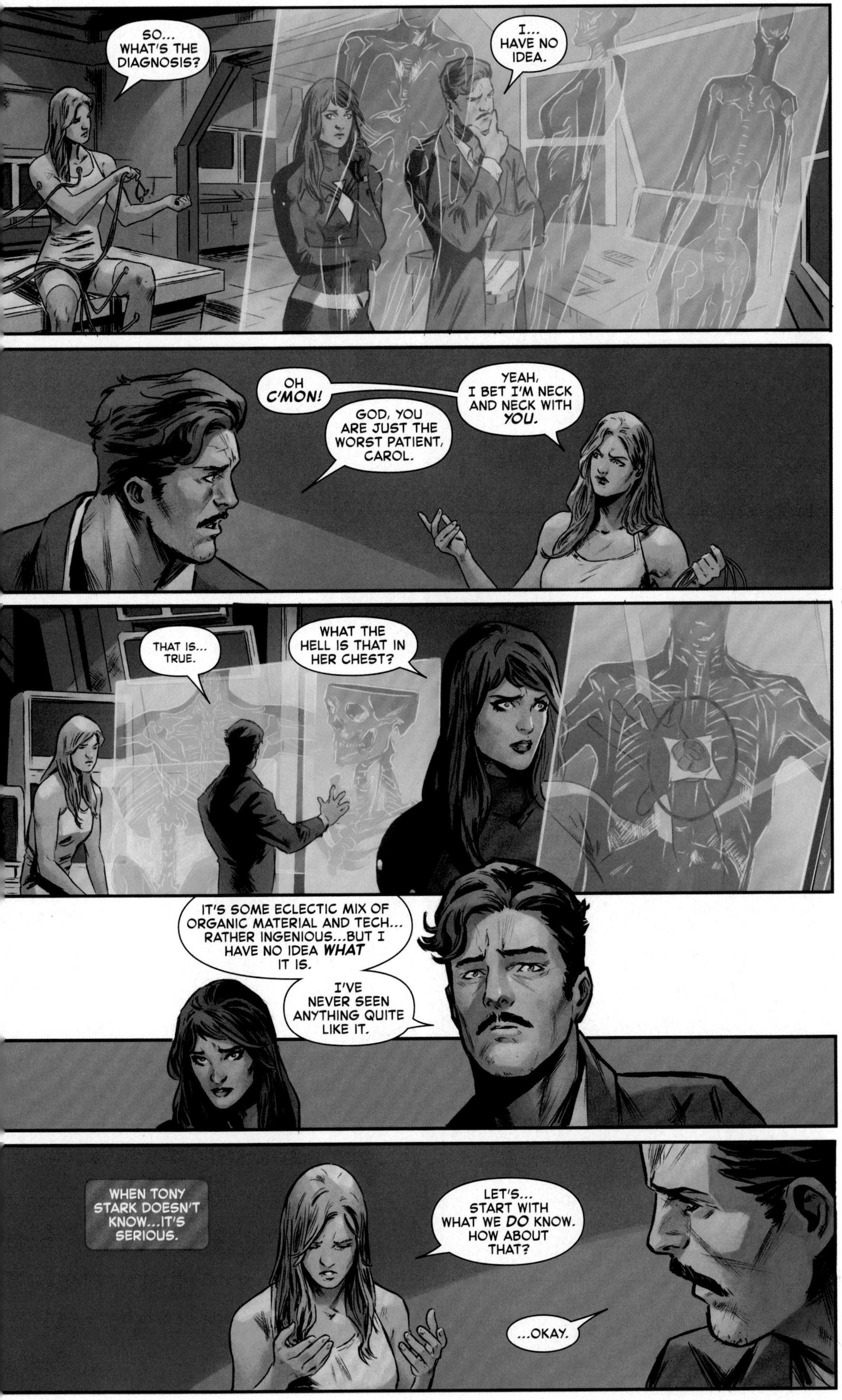

SO... WHAT'S THE DIAGNOSIS?
I... HAVE NO IDEA.
OH C'MON!
GOD, YOU ARE JUST THE WORST PATIENT, CAROL.
YEAH, I BET I'M NECK AND NECK WITH YOU.
THAT IS... TRUE.
WHAT THE HELL IS THAT IN HER CHEST?
IT'S SOME ECLECTIC MIX OF ORGANIC MATERIAL AND TECH... RATHER INGENIOUS...BUT I HAVE NO IDEA WHAT IT IS.
I'VE NEVER SEEN ANYTHING QUITE LIKE IT.
WHEN TONY STARK DOESN'T KNOW...IT'S SERIOUS.
LET'S... START WITH WHAT WE DO KNOW. HOW ABOUT THAT?
...OKAY.

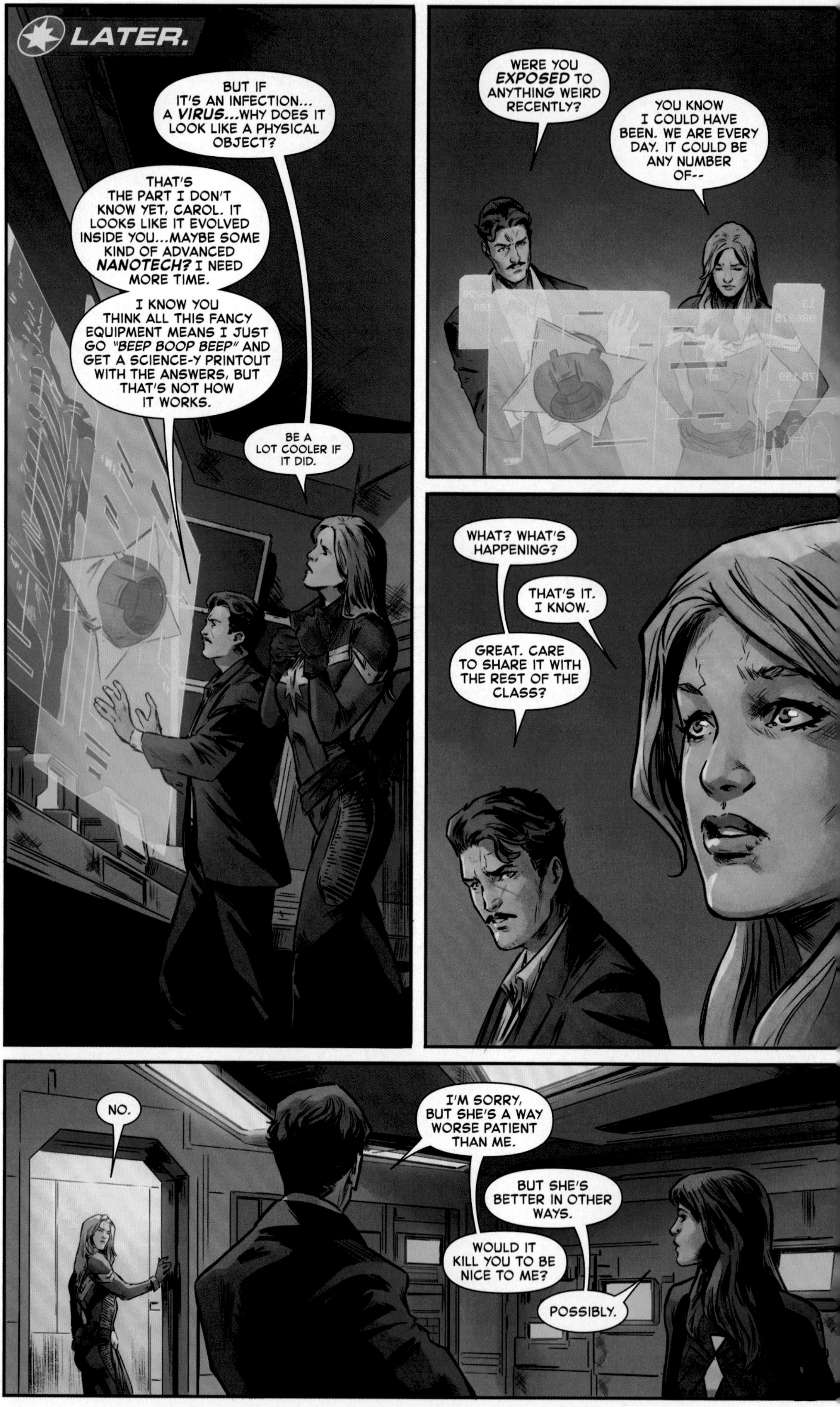
LATER.
BUT IF IT'S AN INFECTION... A VIRUS...WHY DOES IT LOOK LIKE A PHYSICAL OBJECT?
THAT'S THE PART I DON'T KNOW YET, CAROL. IT LOOKS LIKE IT EVOLVED INSIDE YOU...MAYBE SOME KIND OF ADVANCED NANOTECH? I NEED MORE TIME.
I KNOW YOU THINK ALL THIS FANCY EQUIPMENT MEANS I JUST GO "BEEP BOOP BEEP" AND GET A SCIENCE-Y PRINTOUT WITH THE ANSWERS, BUT THAT'S NOT HOW IT WORKS.
BE A LOT COOLER IF IT DID.
WERE YOU EXPOSED TO ANYTHING WEIRD RECENTLY?
YOU KNOW I COULD HAVE BEEN. WE ARE EVERY DAY. IT COULD BE ANY NUMBER OF--
WHAT? WHAT'S HAPPENING?
THAT'S IT. I KNOW.
GREAT. CARE TO SHARE IT WITH THE REST OF THE CLASS?
NO.
I'M SORRY, BUT SHE'S A WAY WORSE PATIENT THAN ME.
BUT SHE'S BETTER IN OTHER WAYS.
WOULD IT KILL YOU TO BE NICE TO ME?
POSSIBLY.

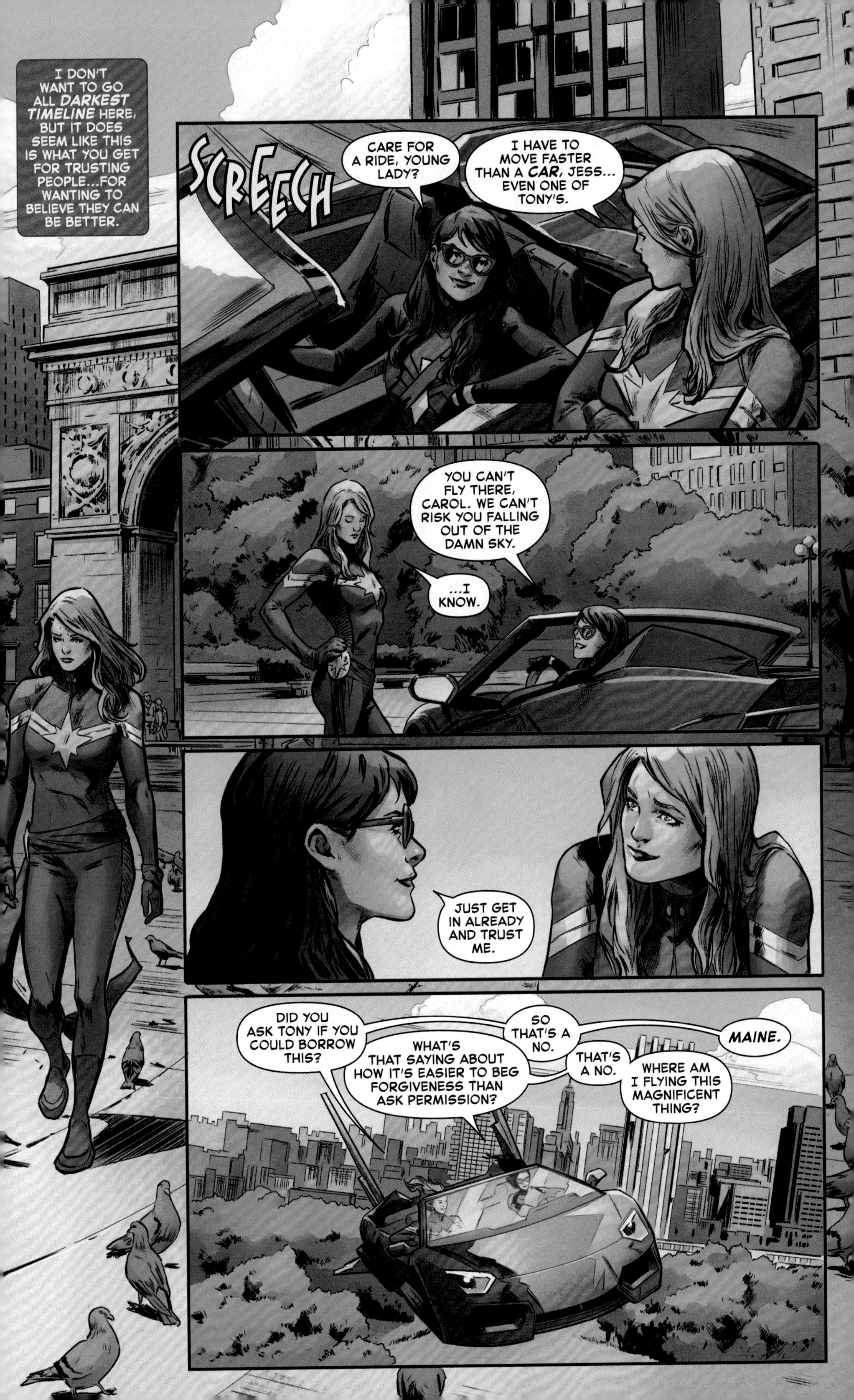
I DON'T WANT TO GO ALL DARKEST TIMELINE HERE, BUT IT DOES SEEM LIKE THIS IS WHAT YOU GET FOR TRUSTING PEOPLE...FOR WANTING TO BELIEVE THEY CAN BE BETTER.
SCREECH
CARE FOR A RIDE, YOUNG LADY?
I HAVE TO MOVE FASTER THAN A CAR, JESS... EVEN ONE OF TONY'S.
YOU CAN'T FLY THERE, CAROL. WE CAN'T RISK YOU FALLING OUT OF THE DAMN SKY.
...I KNOW.
JUST GET IN ALREADY AND TRUST ME.
DID YOU ASK TONY IF YOU COULD BORROW THIS?
WHAT'S THAT SAYING ABOUT HOW IT'S EASIER TO BEG FORGIVENESS THAN ASK PERMISSION?
SO THAT'S A NO.
THAT'S A NO.
WHERE AM I FLYING THIS MAGNIFICENT THING?
MAINE.

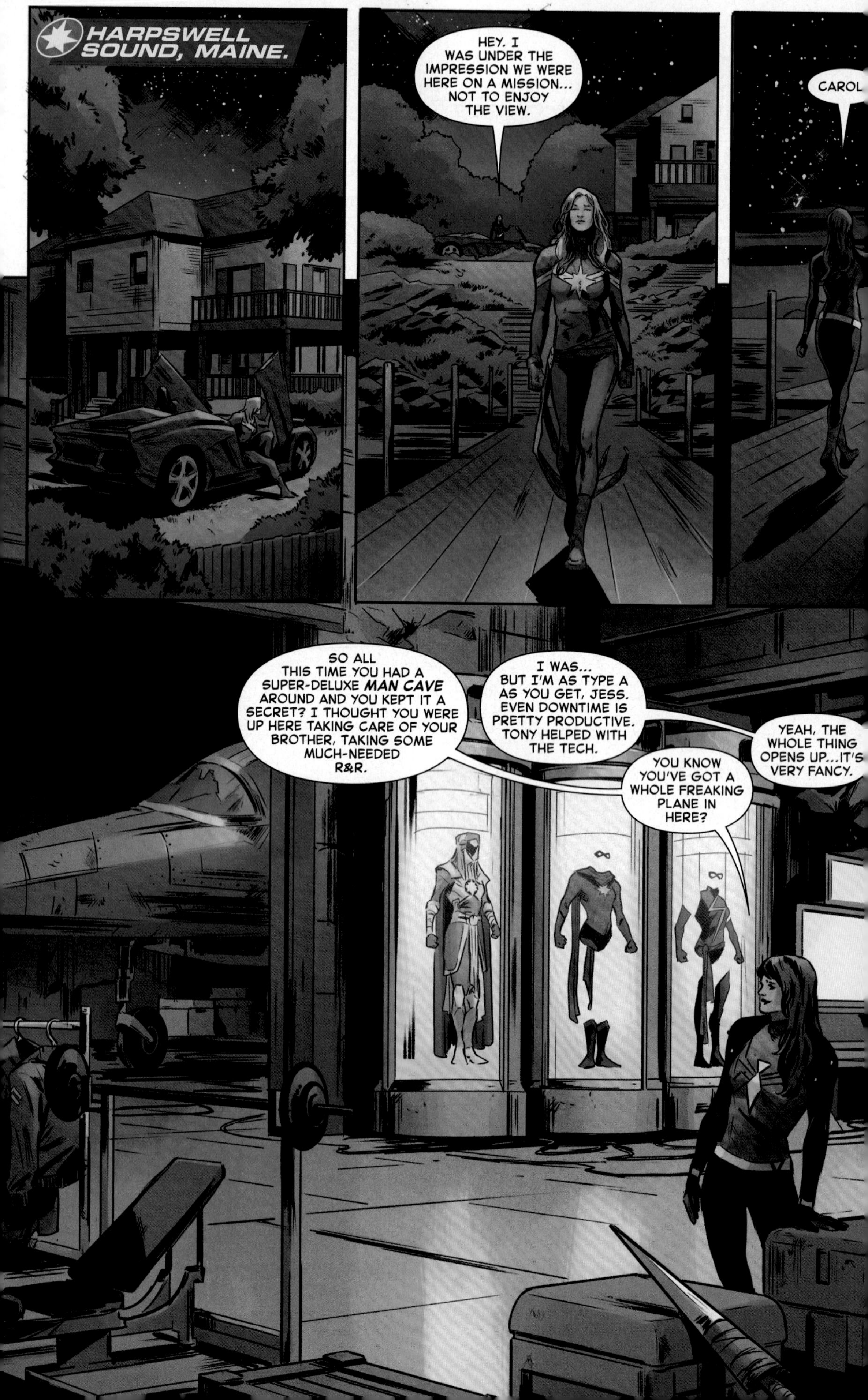
HARPSWELL SOUND, MAINE.
HEY. I WAS UNDER THE IMPRESSION WE WERE HERE ON A MISSION... NOT TO ENJOY THE VIEW.
CAROL
SO ALL THIS TIME YOU HAD A SUPER-DELUXE MAN CAVE AROUND AND YOU KEPT IT A SECRET? I THOUGHT YOU WERE UP HERE TAKING CARE OF YOUR BROTHER, TAKING SOME MUCH-NEEDED R&R.
I WAS... BUT I'M AS TYPE A AS YOU GET, JESS. EVEN DOWNTIME IS PRETTY PRODUCTIVE. TONY HELPED WITH THE TECH.
YOU KNOW YOU'VE GOT A WHOLE FREAKING PLANE IN HERE?
YEAH, THE WHOLE THING OPENS UP...IT'S VERY FANCY.

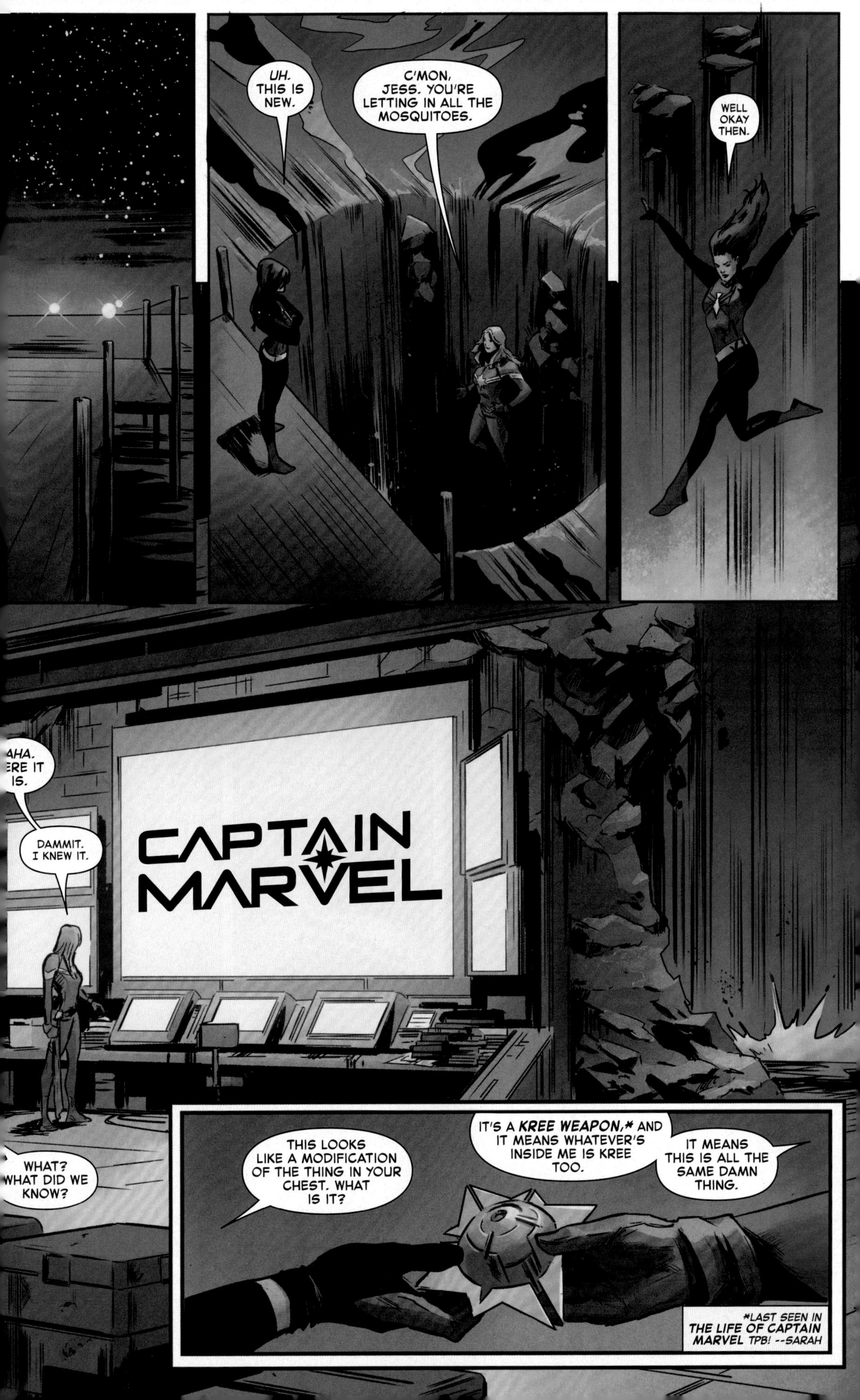
UH. THIS IS NEW.
C'MON, JESS. YOU'RE LETTING IN ALL THE MOSQUITOES.
WELL OKAY THEN.
AHA. ERE IT IS.
DAMMIT. I KNEW IT.
CAPTAIN MARVEL
WHAT? WHAT DID WE KNOW?
THIS LOOKS LIKE A MODIFICATION OF THE THING IN YOUR CHEST. WHAT IS IT?
IT'S A KREE WEAPON,* AND IT MEANS WHATEVER'S INSIDE ME IS KREE TOO.
IT MEANS THIS IS ALL THE SAME DAMN THING.
*LAST SEEN IN THE LIFE OF CAPTAIN MARVEL TPB! --SARAH

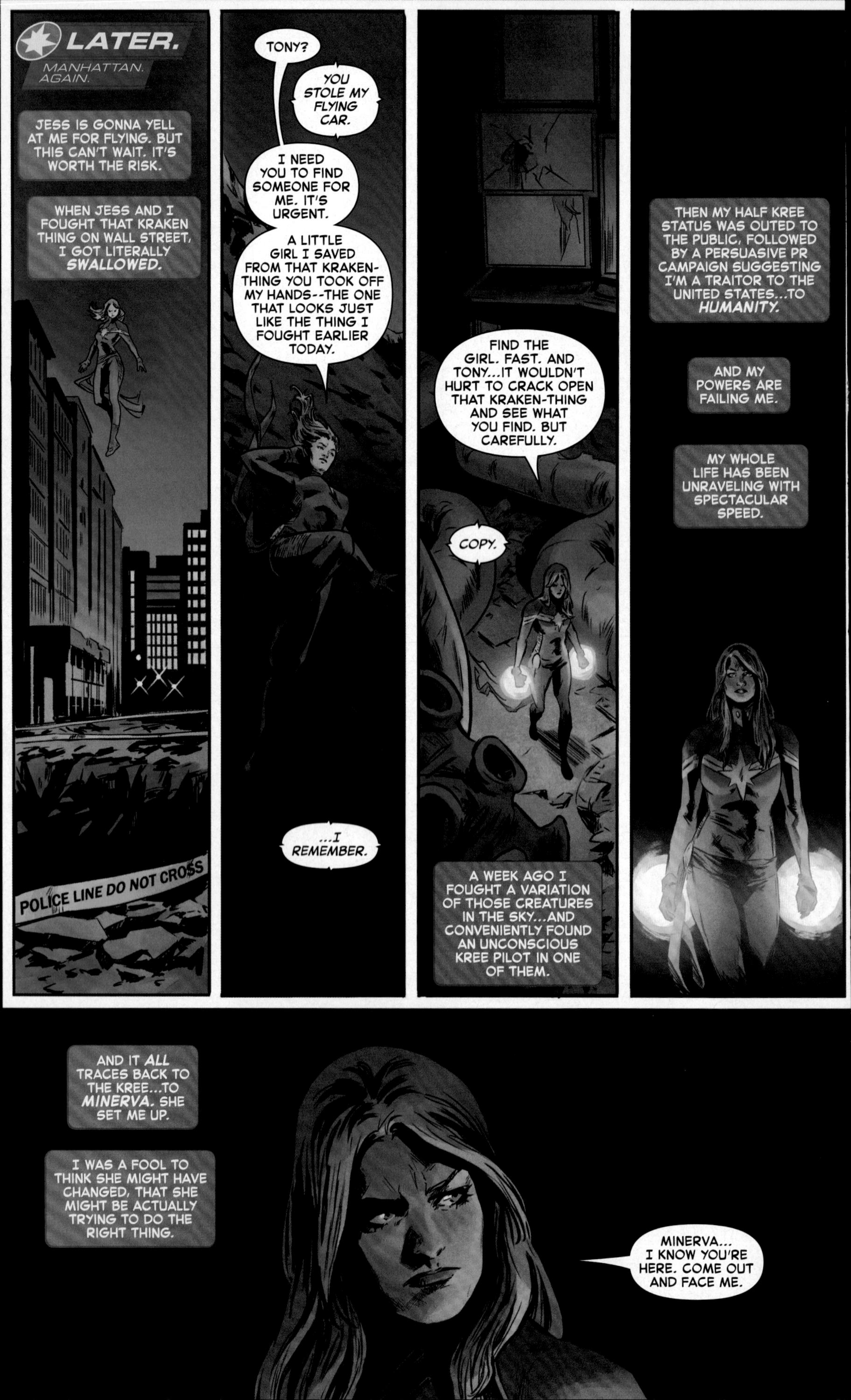
LATER.
MANHATTAN. AGAIN.
JESS IS GONNA YELL AT ME FOR FLYING. BUT THIS CAN'T WAIT. IT'S WORTH THE RISK.
WHEN JESS AND I FOUGHT THAT KRAKEN THING ON WALL STREET, I GOT LITERALLY SWALLOWED.
POLICE LINE DO NOT CROSS
TONY?
YOU STOLE MY FLYING CAR.
I NEED YOU TO FIND SOMEONE FOR ME. IT'S URGENT.
A LITTLE GIRL I SAVED FROM THAT KRAKEN-THING YOU TOOK OFF MY HANDS--THE ONE THAT LOOKS JUST LIKE THE THING I FOUGHT EARLIER TODAY.
...I REMEMBER.
FIND THE GIRL. FAST. AND TONY...IT WOULDN'T HURT TO CRACK OPEN THAT KRAKEN-THING AND SEE WHAT YOU FIND. BUT CAREFULLY.
COPY.
A WEEK AGO I FOUGHT A VARIATION OF THOSE CREATURES IN THE SKY...AND CONVENIENTLY FOUND AN UNCONSCIOUS KREE PILOT IN ONE OF THEM.
THEN MY HALF KREE STATUS WAS OUTED TO THE PUBLIC, FOLLOWED BY A PERSUASIVE PR CAMPAIGN SUGGESTING I'M A TRAITOR TO THE UNITED STATES...TO HUMANITY.
AND MY POWERS ARE FAILING ME.
MY WHOLE LIFE HAS BEEN UNRAVELING WITH SPECTACULAR SPEED.
AND IT ALL TRACES BACK TO THE KREE...TO MINERVA. SHE SET ME UP.
I WAS A FOOL TO THINK SHE MIGHT HAVE CHANGED, THAT SHE MIGHT BE ACTUALLY TRYING TO DO THE RIGHT THING.
MINERVA... I KNOW YOU'RE HERE. COME OUT AND FACE ME.

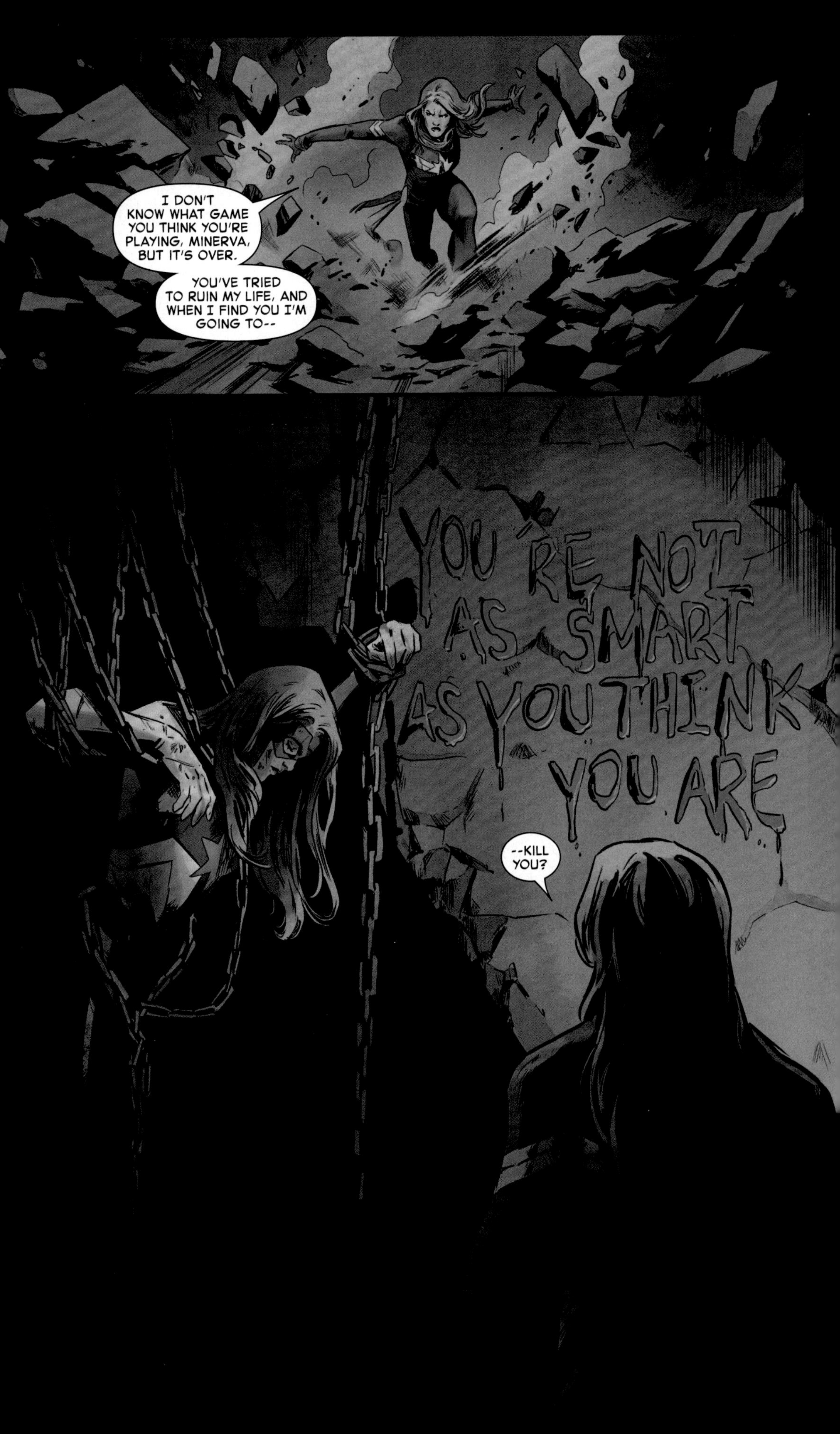
I DON'T KNOW WHAT GAME YOU THINK YOU'RE PLAYING, MINERVA, BUT IT'S OVER.
YOU'VE TRIED TO RUIN MY LIFE, AND WHEN I FIND YOU I'M GOING TO--
YOU'RE NOT AS SMART AS YOU THINK YOU ARE
--KILL YOU?

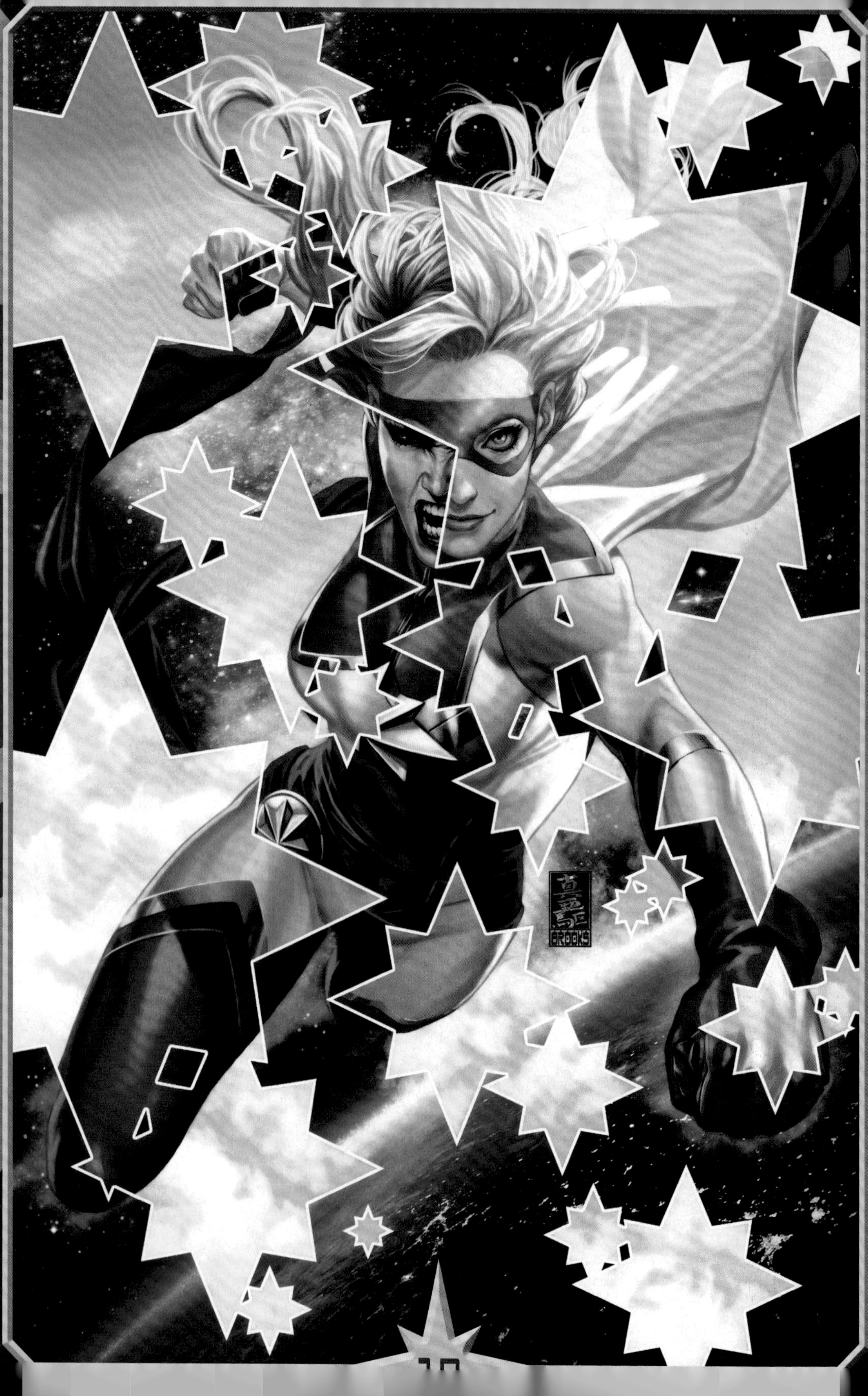

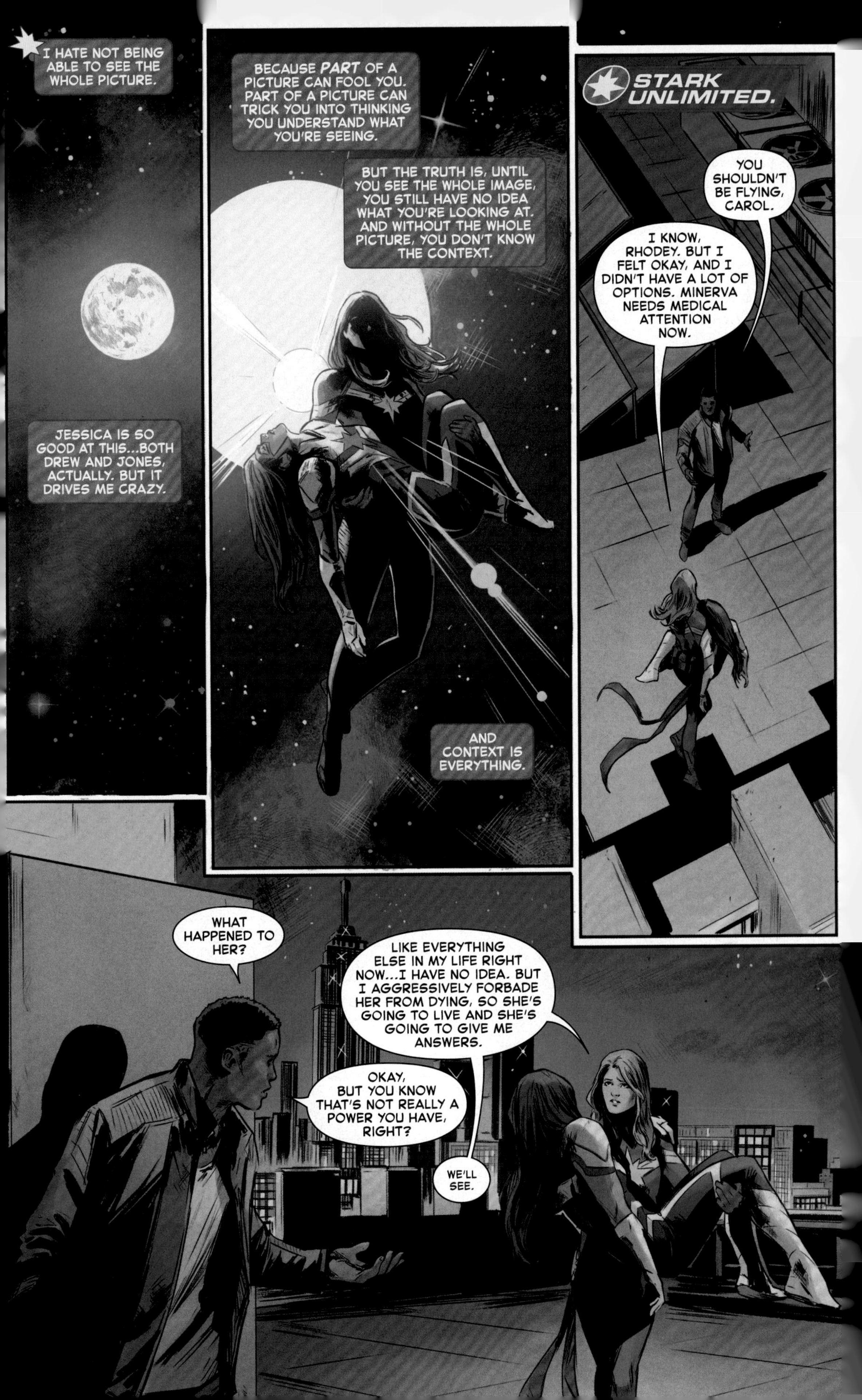
I HATE NOT BEING ABLE TO SEE THE WHOLE PICTURE.
JESSICA IS SO GOOD AT THIS...BOTH DREW AND JONES, ACTUALLY. BUT IT DRIVES ME CRAZY.
BECAUSE PART OF A PICTURE CAN FOOL YOU. PART OF A PICTURE CAN TRICK YOU INTO THINKING YOU UNDERSTAND WHAT YOU'RE SEEING.
BUT THE TRUTH IS, UNTIL YOU SEE THE WHOLE IMAGE, YOU STILL HAVE NO IDEA WHAT YOU'RE LOOKING AT. AND WITHOUT THE WHOLE PICTURE, YOU DON'T KNOW THE CONTEXT.
AND CONTEXT IS EVERYTHING.
STARK UNLIMITED.
YOU SHOULDN'T BE FLYING, CAROL.
I KNOW, RHODEY. BUT I FELT OKAY, AND I DIDN'T HAVE A LOT OF OPTIONS. MINERVA NEEDS MEDICAL ATTENTION NOW.
WHAT HAPPENED TO HER?
LIKE EVERYTHING ELSE IN MY LIFE RIGHT NOW...I HAVE NO IDEA. BUT I AGGRESSIVELY FORBADE HER FROM DYING, SO SHE'S GOING TO LIVE AND SHE'S GOING TO GIVE ME ANSWERS.
OKAY, BUT YOU KNOW THAT'S NOT REALLY A POWER YOU HAVE, RIGHT?
WE'LL SEE.

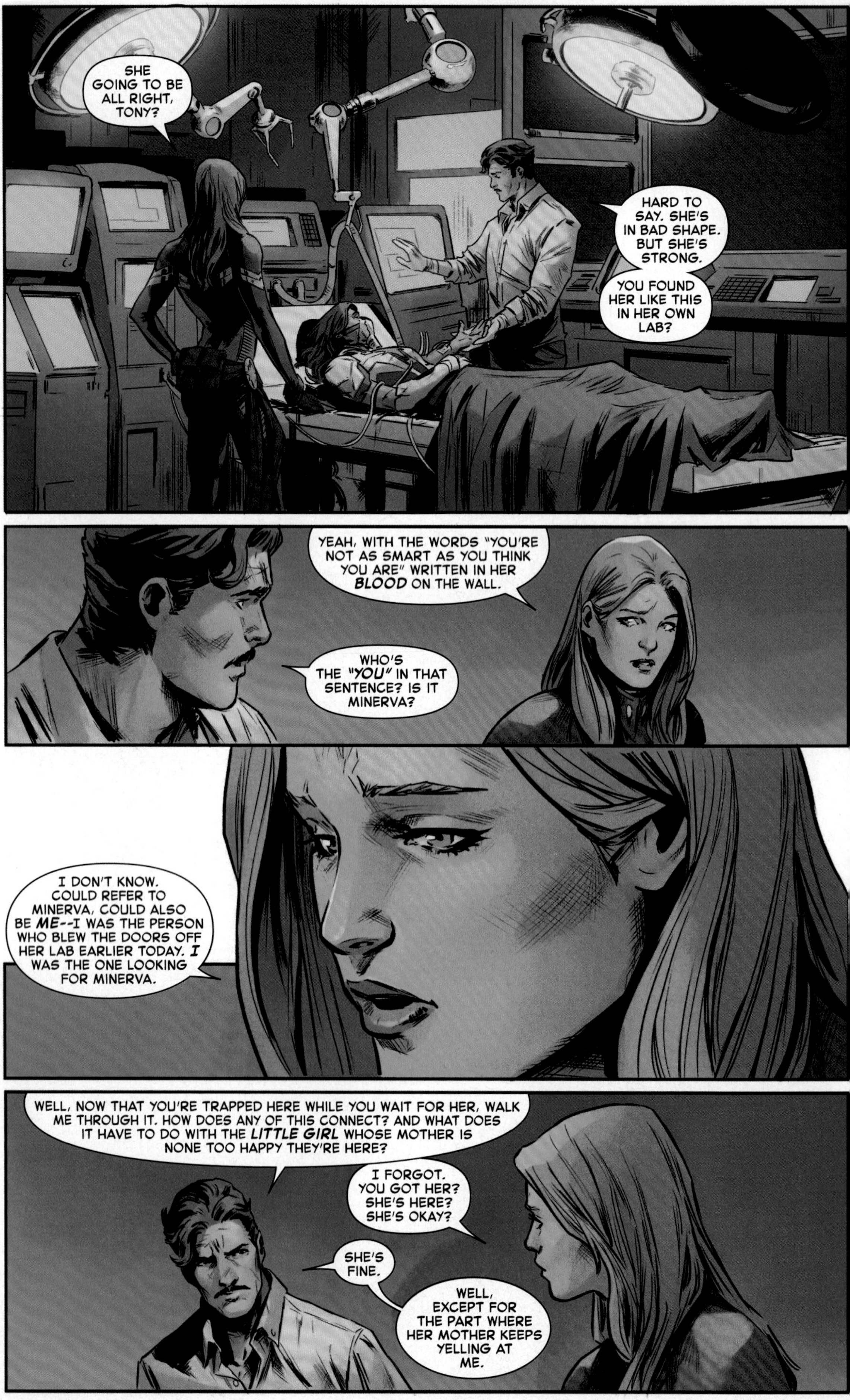
SHE GOING TO BE ALL RIGHT, TONY?
HARD TO SAY. SHE'S IN BAD SHAPE. BUT SHE'S STRONG.
YOU FOUND HER LIKE THIS IN HER OWN LAB?
YEAH, WITH THE WORDS "YOU'RE NOT AS SMART AS YOU THINK YOU ARE" WRITTEN IN HER BLOOD ON THE WALL.
WHO'S THE "YOU" IN THAT SENTENCE? IS IT MINERVA?
I DON'T KNOW. COULD REFER TO MINERVA, COULD ALSO BE ME--I WAS THE PERSON WHO BLEW THE DOORS OFF HER LAB EARLIER TODAY. I WAS THE ONE LOOKING FOR MINERVA.
WELL, NOW THAT YOU'RE TRAPPED HERE WHILE YOU WAIT FOR HER, WALK ME THROUGH IT. HOW DOES ANY OF THIS CONNECT? AND WHAT DOES IT HAVE TO DO WITH THE LITTLE GIRL WHOSE MOTHER IS NONE TOO HAPPY THEY'RE HERE?
I FORGOT. YOU GOT HER? SHE'S HERE? SHE'S OKAY?
SHE'S FINE.
WELL, EXCEPT FOR THE PART WHERE HER MOTHER KEEPS YELLING AT ME.

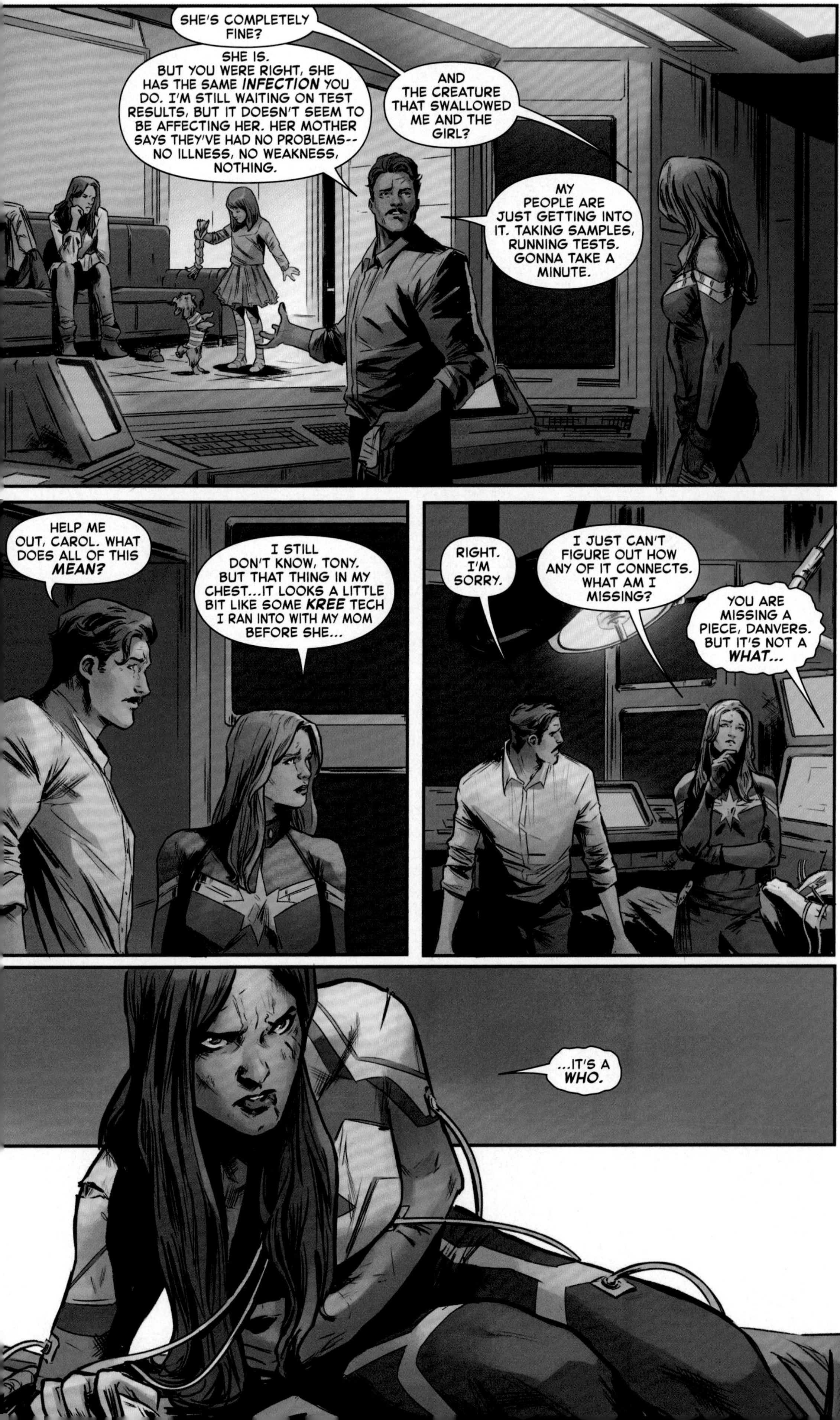
SHE'S COMPLETELY FINE?
SHE IS. BUT YOU WERE RIGHT, SHE HAS THE SAME INFECTION YOU DO. I'M STILL WAITING ON TEST RESULTS, BUT IT DOESN'T SEEM TO BE AFFECTING HER. HER MOTHER SAYS THEY'VE HAD NO PROBLEMS-- NO ILLNESS, NO WEAKNESS, NOTHING.
AND THE CREATURE THAT SWALLOWED ME AND THE GIRL?
MY PEOPLE ARE JUST GETTING INTO IT. TAKING SAMPLES, RUNNING TESTS. GONNA TAKE A MINUTE.
HELP ME OUT, CAROL. WHAT DOES ALL OF THIS MEAN?
I STILL DON'T KNOW, TONY. BUT THAT THING IN MY CHEST...IT LOOKS A LITTLE BIT LIKE SOME KREE TECH I RAN INTO BEFORE WITH MY MOM BEFORE SHE...
RIGHT. I'M SORRY.
I JUST CAN'T FIGURE OUT HOW ANY OF IT CONNECTS. WHAT AM I MISSING?
YOU ARE MISSING A PIECE, DANVERS. BUT IT'S NOT A WHAT...
...IT'S A WHO.

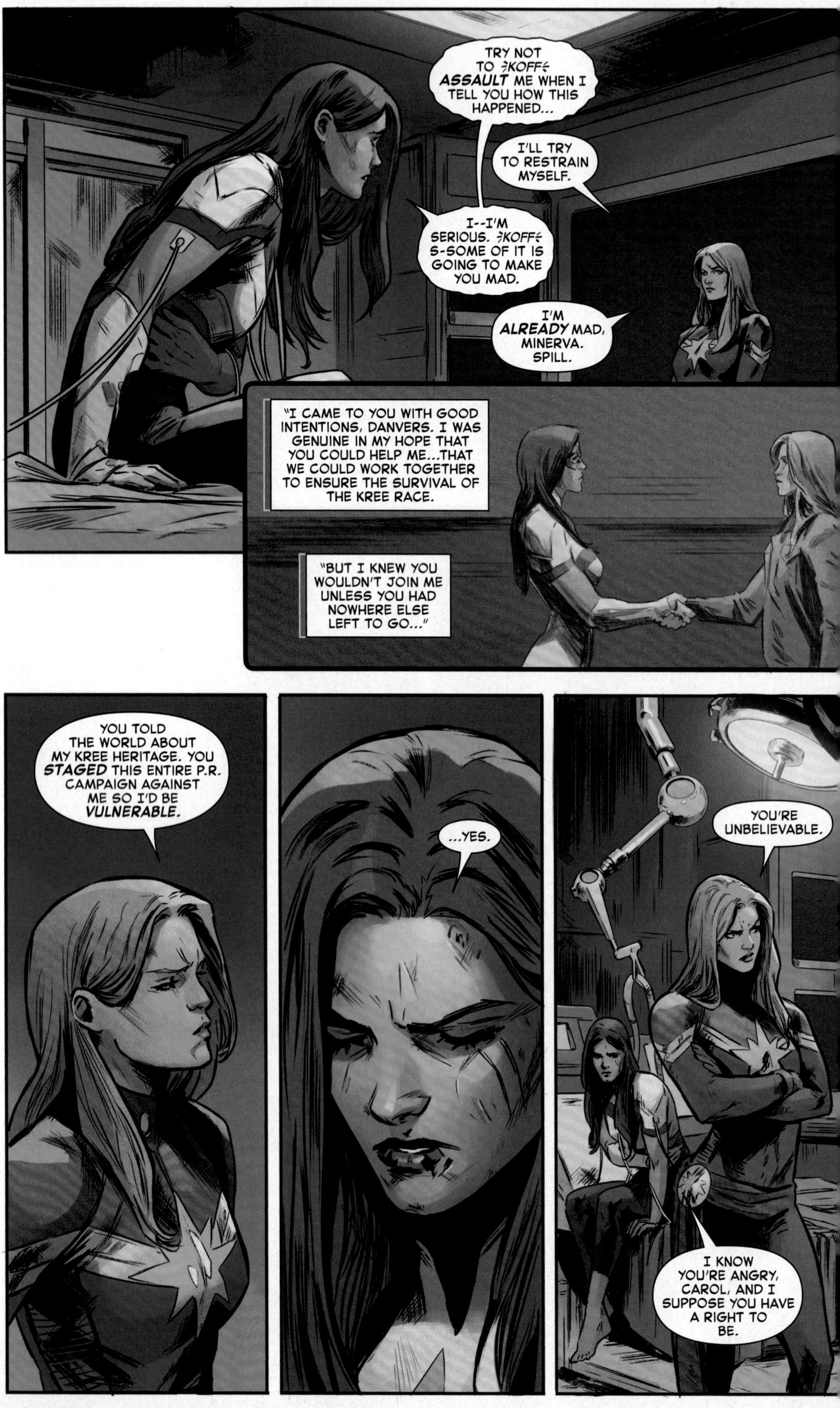
TRY NOT TO ⁑KOFF⁑ **ASSAULT** ME WHEN I TELL YOU HOW THIS HAPPENED...
I'LL TRY TO RESTRAIN MYSELF.
I--I'M SERIOUS. ⁑KOFF⁑ S-SOME OF IT IS GOING TO MAKE YOU MAD.
I'M **ALREADY** MAD, MINERVA. SPILL.
"I CAME TO YOU WITH GOOD INTENTIONS, DANVERS. I WAS GENUINE IN MY HOPE THAT YOU COULD HELP ME...THAT WE COULD WORK TOGETHER TO ENSURE THE SURVIVAL OF THE KREE RACE.
"BUT I KNEW YOU WOULDN'T JOIN ME UNLESS YOU HAD NOWHERE ELSE LEFT TO GO..."
YOU TOLD THE WORLD ABOUT MY KREE HERITAGE. YOU **STAGED** THIS ENTIRE P.R. CAMPAIGN AGAINST ME SO I'D BE **VULNERABLE.**
...YES.
YOU'RE UNBELIEVABLE.
I KNOW YOU'RE ANGRY, CAROL, AND I SUPPOSE YOU HAVE A RIGHT TO BE.

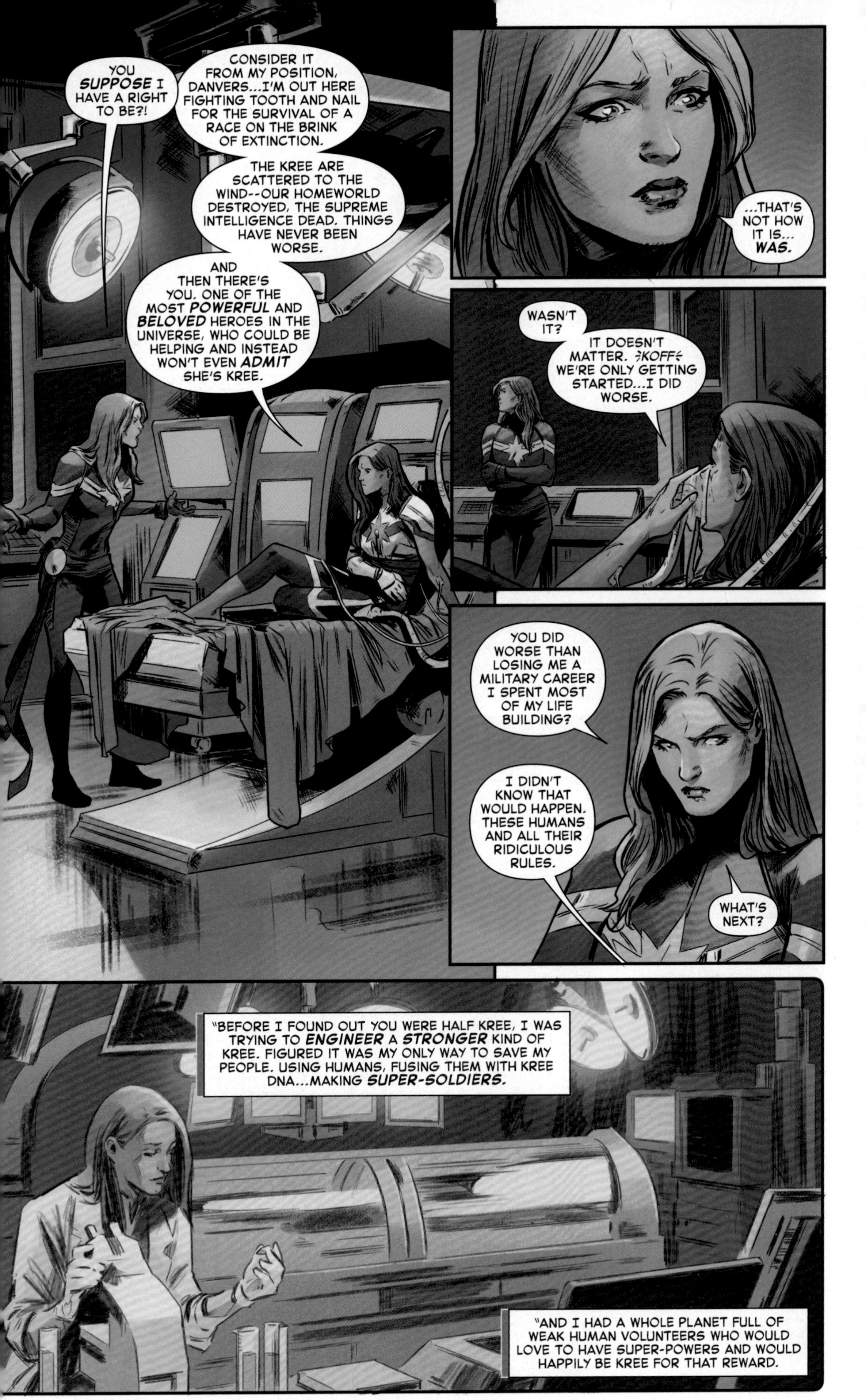
YOU SUPPOSE I HAVE A RIGHT TO BE?!
CONSIDER IT FROM MY POSITION, DANVERS...I'M OUT HERE FIGHTING TOOTH AND NAIL FOR THE SURVIVAL OF A RACE ON THE BRINK OF EXTINCTION.
THE KREE ARE SCATTERED TO THE WIND--OUR HOMEWORLD DESTROYED, THE SUPREME INTELLIGENCE DEAD. THINGS HAVE NEVER BEEN WORSE.
AND THEN THERE'S YOU. ONE OF THE MOST POWERFUL AND BELOVED HEROES IN THE UNIVERSE, WHO COULD BE HELPING AND INSTEAD WON'T EVEN ADMIT SHE'S KREE.
...THAT'S NOT HOW IT IS... WAS.
WASN'T IT?
IT DOESN'T MATTER. ⚡KOFF⚡ WE'RE ONLY GETTING STARTED...I DID WORSE.
YOU DID WORSE THAN LOSING ME A MILITARY CAREER I SPENT MOST OF MY LIFE BUILDING?
I DIDN'T KNOW THAT WOULD HAPPEN. THESE HUMANS AND ALL THEIR RIDICULOUS RULES.
WHAT'S NEXT?
"BEFORE I FOUND OUT YOU WERE HALF KREE, I WAS TRYING TO ENGINEER A STRONGER KIND OF KREE. FIGURED IT WAS MY ONLY WAY TO SAVE MY PEOPLE. USING HUMANS, FUSING THEM WITH KREE DNA...MAKING SUPER-SOLDIERS.
"AND I HAD A WHOLE PLANET FULL OF WEAK HUMAN VOLUNTEERS WHO WOULD LOVE TO HAVE SUPER-POWERS AND WOULD HAPPILY BE KREE FOR THAT REWARD.

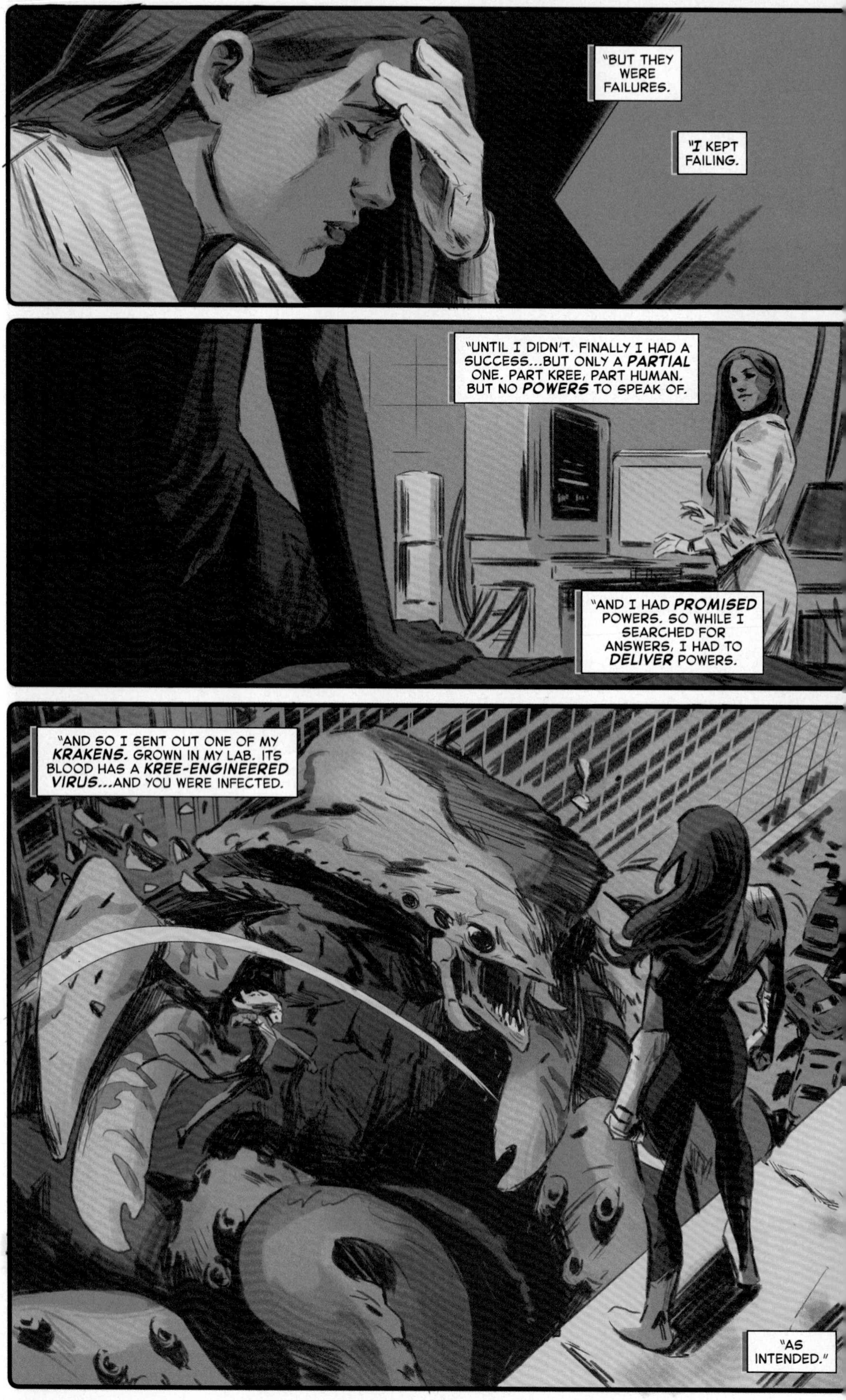
"BUT THEY WERE FAILURES.
"I KEPT FAILING.
"UNTIL I DIDN'T. FINALLY I HAD A SUCCESS...BUT ONLY A PARTIAL ONE. PART KREE, PART HUMAN. BUT NO POWERS TO SPEAK OF.
"AND I HAD PROMISED POWERS. SO WHILE I SEARCHED FOR ANSWERS, I HAD TO DELIVER POWERS.
"AND SO I SENT OUT ONE OF MY KRAKENS. GROWN IN MY LAB. ITS BLOOD HAS A KREE-ENGINEERED VIRUS...AND YOU WERE INFECTED.
"AS INTENDED."

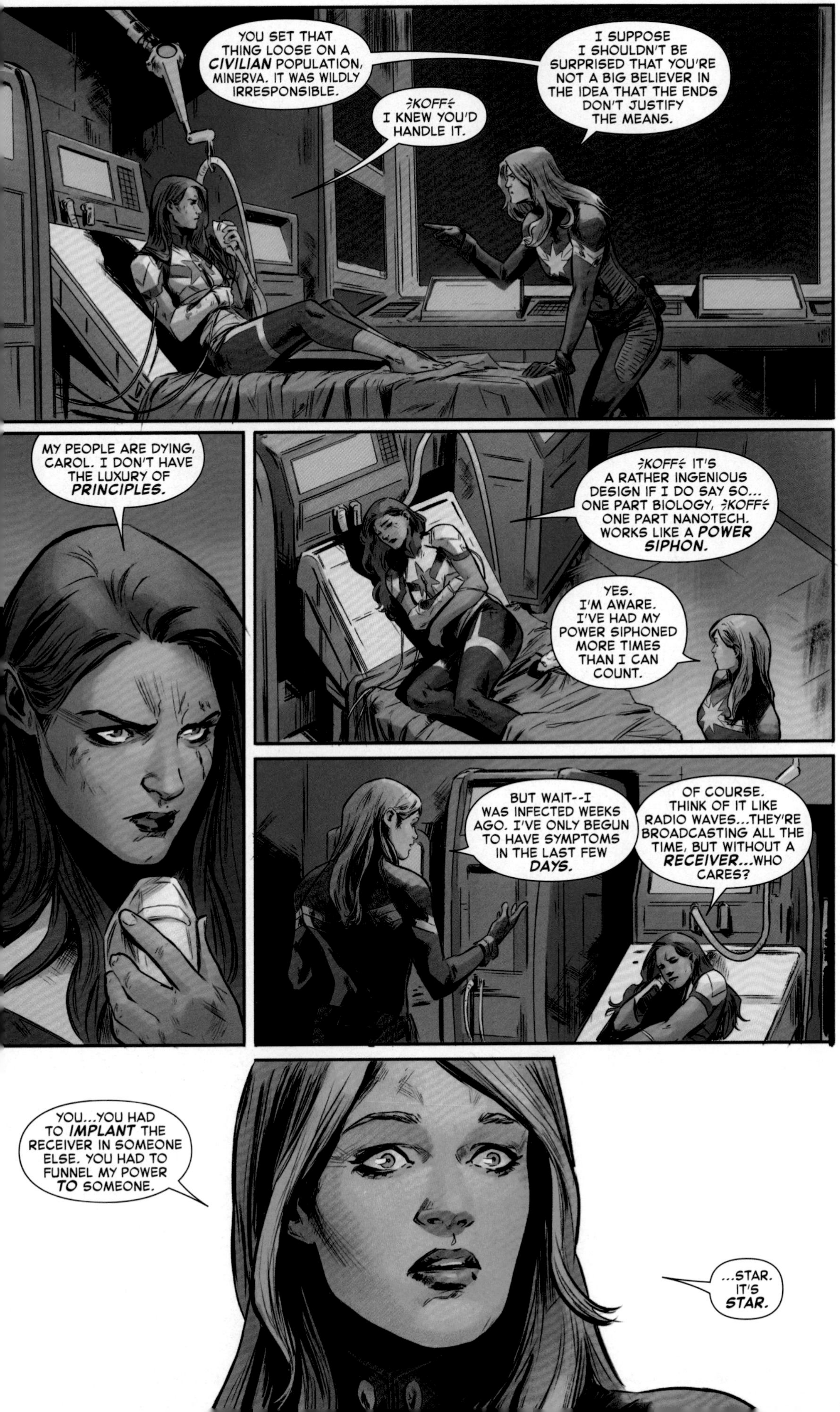
YOU SET THAT THING LOOSE ON A CIVILIAN POPULATION, MINERVA. IT WAS WILDLY IRRESPONSIBLE.
≠KOFF≠ I KNEW YOU'D HANDLE IT.
I SUPPOSE I SHOULDN'T BE SURPRISED THAT YOU'RE NOT A BIG BELIEVER IN THE IDEA THAT THE ENDS DON'T JUSTIFY THE MEANS.
MY PEOPLE ARE DYING, CAROL. I DON'T HAVE THE LUXURY OF PRINCIPLES.
≠KOFF≠ IT'S A RATHER INGENIOUS DESIGN IF I DO SAY SO... ONE PART BIOLOGY, ≠KOFF≠ ONE PART NANOTECH. WORKS LIKE A POWER SIPHON.
YES. I'M AWARE. I'VE HAD MY POWER SIPHONED MORE TIMES THAN I CAN COUNT.
BUT WAIT--I WAS INFECTED WEEKS AGO. I'VE ONLY BEGUN TO HAVE SYMPTOMS IN THE LAST FEW DAYS.
OF COURSE. THINK OF IT LIKE RADIO WAVES...THEY'RE BROADCASTING ALL THE TIME, BUT WITHOUT A RECEIVER...WHO CARES?
YOU...YOU HAD TO IMPLANT THE RECEIVER IN SOMEONE ELSE. YOU HAD TO FUNNEL MY POWER TO SOMEONE.
...STAR. IT'S STAR.

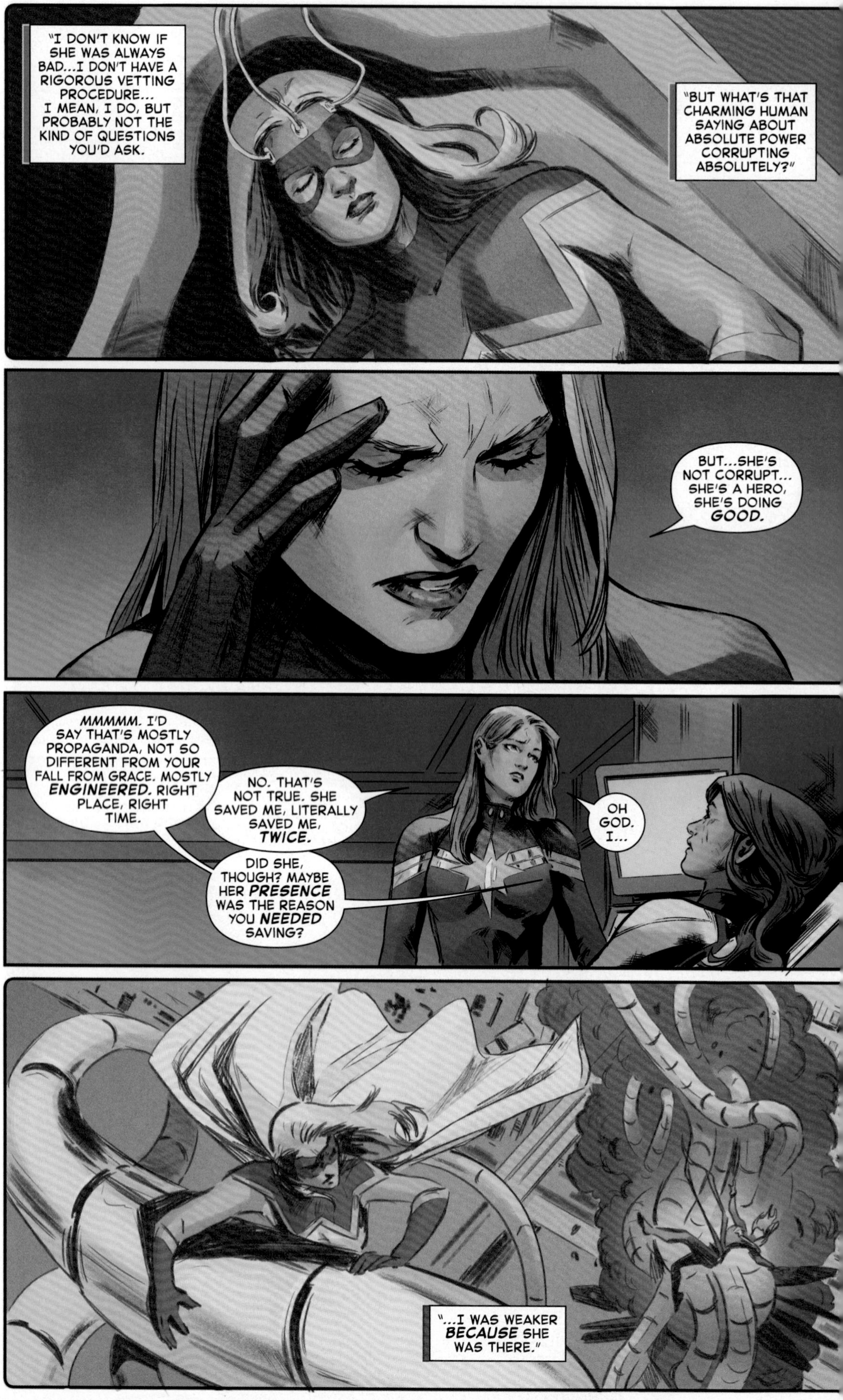
"I DON'T KNOW IF SHE WAS ALWAYS BAD...I DON'T HAVE A RIGOROUS VETTING PROCEDURE... I MEAN, I DO, BUT PROBABLY NOT THE KIND OF QUESTIONS YOU'D ASK.
"BUT WHAT'S THAT CHARMING HUMAN SAYING ABOUT ABSOLUTE POWER CORRUPTING ABSOLUTELY?"
BUT...SHE'S NOT CORRUPT... SHE'S A HERO, SHE'S DOING GOOD.
MMMMM. I'D SAY THAT'S MOSTLY PROPAGANDA, NOT SO DIFFERENT FROM YOUR FALL FROM GRACE. MOSTLY ENGINEERED. RIGHT PLACE, RIGHT TIME.
NO. THAT'S NOT TRUE. SHE SAVED ME, LITERALLY SAVED ME, TWICE.
DID SHE, THOUGH? MAYBE HER PRESENCE WAS THE REASON YOU NEEDED SAVING?
OH GOD. I...
"...I WAS WEAKER BECAUSE SHE WAS THERE."

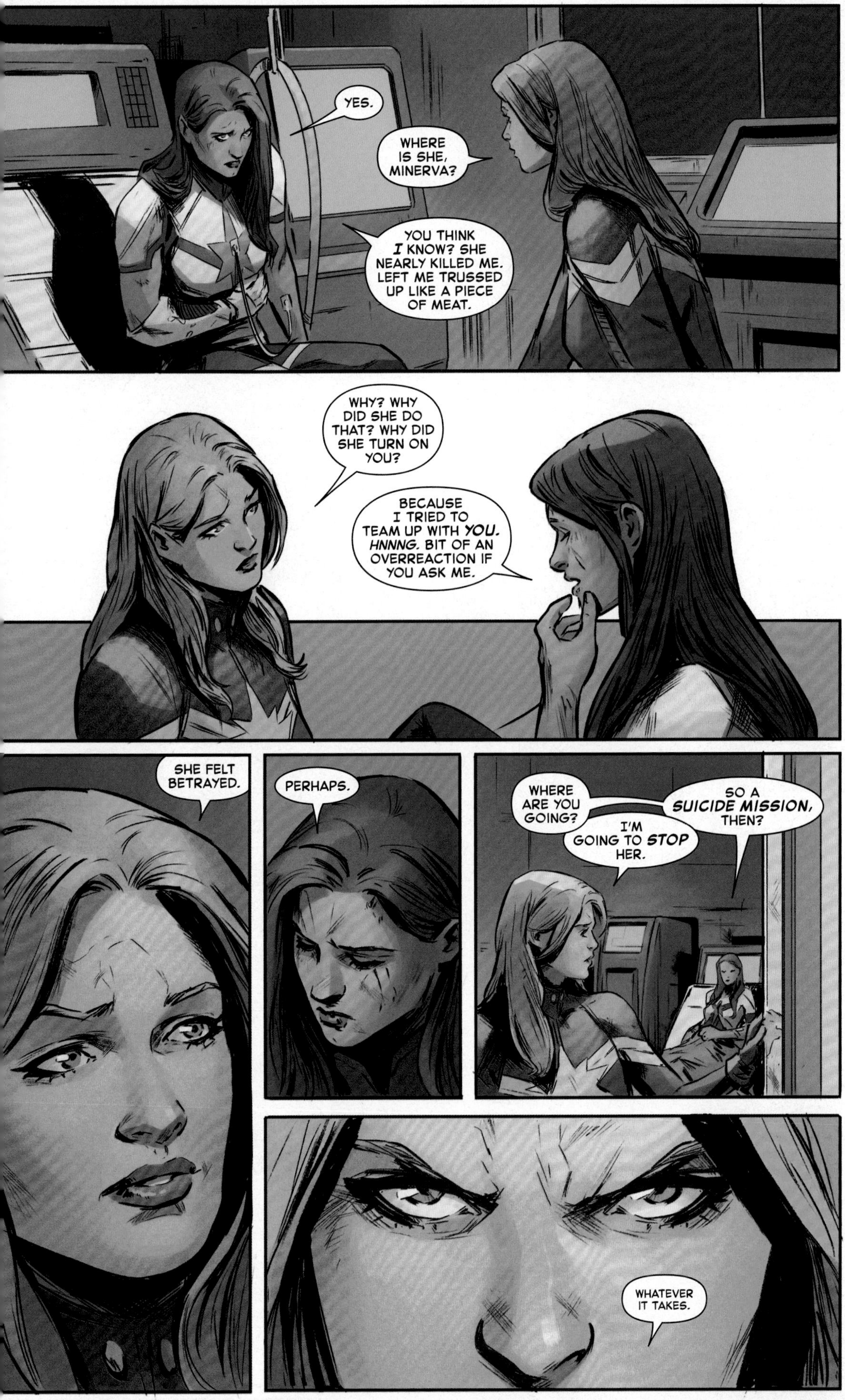
YES.
WHERE IS SHE, MINERVA?
YOU THINK I KNOW? SHE NEARLY KILLED ME. LEFT ME TRUSSED UP LIKE A PIECE OF MEAT.
WHY? WHY DID SHE DO THAT? WHY DID SHE TURN ON YOU?
BECAUSE I TRIED TO TEAM UP WITH YOU. HNNNG. BIT OF AN OVERREACTION IF YOU ASK ME.
SHE FELT BETRAYED.
PERHAPS.
WHERE ARE YOU GOING?
I'M GOING TO STOP HER.
SO A SUICIDE MISSION, THEN?
WHATEVER IT TAKES.

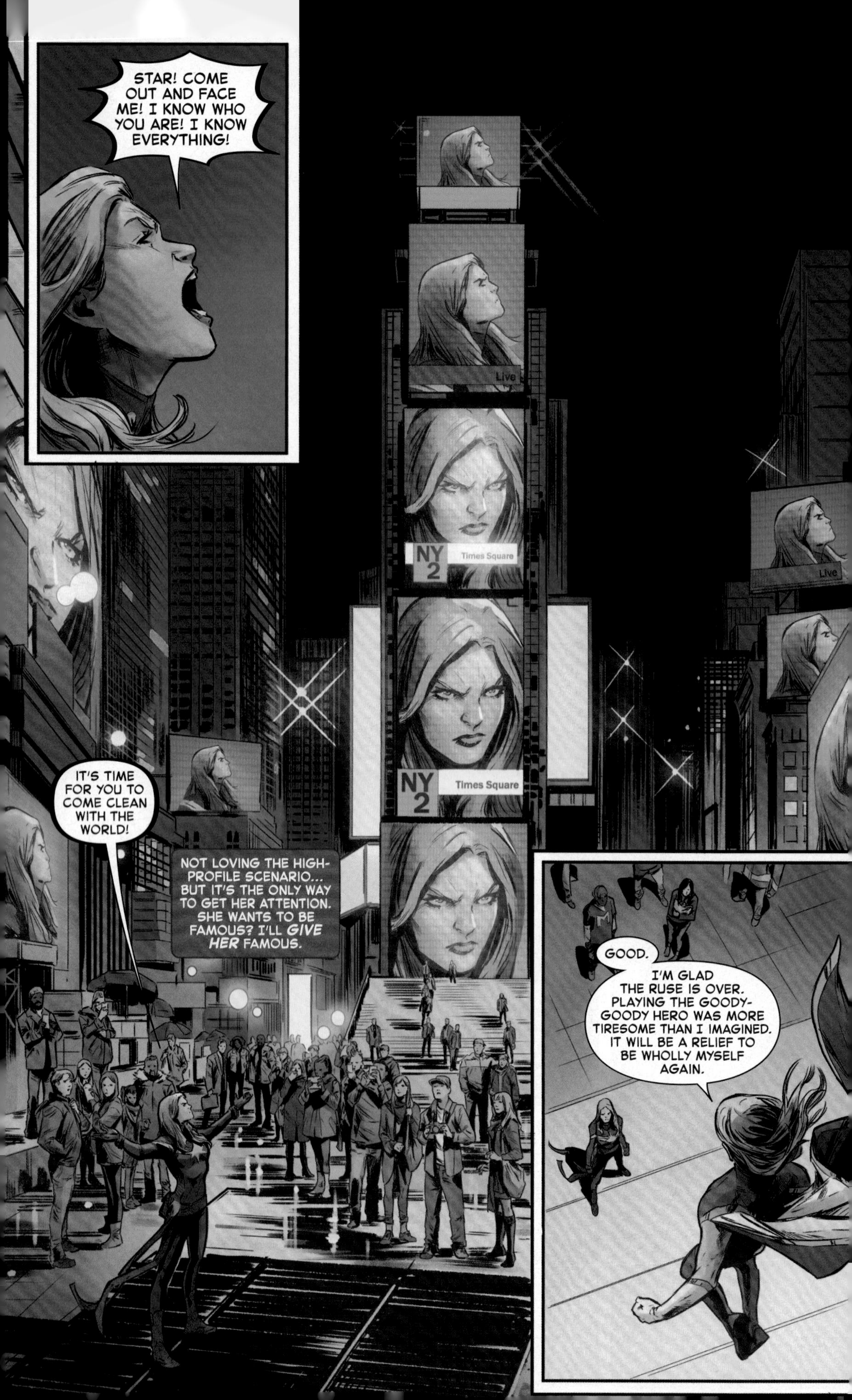
STAR! COME OUT AND FACE ME! I KNOW WHO YOU ARE! I KNOW EVERYTHING!
Live
NY 2 Times Square
NY 2 Times Square
Live
IT'S TIME FOR YOU TO COME CLEAN WITH THE WORLD!
NOT LOVING THE HIGH-PROFILE SCENARIO... BUT IT'S THE ONLY WAY TO GET HER ATTENTION. SHE WANTS TO BE FAMOUS? I'LL *GIVE HER* FAMOUS.
GOOD.
I'M GLAD THE RUSE IS OVER. PLAYING THE GOODY-GOODY HERO WAS MORE TIRESOME THAN I IMAGINED. IT WILL BE A RELIEF TO BE WHOLLY MYSELF AGAIN.

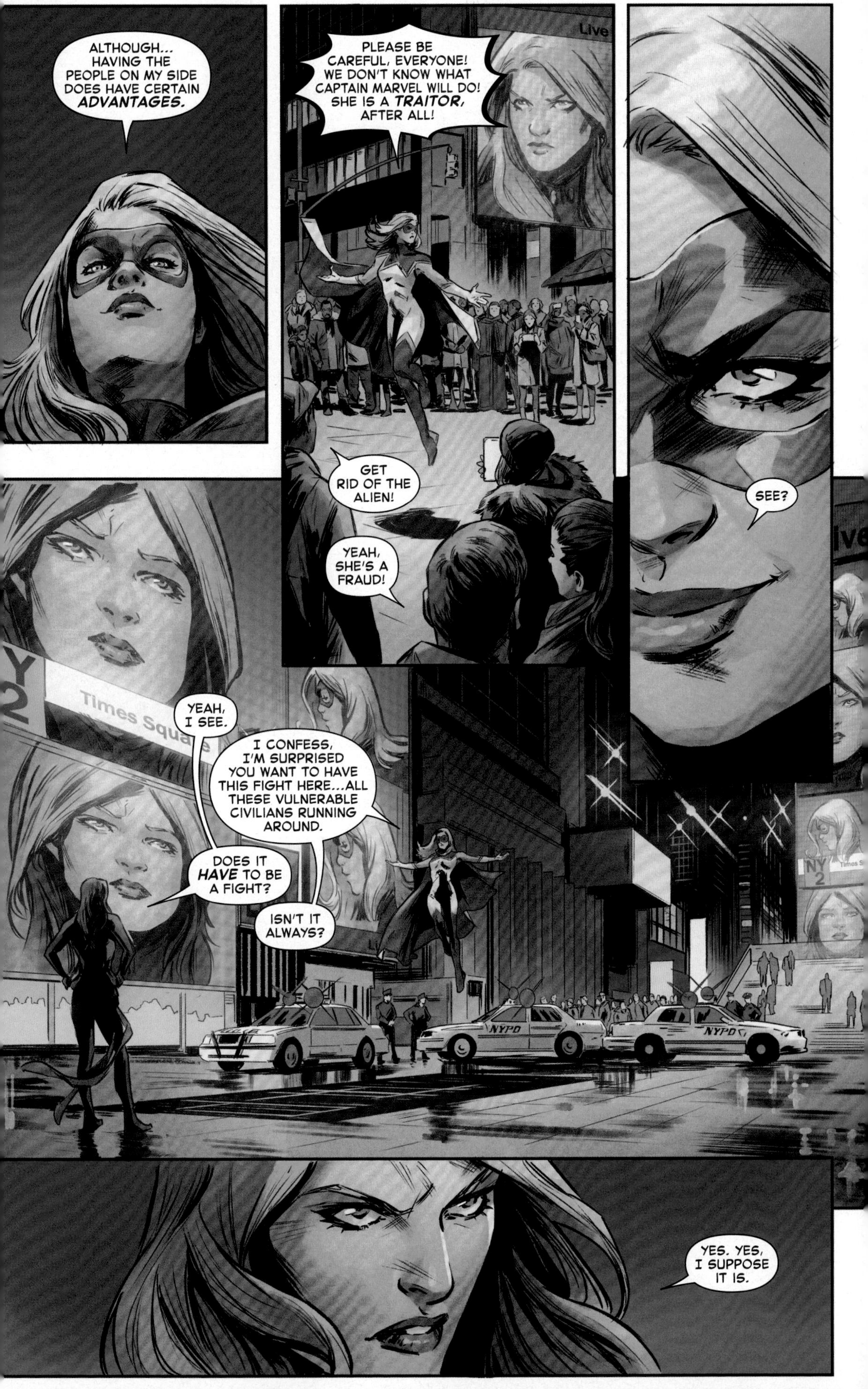

ALTHOUGH... HAVING THE PEOPLE ON MY SIDE DOES HAVE CERTAIN ADVANTAGES.
Live
PLEASE BE CAREFUL, EVERYONE! WE DON'T KNOW WHAT CAPTAIN MARVEL WILL DO! SHE IS A TRAITOR, AFTER ALL!
GET RID OF THE ALIEN!
YEAH, SHE'S A FRAUD!
SEE?
Times Square
YEAH, I SEE.
I CONFESS, I'M SURPRISED YOU WANT TO HAVE THIS FIGHT HERE...ALL THESE VULNERABLE CIVILIANS RUNNING AROUND.
DOES IT HAVE TO BE A FIGHT?
ISN'T IT ALWAYS?
NYPD
NYPD
YES. YES, I SUPPOSE IT IS.

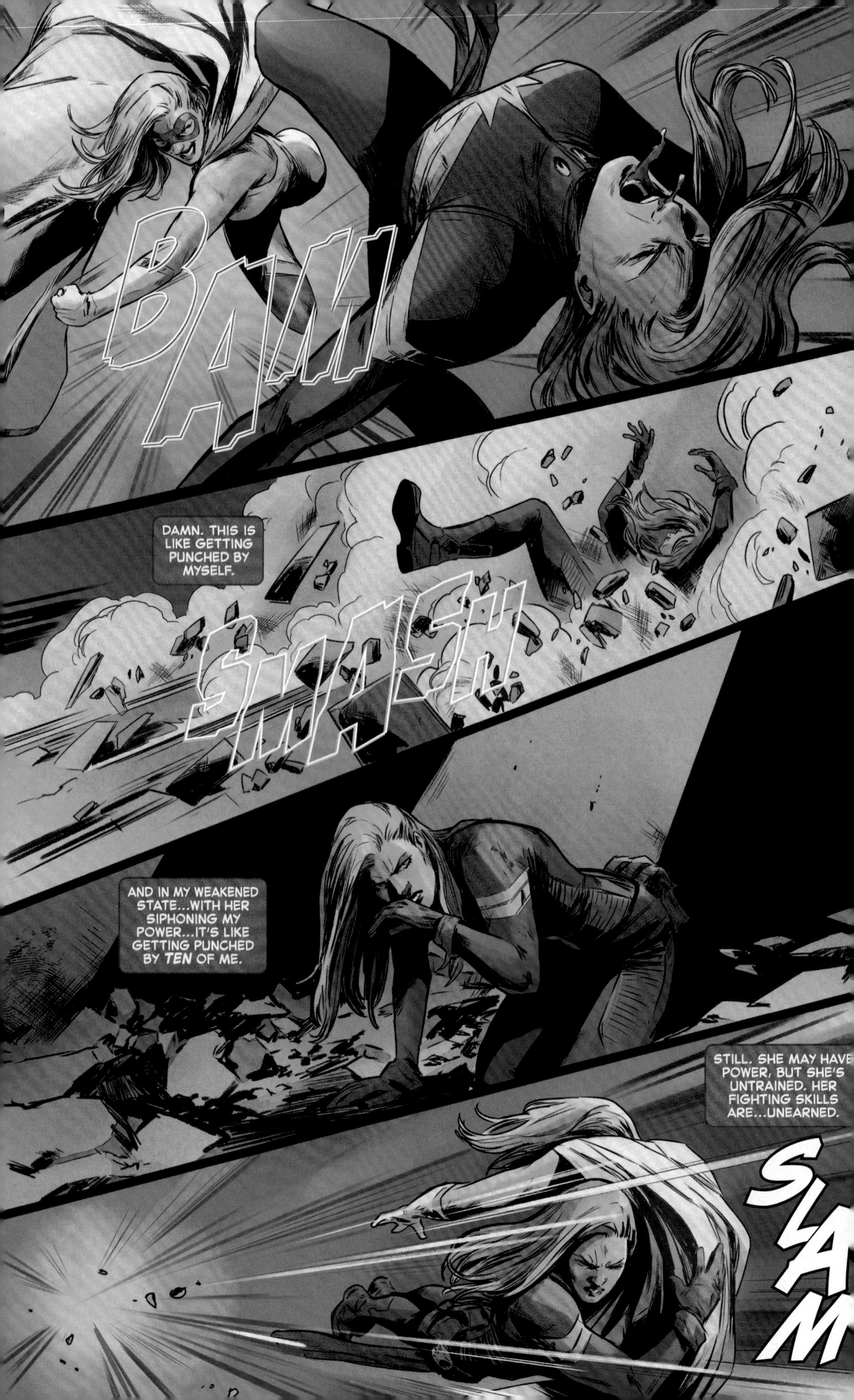
BAM
DAMN. THIS IS LIKE GETTING PUNCHED BY MYSELF.
SMASH
AND IN MY WEAKENED STATE...WITH HER SIPHONING MY POWER...IT'S LIKE GETTING PUNCHED BY TEN OF ME.
STILL. SHE MAY HAVE POWER, BUT SHE'S UNTRAINED. HER FIGHTING SKILLS ARE...UNEARNED.
SLAM

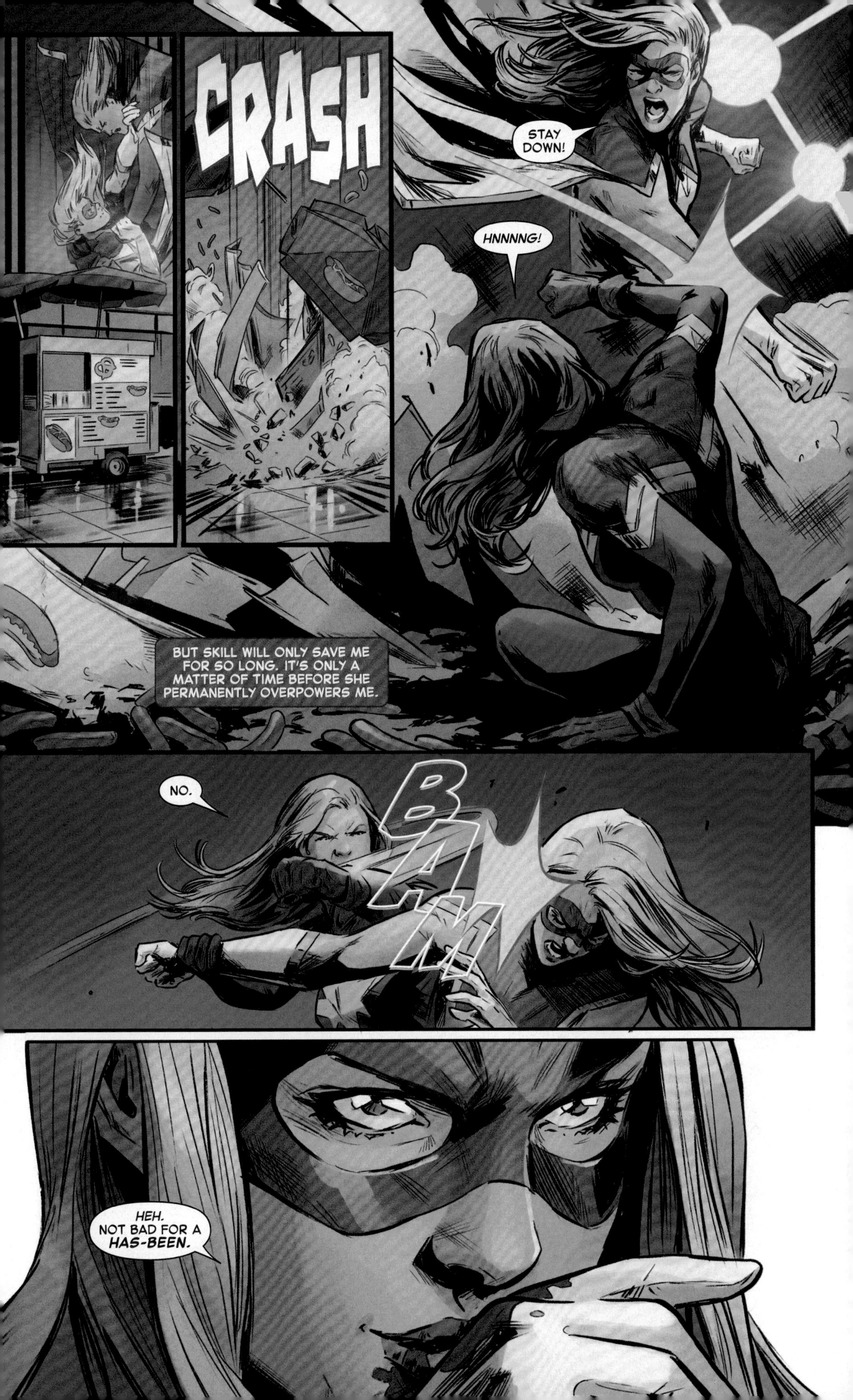
CRASH
STAY DOWN!
HNNNNG!
BUT SKILL WILL ONLY SAVE ME FOR SO LONG. IT'S ONLY A MATTER OF TIME BEFORE SHE PERMANENTLY OVERPOWERS ME.
NO.
BAM
HEH. NOT BAD FOR A HAS-BEEN.

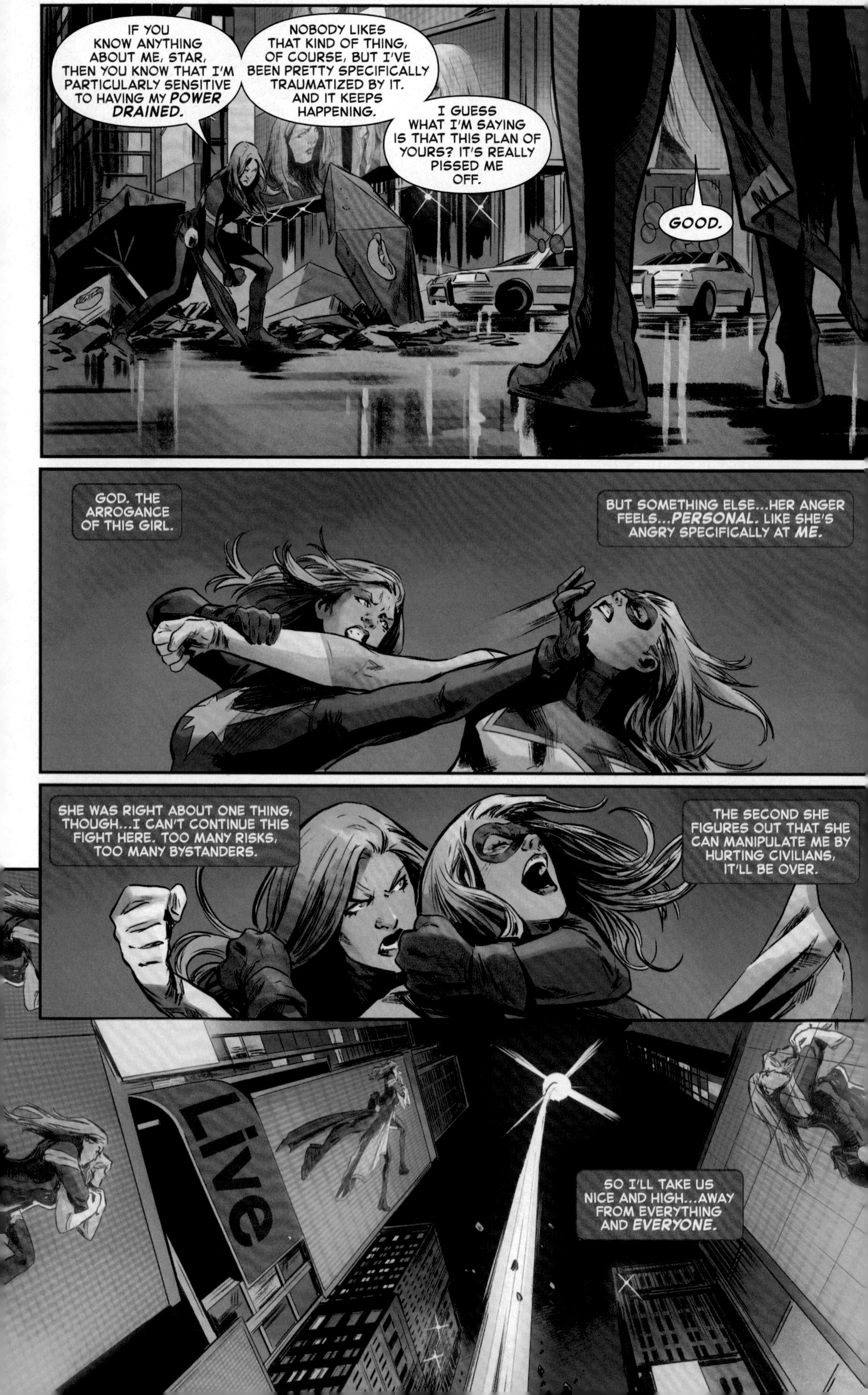
IF YOU KNOW ANYTHING ABOUT ME, STAR, THEN YOU KNOW THAT I'M PARTICULARLY SENSITIVE TO HAVING MY POWER DRAINED.
NOBODY LIKES THAT KIND OF THING, OF COURSE, BUT I'VE BEEN PRETTY SPECIFICALLY TRAUMATIZED BY IT. AND IT KEEPS HAPPENING.
I GUESS WHAT I'M SAYING IS THAT THIS PLAN OF YOURS? IT'S REALLY PISSED ME OFF.
GOOD.
GOD. THE ARROGANCE OF THIS GIRL.
BUT SOMETHING ELSE...HER ANGER FEELS...PERSONAL. LIKE SHE'S ANGRY SPECIFICALLY AT ME.
SHE WAS RIGHT ABOUT ONE THING, THOUGH...I CAN'T CONTINUE THIS FIGHT HERE. TOO MANY RISKS, TOO MANY BYSTANDERS.
THE SECOND SHE FIGURES OUT THAT SHE CAN MANIPULATE ME BY HURTING CIVILIANS, IT'LL BE OVER.
Live
SO I'LL TAKE US NICE AND HIGH...AWAY FROM EVERYTHING AND EVERYONE.

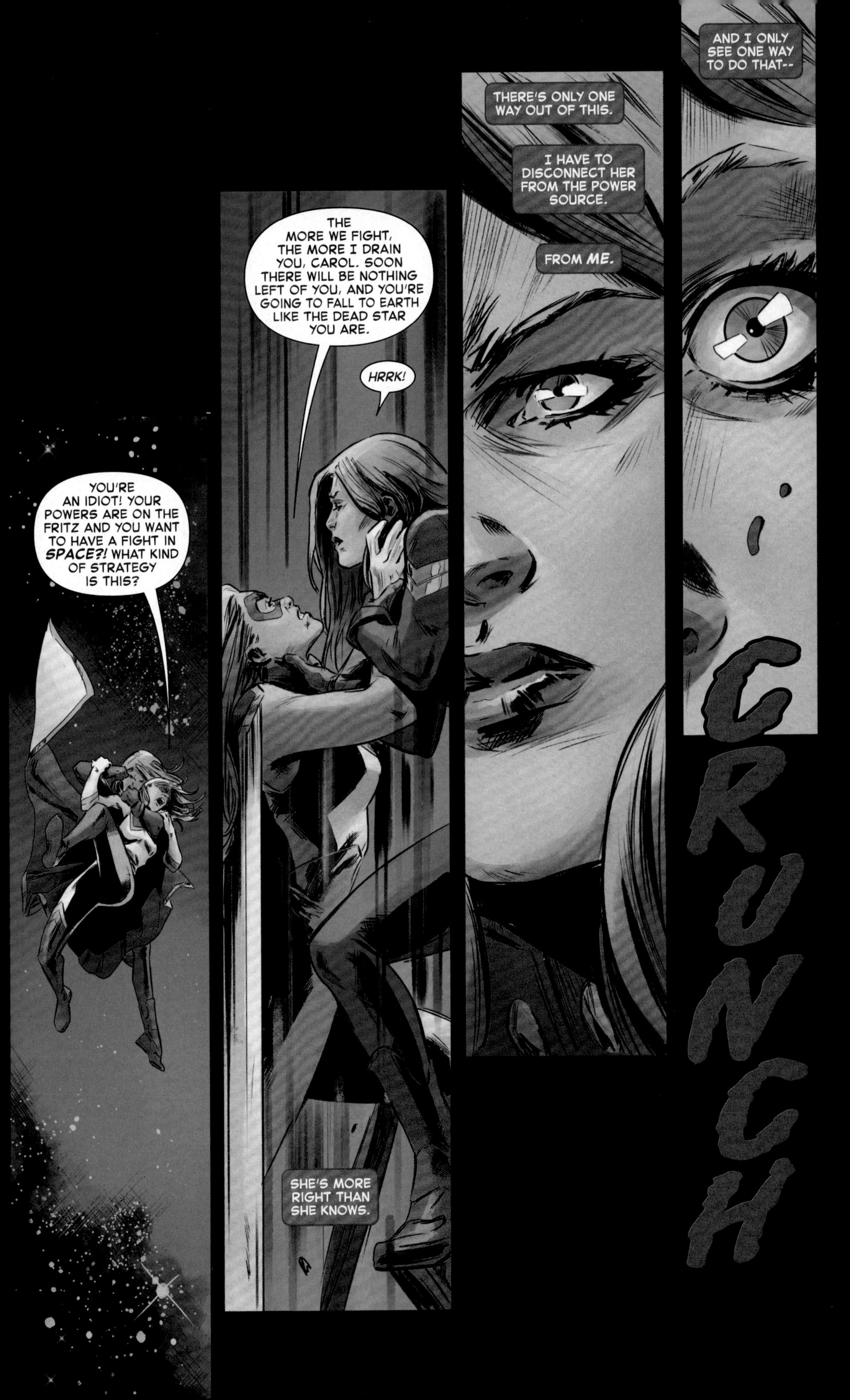
YOU'RE AN IDIOT! YOUR POWERS ARE ON THE FRITZ AND YOU WANT TO HAVE A FIGHT IN SPACE?! WHAT KIND OF STRATEGY IS THIS?
THE MORE WE FIGHT, THE MORE I DRAIN YOU, CAROL. SOON THERE WILL BE NOTHING LEFT OF YOU, AND YOU'RE GOING TO FALL TO EARTH LIKE THE DEAD STAR YOU ARE.
HRRK!
SHE'S MORE RIGHT THAN SHE KNOWS.
THERE'S ONLY ONE WAY OUT OF THIS.
I HAVE TO DISCONNECT HER FROM THE POWER SOURCE.
FROM ME.
AND I ONLY SEE ONE WAY TO DO THAT--
CRUNCH

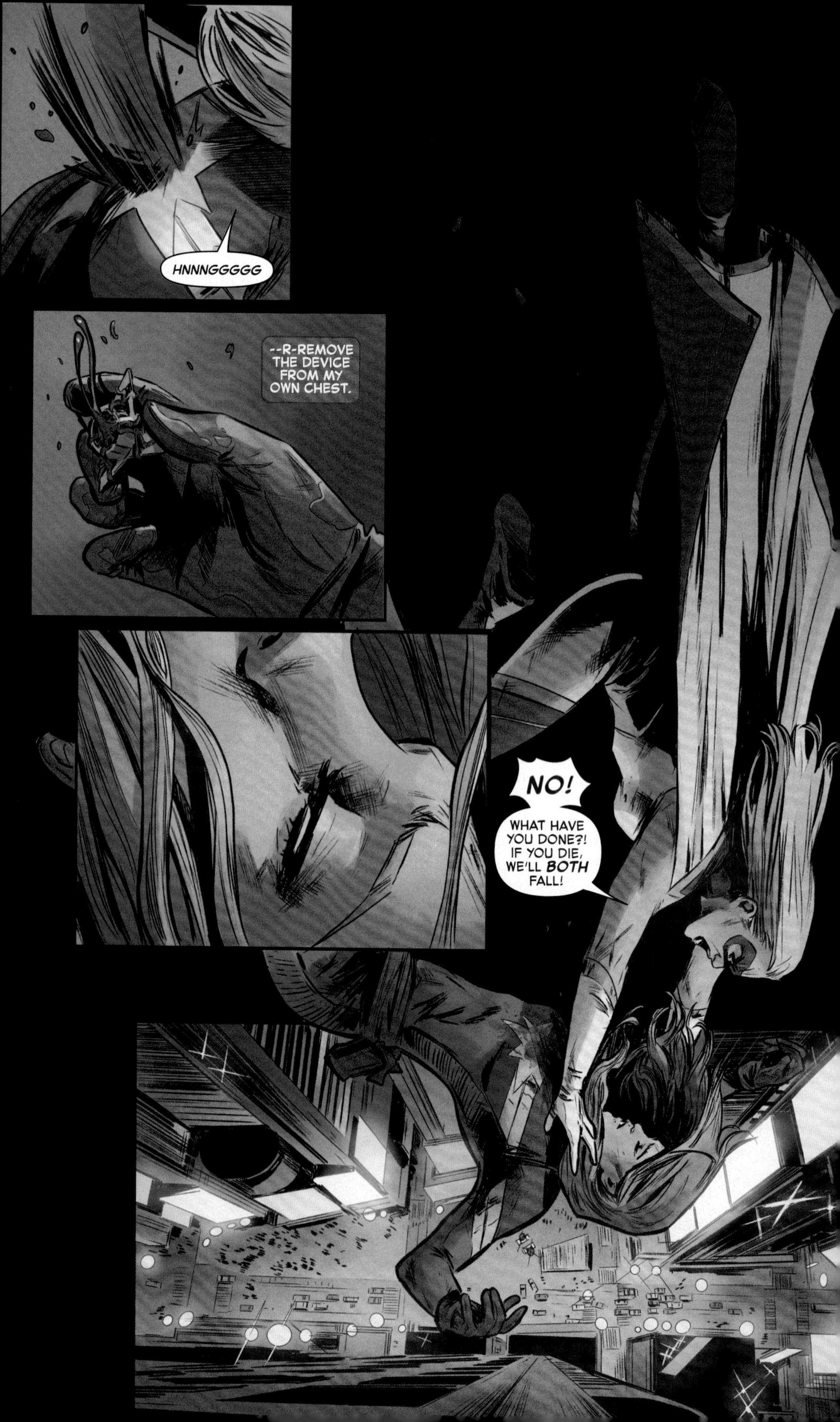
HNNNGGGGG
--R-REMOVE THE DEVICE FROM MY OWN CHEST.
NO!
WHAT HAVE YOU DONE?! IF YOU DIE, WE'LL *BOTH* FALL!

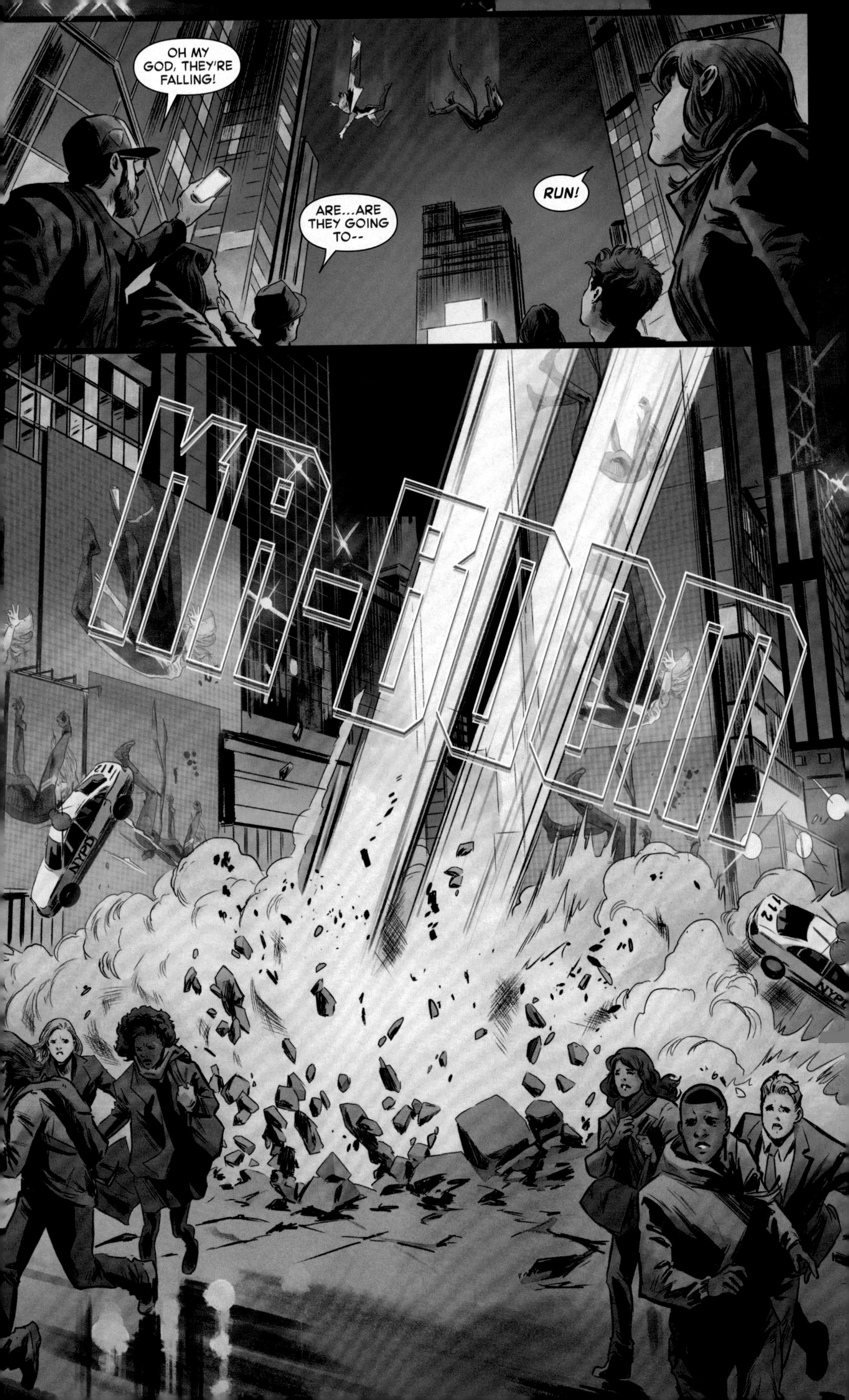
OH MY GOD, THEY'RE FALLING!
ARE...ARE THEY GOING TO--
RUN!
NYPD

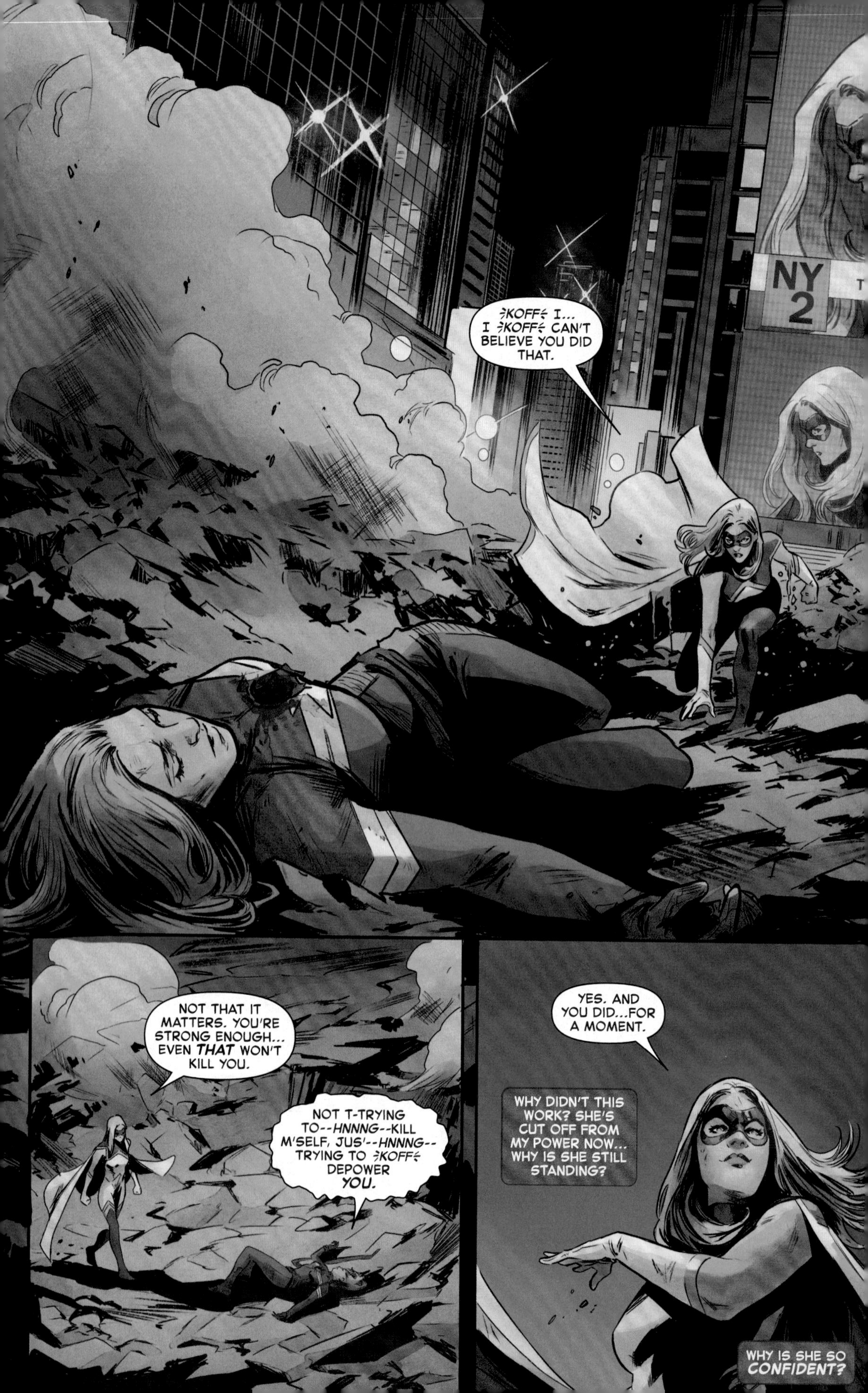
NY 2
KOFF I... I *KOFF* CAN'T BELIEVE YOU DID THAT.
NOT THAT IT MATTERS. YOU'RE STRONG ENOUGH... EVEN **THAT** WON'T KILL YOU.
NOT T-TRYING TO--*HNNNG*--KILL M'SELF, JUS'--*HNNNG*--TRYING TO *KOFF* DEPOWER ***YOU.***
YES. AND YOU DID...FOR A MOMENT.
WHY DIDN'T THIS WORK? SHE'S CUT OFF FROM MY POWER NOW... WHY IS SHE STILL STANDING?
WHY IS SHE SO ***CONFIDENT?***

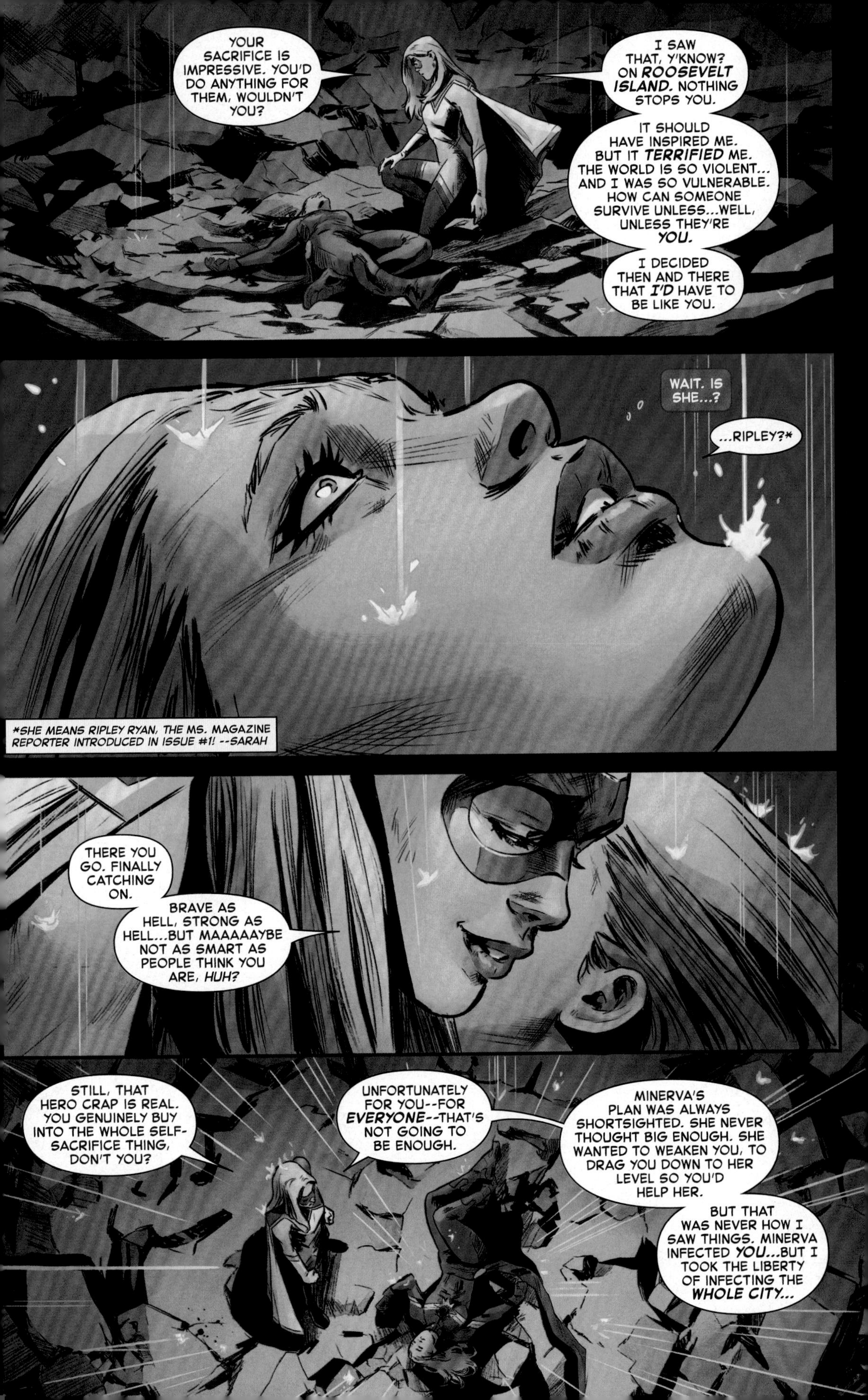
YOUR SACRIFICE IS IMPRESSIVE. YOU'D DO ANYTHING FOR THEM, WOULDN'T YOU?
I SAW THAT, Y'KNOW? ON ROOSEVELT ISLAND. NOTHING STOPS YOU.
IT SHOULD HAVE INSPIRED ME. BUT IT TERRIFIED ME. THE WORLD IS SO VIOLENT... AND I WAS SO VULNERABLE. HOW CAN SOMEONE SURVIVE UNLESS...WELL, UNLESS THEY'RE YOU.
I DECIDED THEN AND THERE THAT I'D HAVE TO BE LIKE YOU.
WAIT. IS SHE...?
...RIPLEY?*
*SHE MEANS RIPLEY RYAN, THE MS. MAGAZINE REPORTER INTRODUCED IN ISSUE #1! --SARAH
THERE YOU GO. FINALLY CATCHING ON.
BRAVE AS HELL, STRONG AS HELL...BUT MAAAAAYBE NOT AS SMART AS PEOPLE THINK YOU ARE, HUH?
STILL, THAT HERO CRAP IS REAL. YOU GENUINELY BUY INTO THE WHOLE SELF-SACRIFICE THING, DON'T YOU?
UNFORTUNATELY FOR YOU--FOR EVERYONE--THAT'S NOT GOING TO BE ENOUGH.
MINERVA'S PLAN WAS ALWAYS SHORTSIGHTED. SHE NEVER THOUGHT BIG ENOUGH. SHE WANTED TO WEAKEN YOU, TO DRAG YOU DOWN TO HER LEVEL SO YOU'D HELP HER.
BUT THAT WAS NEVER HOW I SAW THINGS. MINERVA INFECTED YOU...BUT I TOOK THE LIBERTY OF INFECTING THE WHOLE CITY...

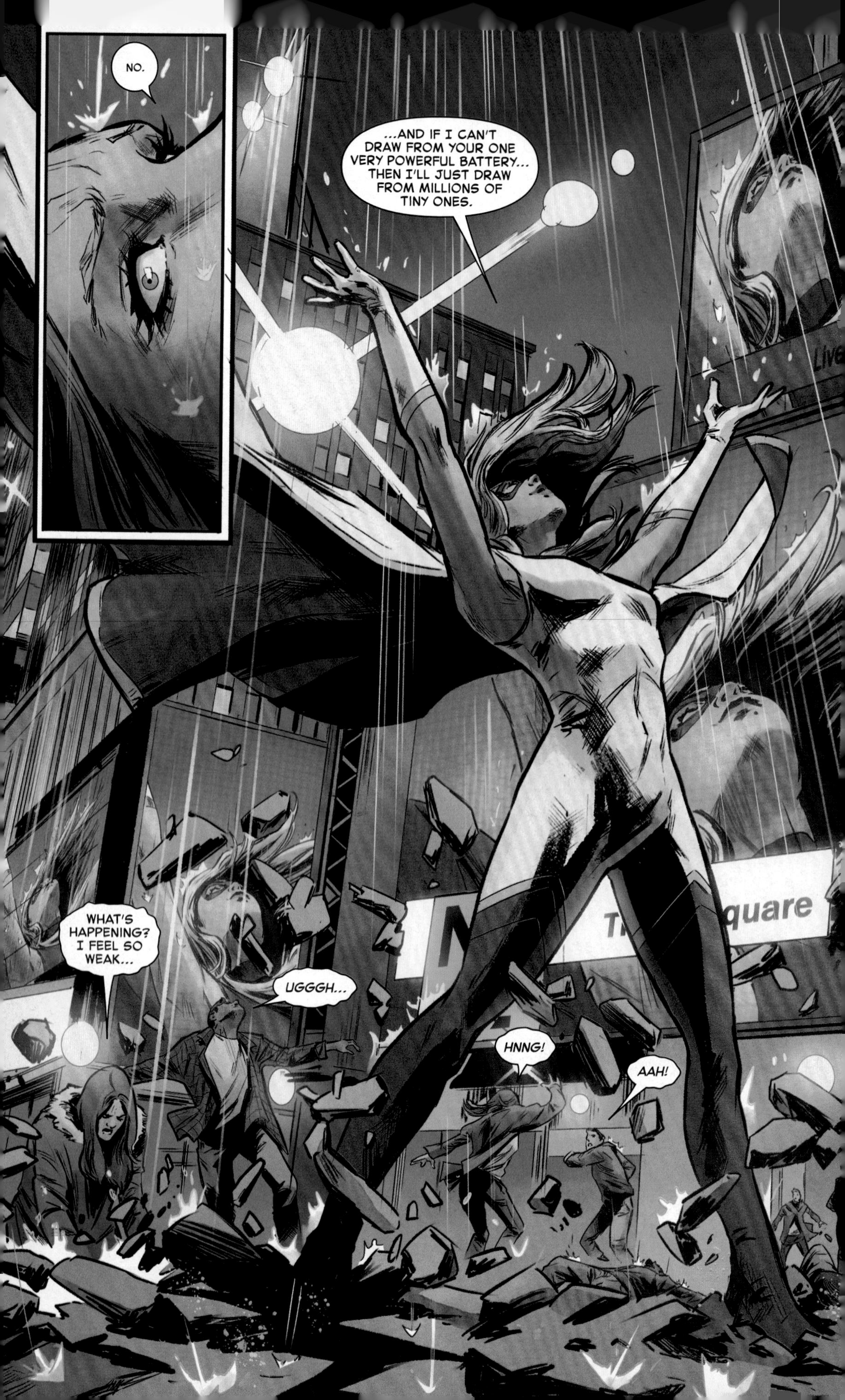
NO.
...AND IF I CAN'T DRAW FROM YOUR ONE VERY POWERFUL BATTERY... THEN I'LL JUST DRAW FROM MILLIONS OF TINY ONES.
WHAT'S HAPPENING? I FEEL SO WEAK...
UGGGH...
HNNG!
AAH!

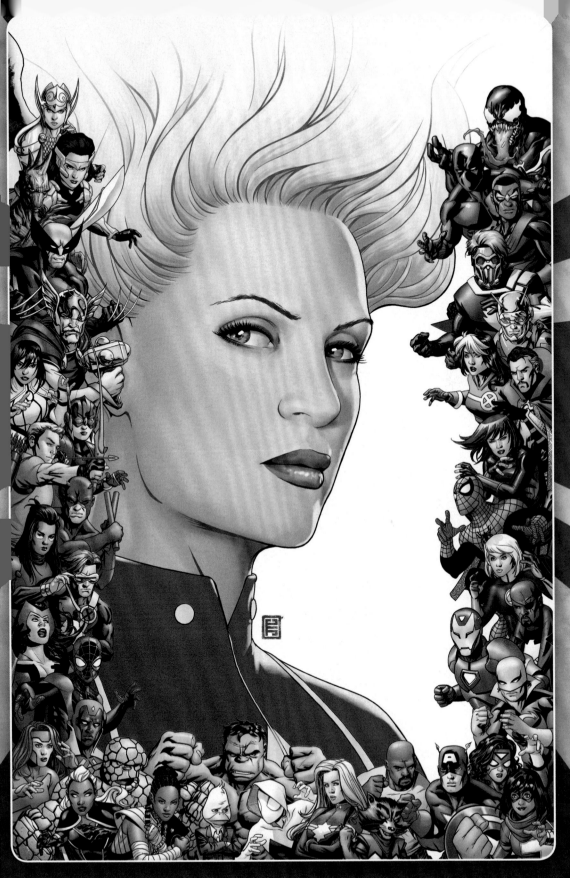

JOHN TYLER CHRISTOPHER

WITH FRAME BY MIKE McKONE & EDGAR DELGADO

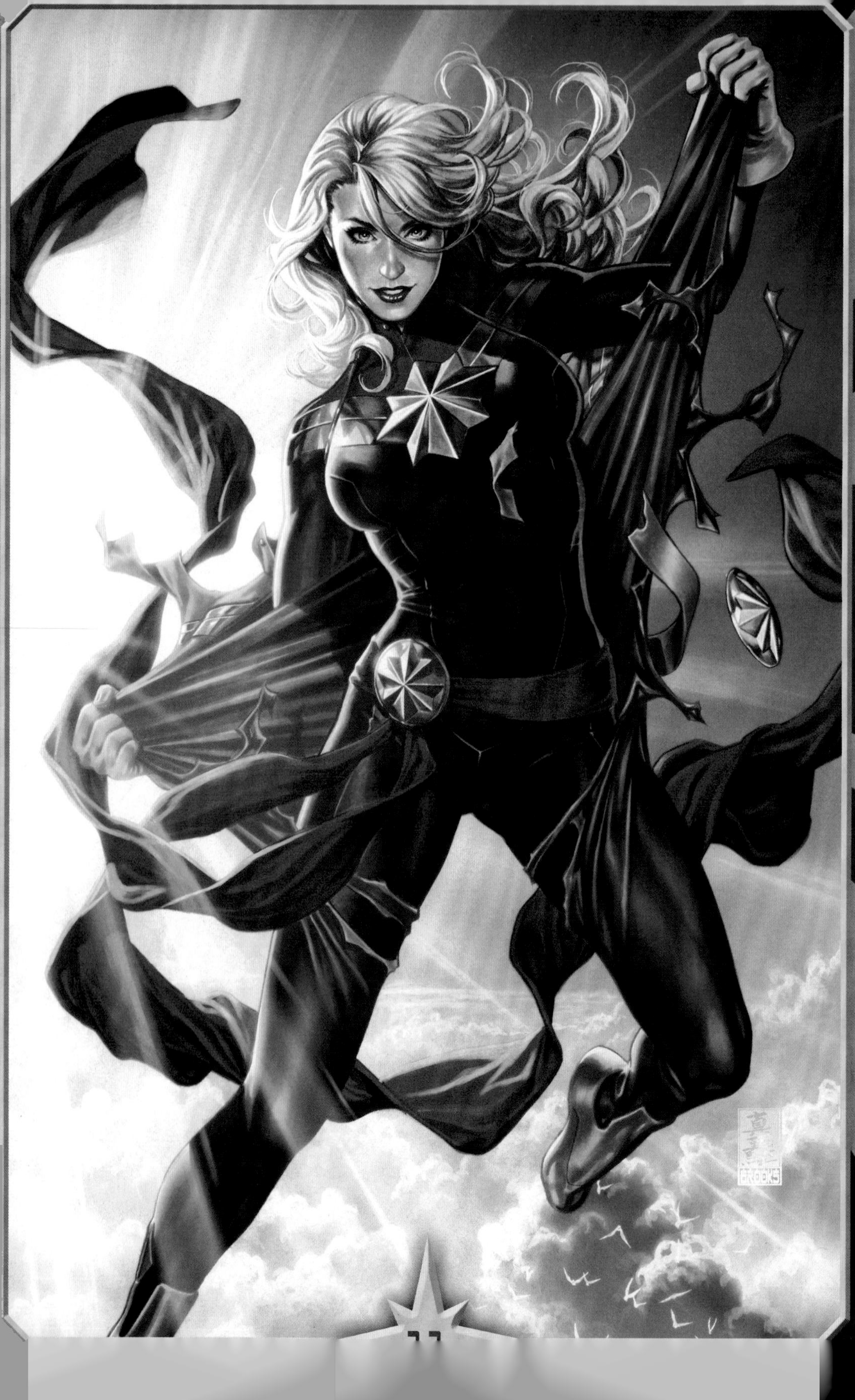

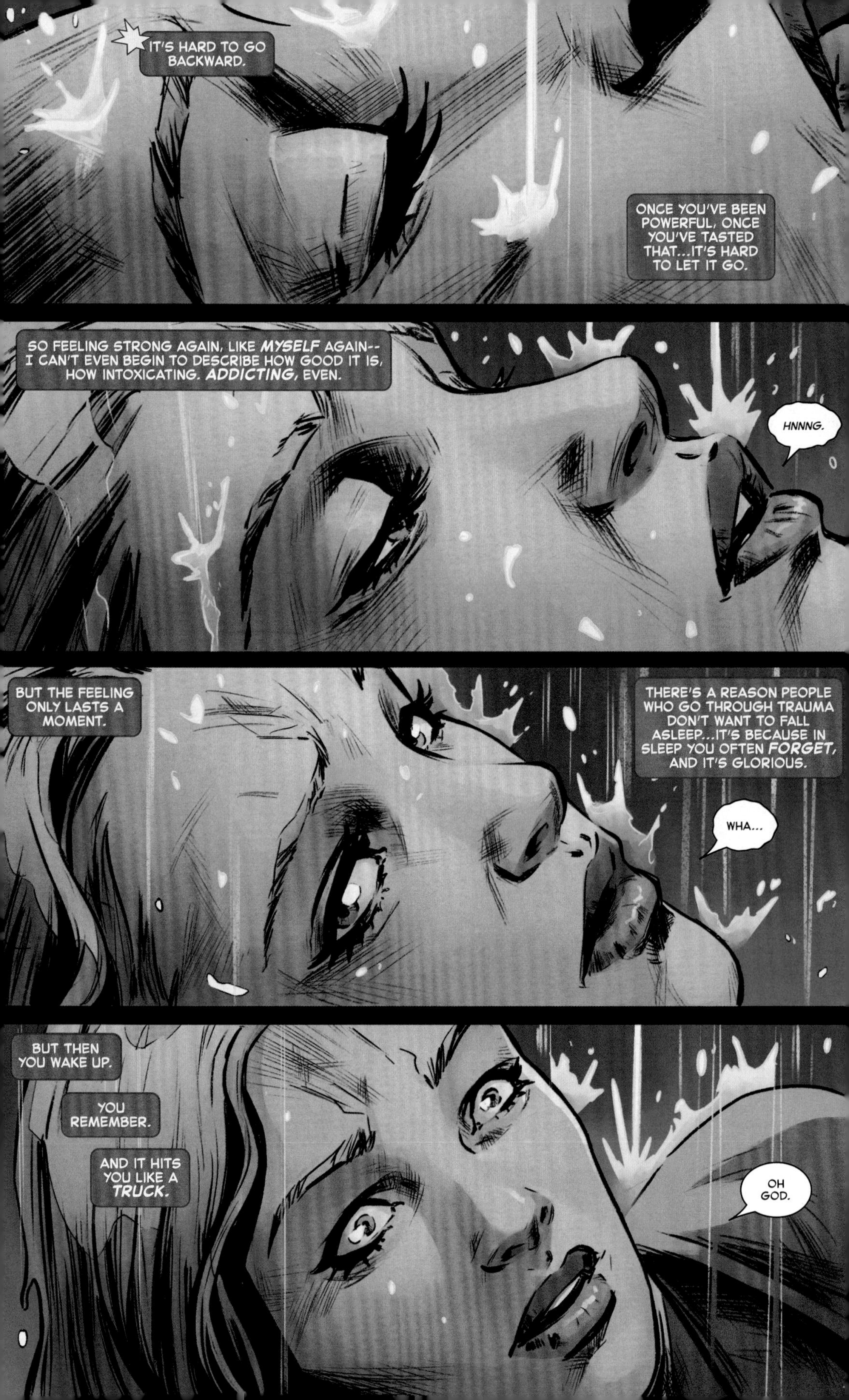
IT'S HARD TO GO BACKWARD.
ONCE YOU'VE BEEN POWERFUL, ONCE YOU'VE TASTED THAT...IT'S HARD TO LET IT GO.
SO FEELING STRONG AGAIN, LIKE MYSELF AGAIN-- I CAN'T EVEN BEGIN TO DESCRIBE HOW GOOD IT IS, HOW INTOXICATING. ADDICTING, EVEN.
HNNNG.
BUT THE FEELING ONLY LASTS A MOMENT.
THERE'S A REASON PEOPLE WHO GO THROUGH TRAUMA DON'T WANT TO FALL ASLEEP...IT'S BECAUSE IN SLEEP YOU OFTEN FORGET, AND IT'S GLORIOUS.
WHA...
BUT THEN YOU WAKE UP.
YOU REMEMBER.
AND IT HITS YOU LIKE A TRUCK.
OH GOD.

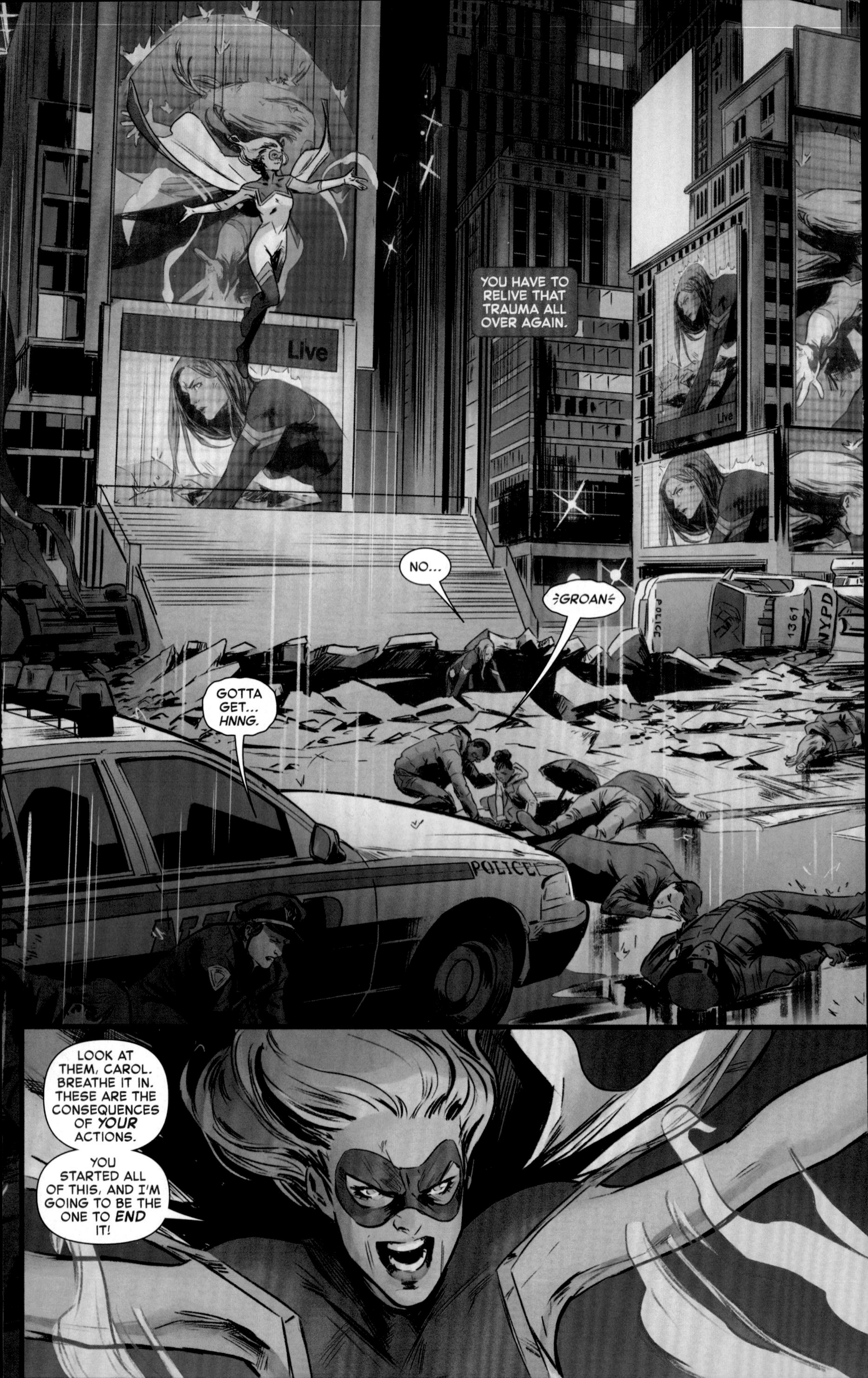
Live
YOU HAVE TO RELIVE THAT TRAUMA ALL OVER AGAIN.
Live
NO...
GROAN
POLICE
1361
NYPD
GOTTA GET... HNNG.
POLICE
LOOK AT THEM, CAROL. BREATHE IT IN. THESE ARE THE CONSEQUENCES OF YOUR ACTIONS.
YOU STARTED ALL OF THIS, AND I'M GOING TO BE THE ONE TO END IT!

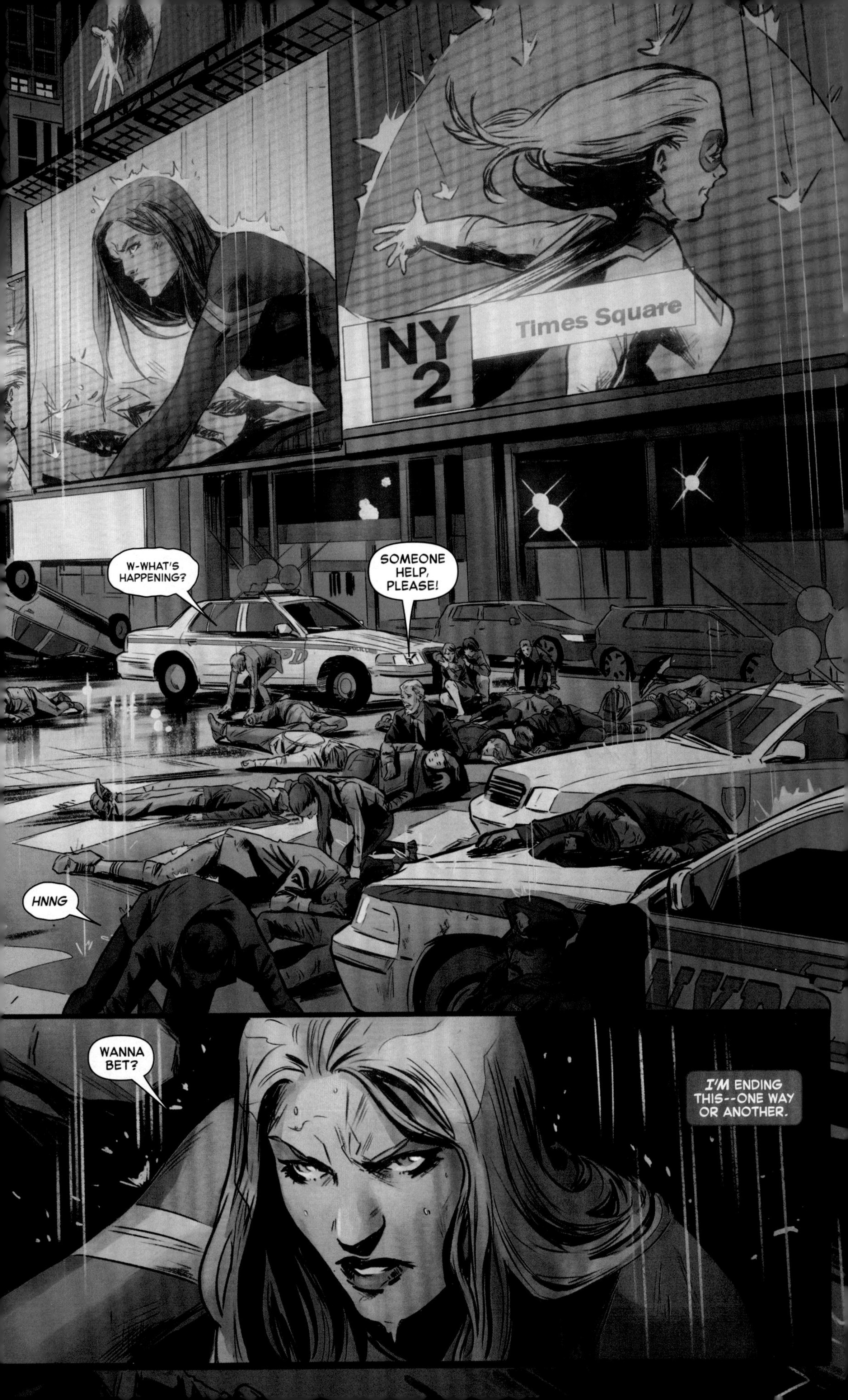
NY 2
Times Square
W-WHAT'S HAPPENING?
SOMEONE HELP, PLEASE!
HNNG
WANNA BET?
I'M ENDING THIS--ONE WAY OR ANOTHER.

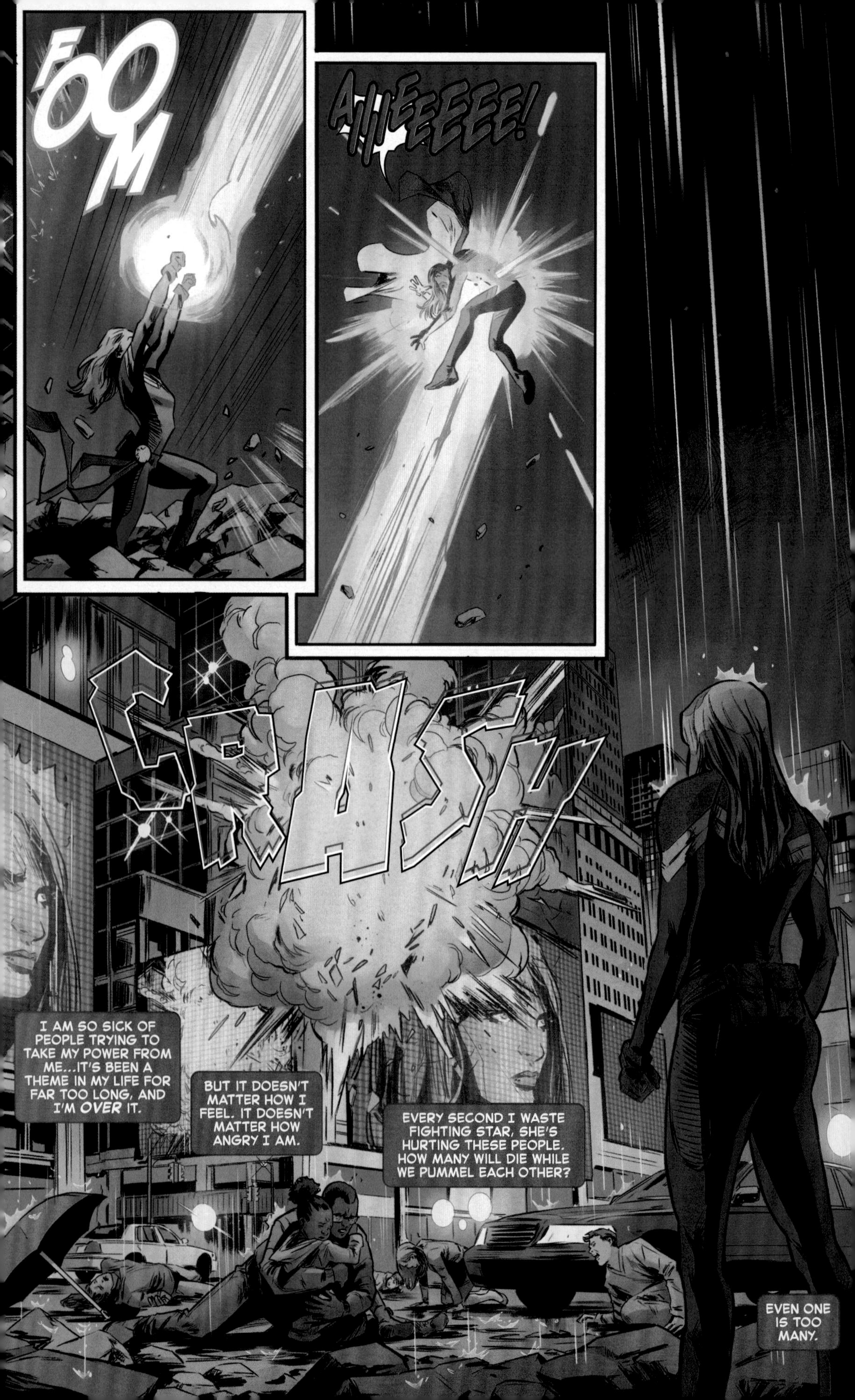
FOOM
AIIIEEEEEE!
CRASH
I AM SO SICK OF PEOPLE TRYING TO TAKE MY POWER FROM ME...IT'S BEEN A THEME IN MY LIFE FOR FAR TOO LONG, AND I'M OVER IT.
BUT IT DOESN'T MATTER HOW I FEEL. IT DOESN'T MATTER HOW ANGRY I AM.
EVERY SECOND I WASTE FIGHTING STAR, SHE'S HURTING THESE PEOPLE. HOW MANY WILL DIE WHILE WE PUMMEL EACH OTHER?
EVEN ONE IS TOO MANY.

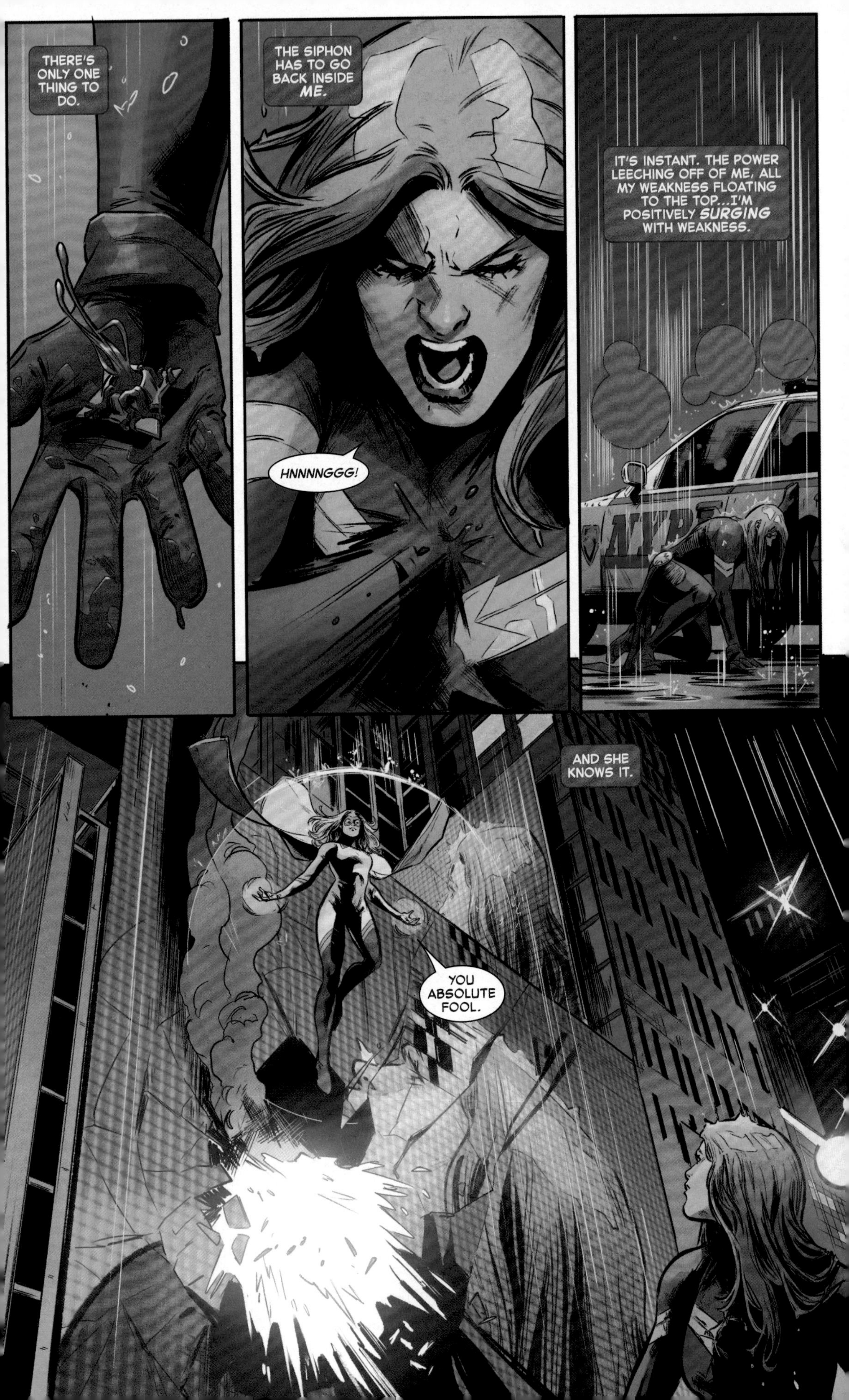
THERE'S ONLY ONE THING TO DO.
THE SIPHON HAS TO GO BACK INSIDE ME.
HNNNNGGG!
IT'S INSTANT. THE POWER LEECHING OFF OF ME, ALL MY WEAKNESS FLOATING TO THE TOP...I'M POSITIVELY SURGING WITH WEAKNESS.
AND SHE KNOWS IT.
YOU ABSOLUTE FOOL.

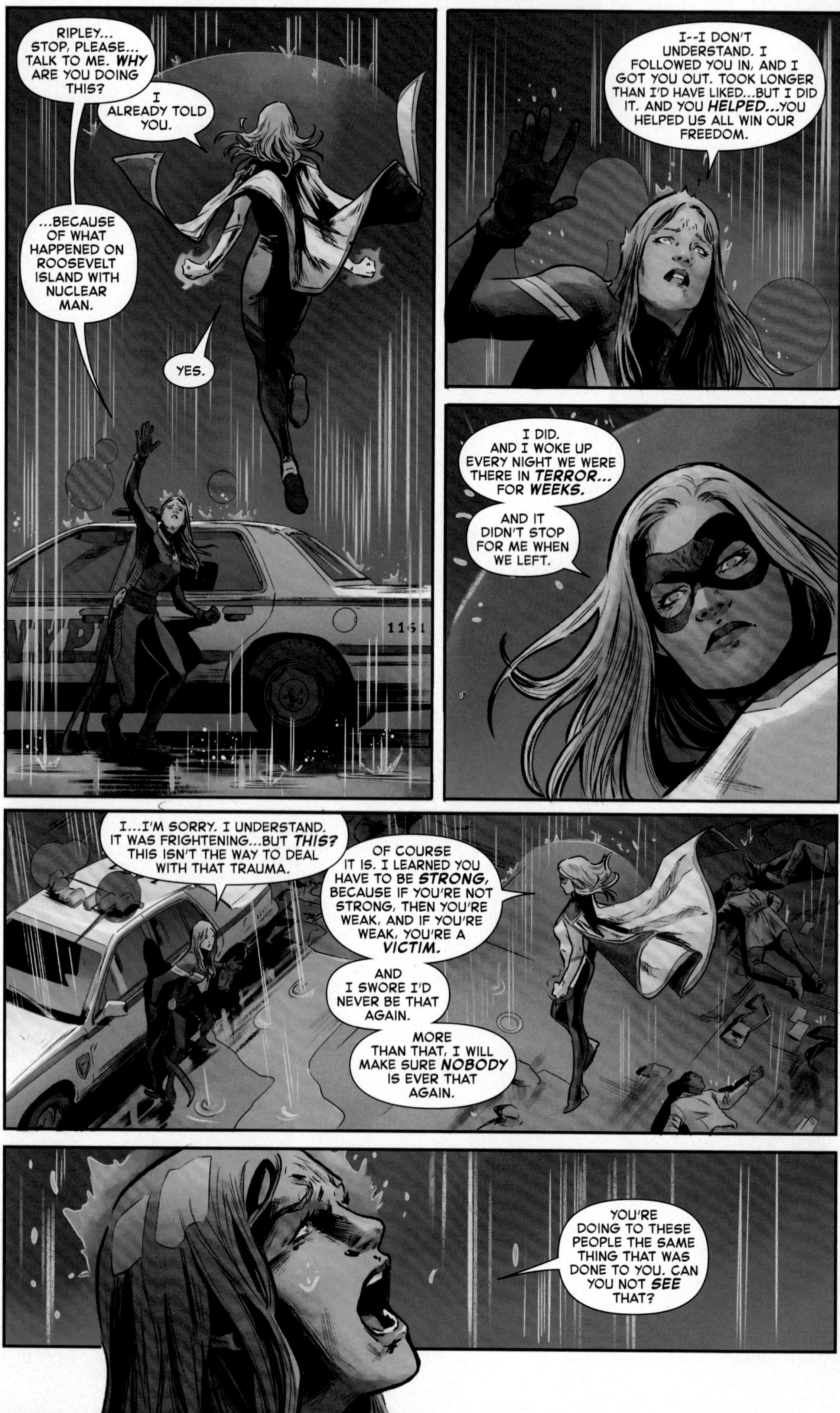
RIPLEY... STOP, PLEASE... TALK TO ME. WHY ARE YOU DOING THIS?
I ALREADY TOLD YOU.
...BECAUSE OF WHAT HAPPENED ON ROOSEVELT ISLAND WITH NUCLEAR MAN.
YES.
1161
I--I DON'T UNDERSTAND. I FOLLOWED YOU IN, AND I GOT YOU OUT. TOOK LONGER THAN I'D HAVE LIKED...BUT I DID IT. AND YOU HELPED...YOU HELPED US ALL WIN OUR FREEDOM.
I DID. AND I WOKE UP EVERY NIGHT WE WERE THERE IN TERROR... FOR WEEKS.
AND IT DIDN'T STOP FOR ME WHEN WE LEFT.
I...I'M SORRY. I UNDERSTAND. IT WAS FRIGHTENING...BUT THIS? THIS ISN'T THE WAY TO DEAL WITH THAT TRAUMA.
OF COURSE IT IS. I LEARNED YOU HAVE TO BE STRONG, BECAUSE IF YOU'RE NOT STRONG, THEN YOU'RE WEAK, AND IF YOU'RE WEAK, YOU'RE A VICTIM.
AND I SWORE I'D NEVER BE THAT AGAIN.
MORE THAN THAT, I WILL MAKE SURE NOBODY IS EVER THAT AGAIN.
YOU'RE DOING TO THESE PEOPLE THE SAME THING THAT WAS DONE TO YOU. CAN YOU NOT SEE THAT?

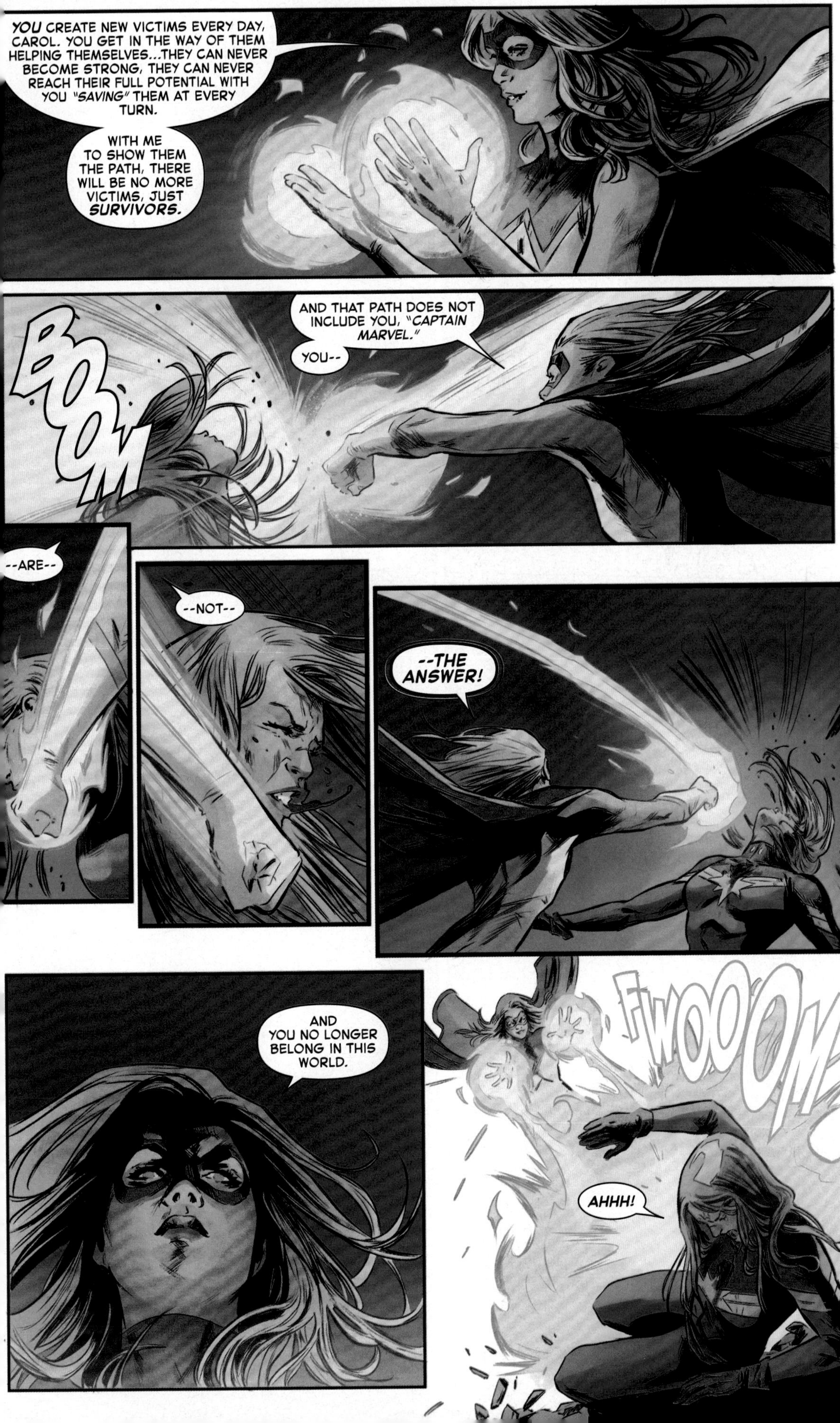
YOU CREATE NEW VICTIMS EVERY DAY, CAROL. YOU GET IN THE WAY OF THEM HELPING THEMSELVES...THEY CAN NEVER BECOME STRONG, THEY CAN NEVER REACH THEIR FULL POTENTIAL WITH YOU "SAVING" THEM AT EVERY TURN.
WITH ME TO SHOW THEM THE PATH, THERE WILL BE NO MORE VICTIMS, JUST SURVIVORS.
BOOM
AND THAT PATH DOES NOT INCLUDE YOU, "CAPTAIN MARVEL."
YOU--
--ARE--
--NOT--
--THE ANSWER!
AND YOU NO LONGER BELONG IN THIS WORLD.
FWOOOM
AHHH!

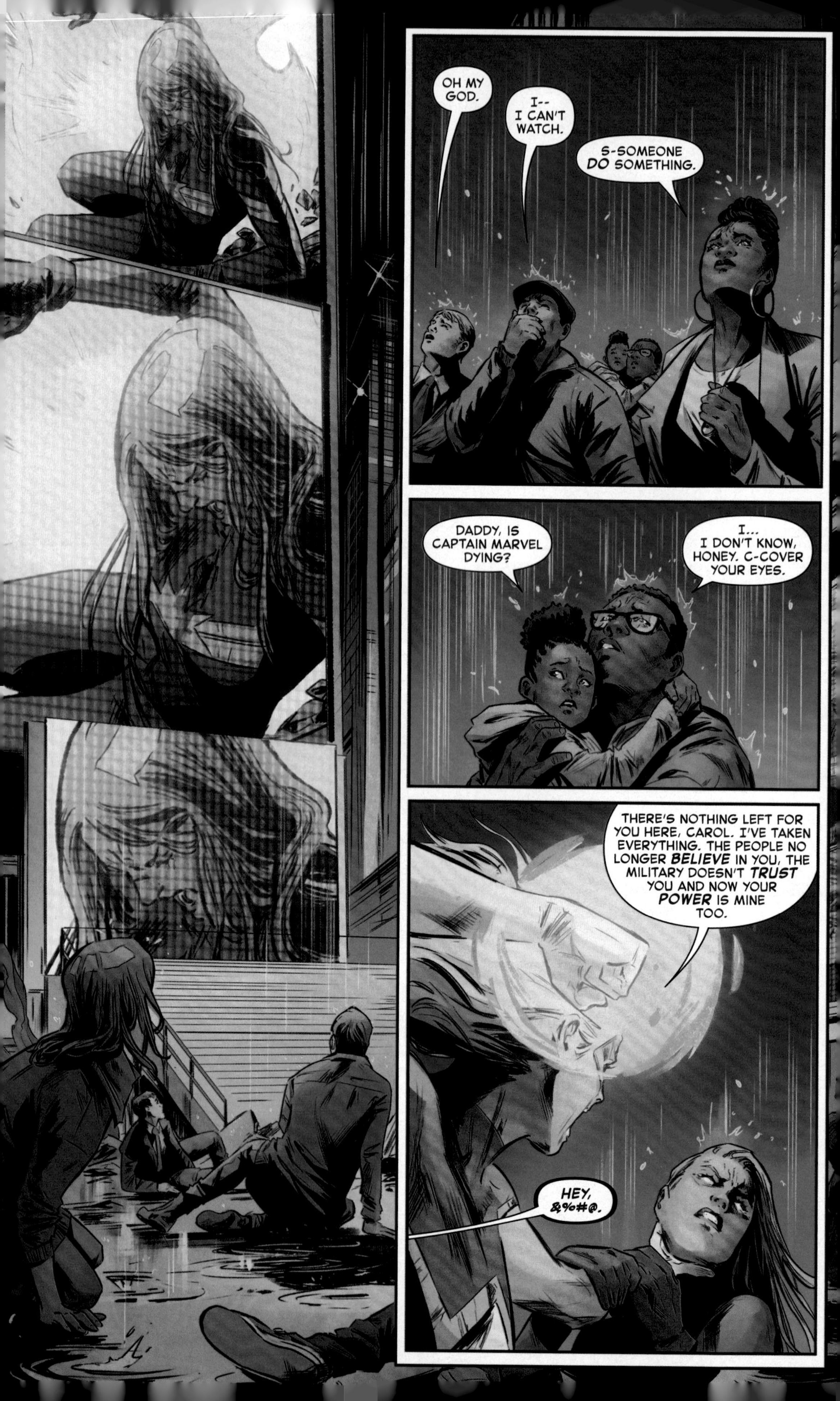

OH MY GOD.
I-- I CAN'T WATCH.
S-SOMEONE DO SOMETHING.
DADDY, IS CAPTAIN MARVEL DYING?
I... I DON'T KNOW, HONEY. C-COVER YOUR EYES.
THERE'S NOTHING LEFT FOR YOU HERE, CAROL. I'VE TAKEN EVERYTHING. THE PEOPLE NO LONGER BELIEVE IN YOU, THE MILITARY DOESN'T TRUST YOU AND NOW YOUR POWER IS MINE TOO.
HEY, &%#@.

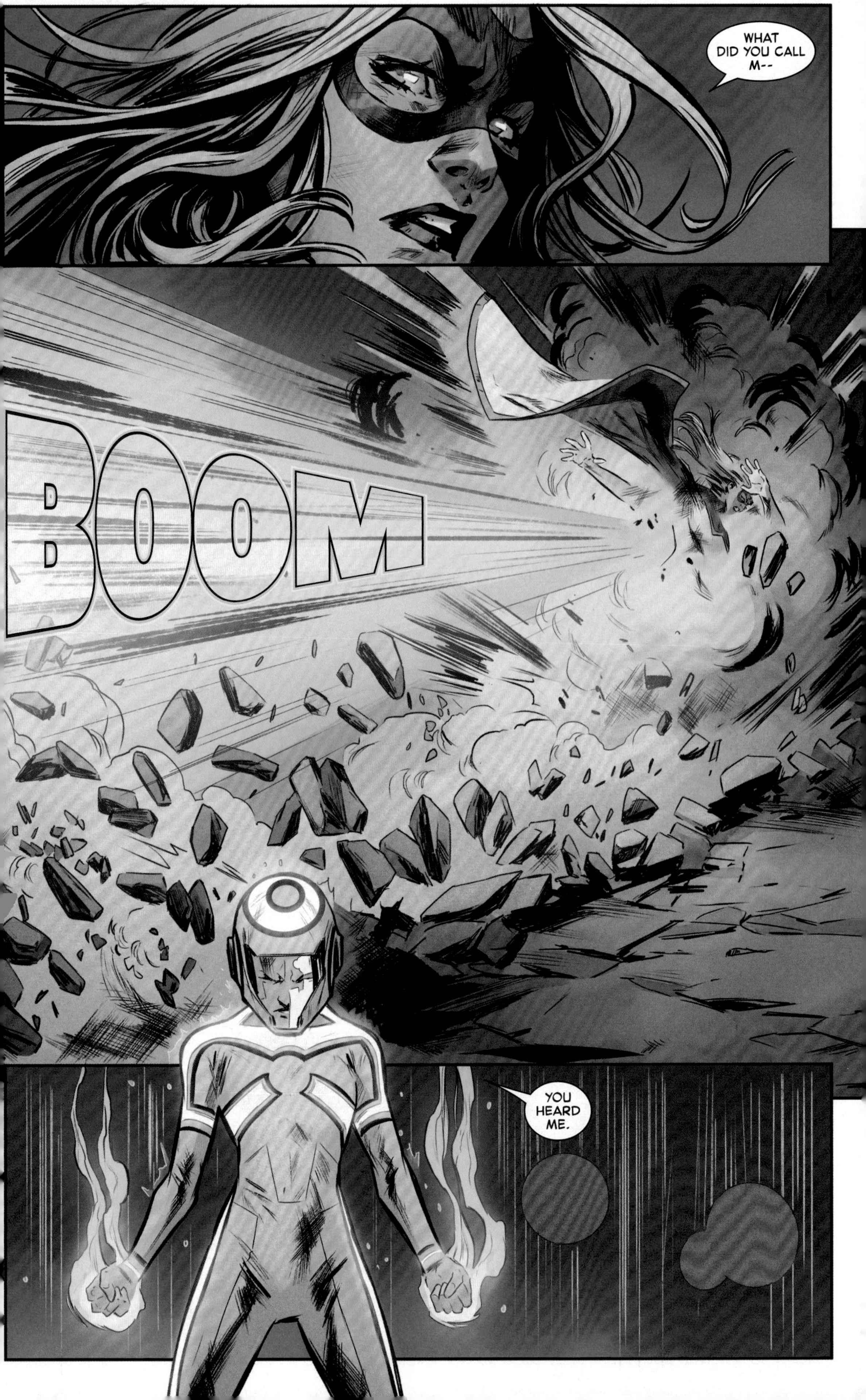
WHAT DID YOU CALL M--
BOOM
YOU HEARD ME.

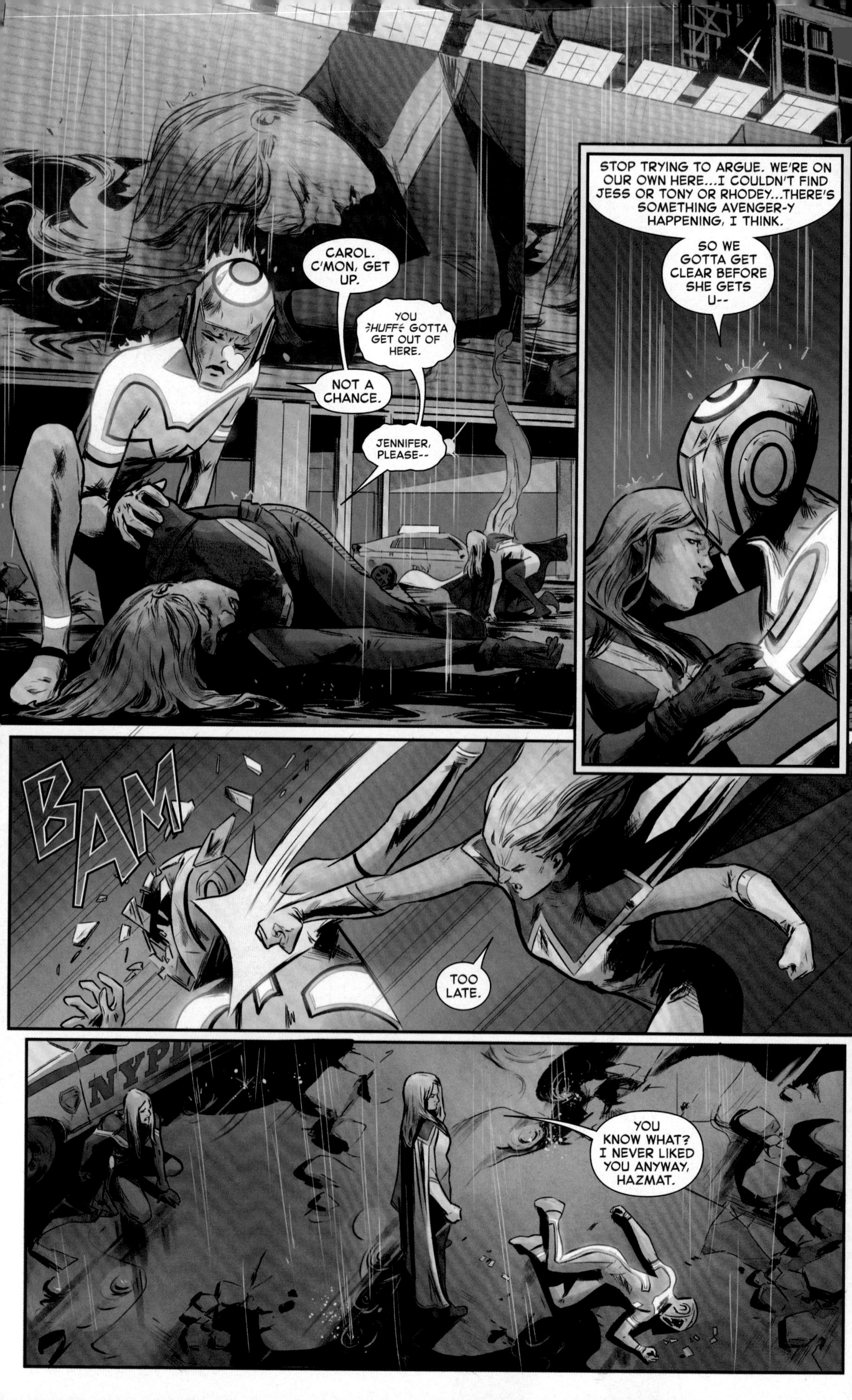
CAROL. C'MON, GET UP.
YOU ≠HUFF≠ GOTTA GET OUT OF HERE.
NOT A CHANCE.
JENNIFER, PLEASE--
STOP TRYING TO ARGUE. WE'RE ON OUR OWN HERE... I COULDN'T FIND JESS OR TONY OR RHODEY... THERE'S SOMETHING AVENGER-Y HAPPENING, I THINK.
SO WE GOTTA GET CLEAR BEFORE SHE GETS U--
BAM
TOO LATE.
YOU KNOW WHAT? I NEVER LIKED YOU ANYWAY, HAZMAT.

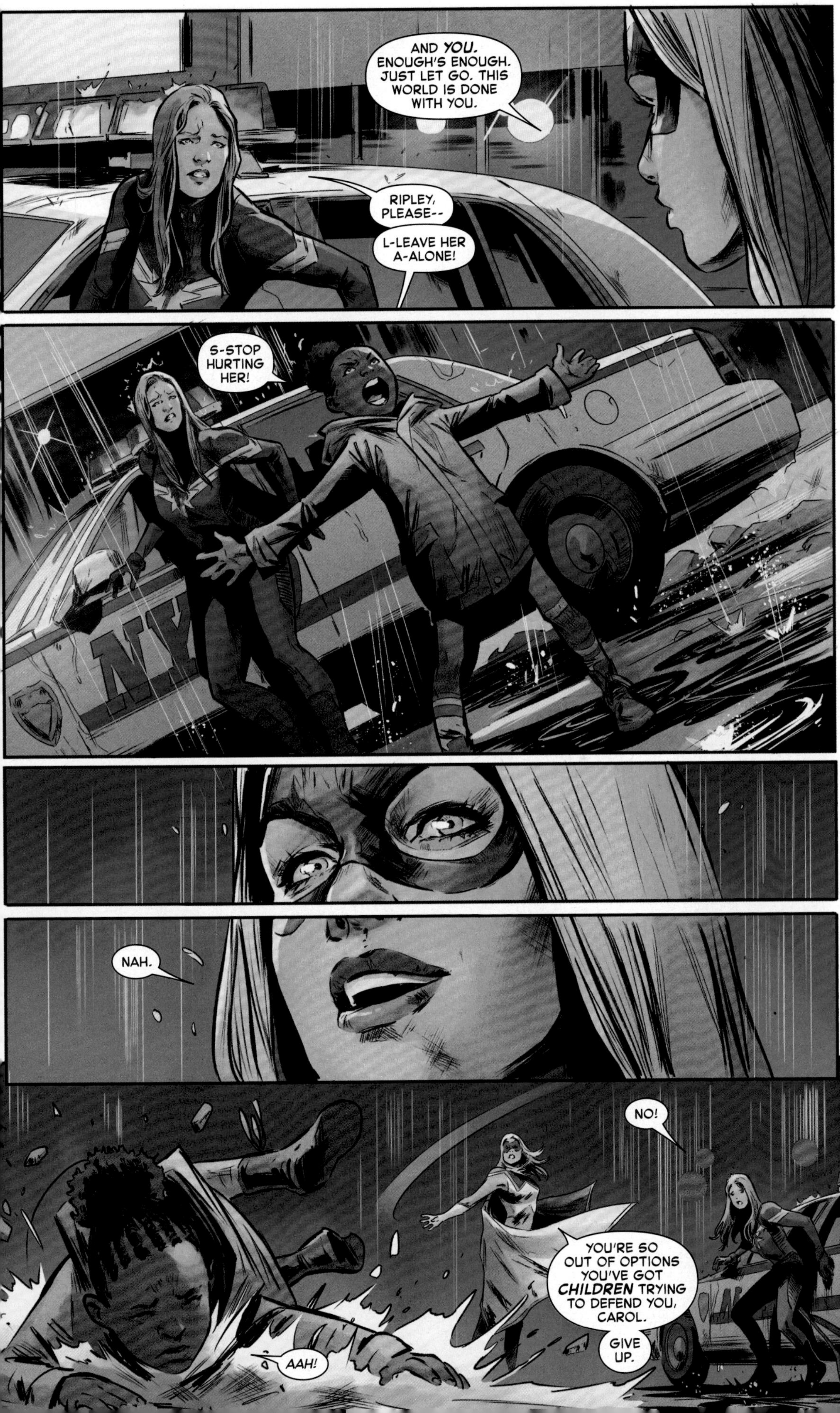
AND YOU. ENOUGH'S ENOUGH. JUST LET GO. THIS WORLD IS DONE WITH YOU.
RIPLEY, PLEASE--
L-LEAVE HER A-ALONE!
S-STOP HURTING HER!
NAH.
NO!
YOU'RE SO OUT OF OPTIONS YOU'VE GOT CHILDREN TRYING TO DEFEND YOU, CAROL.
GIVE UP.
AAH!

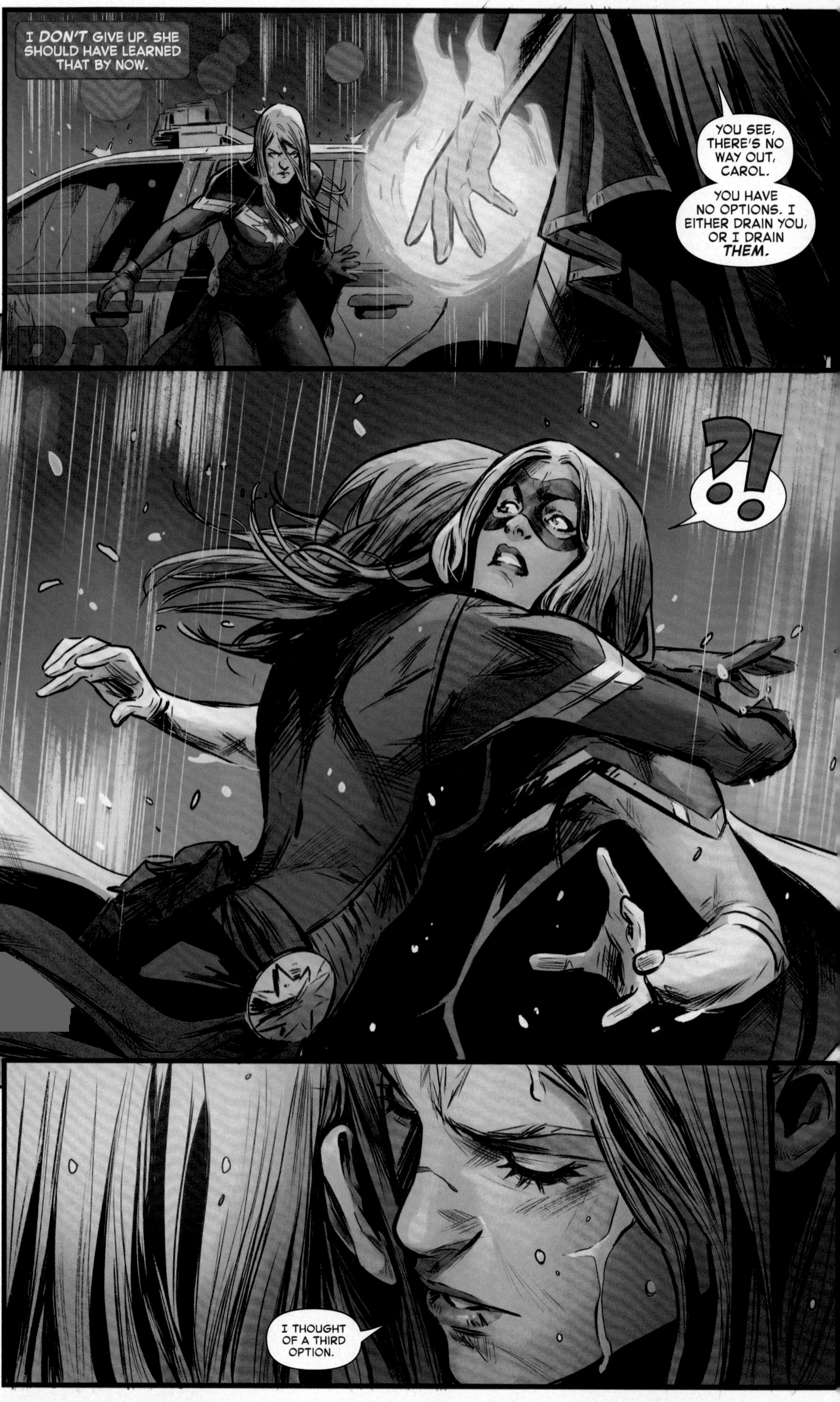
I DON'T GIVE UP. SHE SHOULD HAVE LEARNED THAT BY NOW.
YOU SEE, THERE'S NO WAY OUT, CAROL.
YOU HAVE NO OPTIONS. I EITHER DRAIN YOU, OR I DRAIN THEM.
?!
I THOUGHT OF A THIRD OPTION.

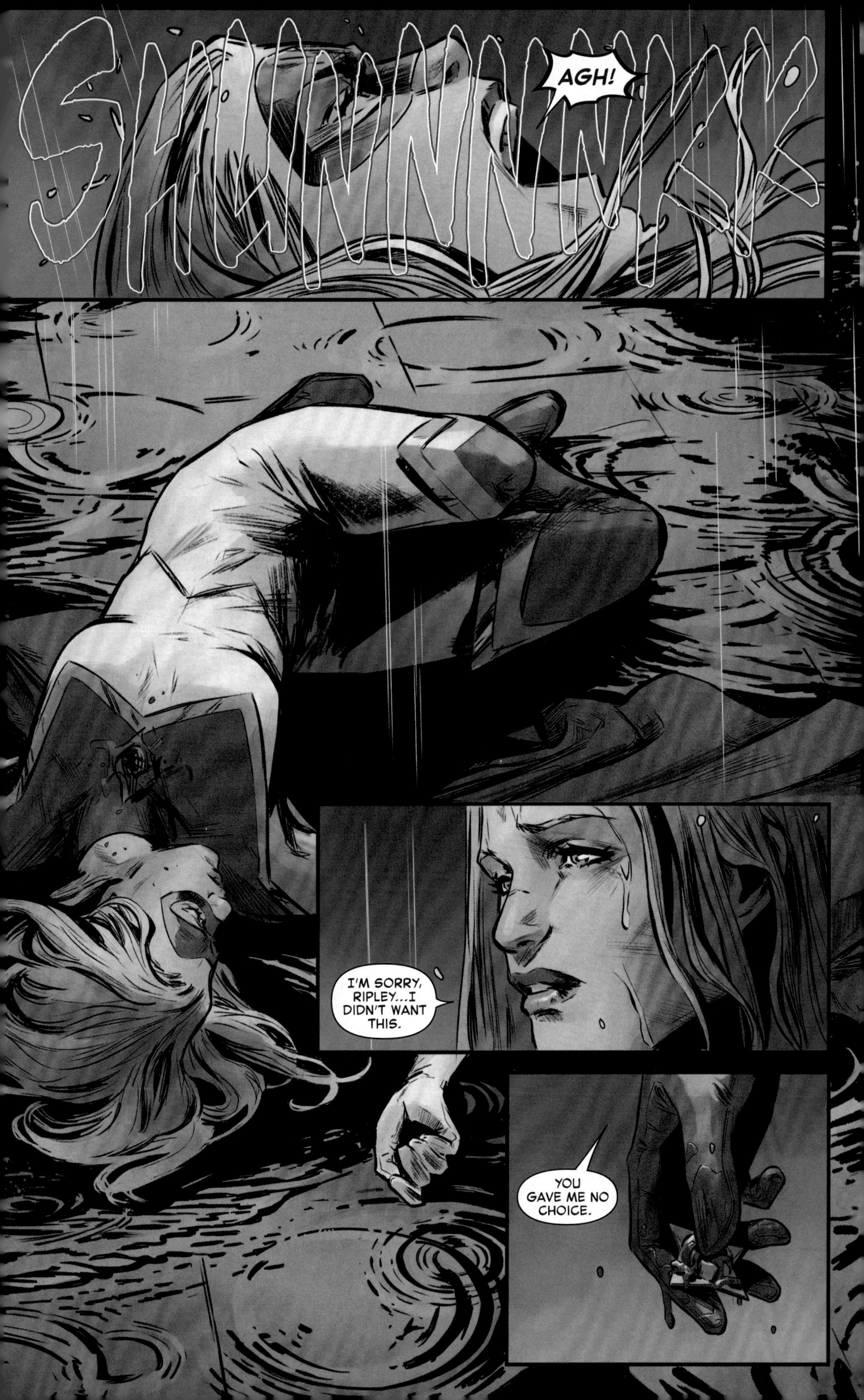
AGH!
I'M SORRY, RIPLEY...I DIDN'T WANT THIS.
YOU GAVE ME NO CHOICE.

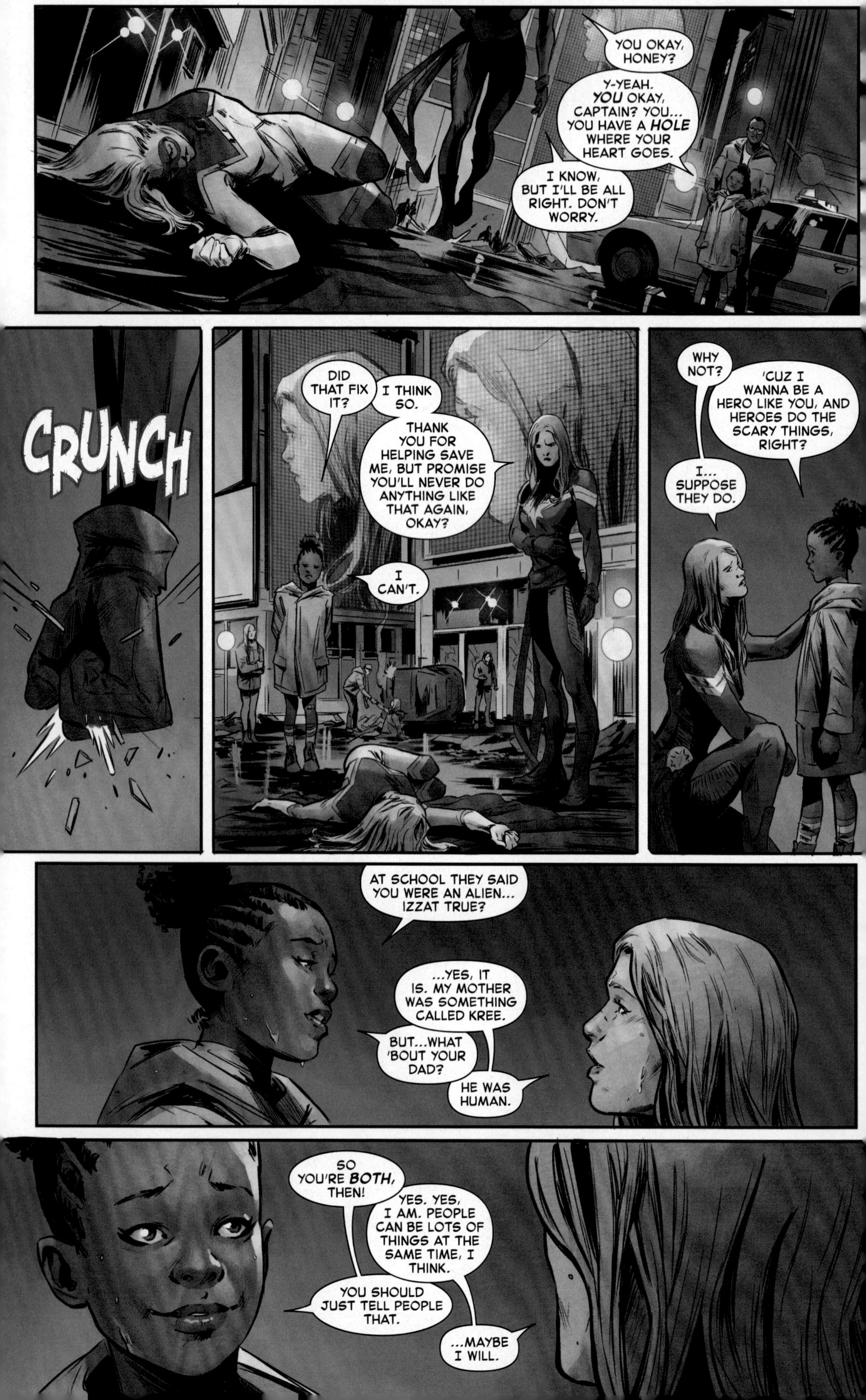
YOU OKAY, HONEY?
Y-YEAH. YOU OKAY, CAPTAIN? YOU... YOU HAVE A HOLE WHERE YOUR HEART GOES.
I KNOW, BUT I'LL BE ALL RIGHT. DON'T WORRY.
CRUNCH
DID THAT FIX IT?
I THINK SO.
THANK YOU FOR HELPING SAVE ME, BUT PROMISE YOU'LL NEVER DO ANYTHING LIKE THAT AGAIN, OKAY?
I CAN'T.
WHY NOT?
'CUZ I WANNA BE A HERO LIKE YOU, AND HEROES DO THE SCARY THINGS, RIGHT?
I... SUPPOSE THEY DO.
AT SCHOOL THEY SAID YOU WERE AN ALIEN... IZZAT TRUE?
...YES, IT IS. MY MOTHER WAS SOMETHING CALLED KREE.
BUT...WHAT 'BOUT YOUR DAD?
HE WAS HUMAN.
SO YOU'RE BOTH, THEN!
YES. YES, I AM. PEOPLE CAN BE LOTS OF THINGS AT THE SAME TIME, I THINK.
YOU SHOULD JUST TELL PEOPLE THAT.
...MAYBE I WILL.

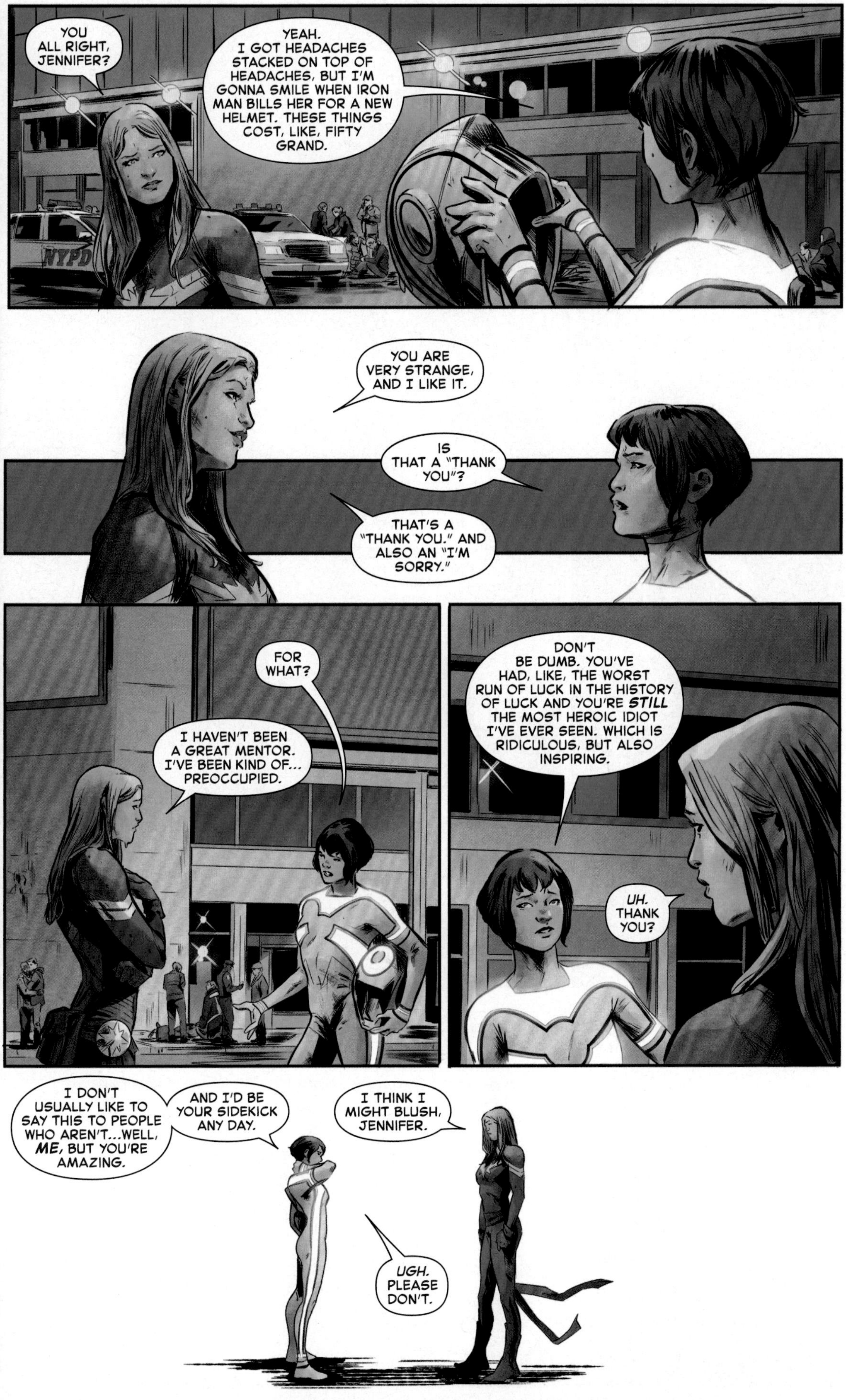
YOU ALL RIGHT, JENNIFER?
YEAH. I GOT HEADACHES STACKED ON TOP OF HEADACHES, BUT I'M GONNA SMILE WHEN IRON MAN BILLS HER FOR A NEW HELMET. THESE THINGS COST, LIKE, FIFTY GRAND.
NYPD
YOU ARE VERY STRANGE, AND I LIKE IT.
IS THAT A "THANK YOU"?
THAT'S A "THANK YOU." AND ALSO AN "I'M SORRY."
FOR WHAT?
I HAVEN'T BEEN A GREAT MENTOR. I'VE BEEN KIND OF... PREOCCUPIED.
DON'T BE DUMB. YOU'VE HAD, LIKE, THE WORST RUN OF LUCK IN THE HISTORY OF LUCK AND YOU'RE *STILL* THE MOST HEROIC IDIOT I'VE EVER SEEN. WHICH IS RIDICULOUS, BUT ALSO INSPIRING.
UH. THANK YOU?
I DON'T USUALLY LIKE TO SAY THIS TO PEOPLE WHO AREN'T...WELL, *ME*, BUT YOU'RE AMAZING.
AND I'D BE YOUR SIDEKICK ANY DAY.
I THINK I MIGHT BLUSH, JENNIFER.
UGH. PLEASE DON'T.

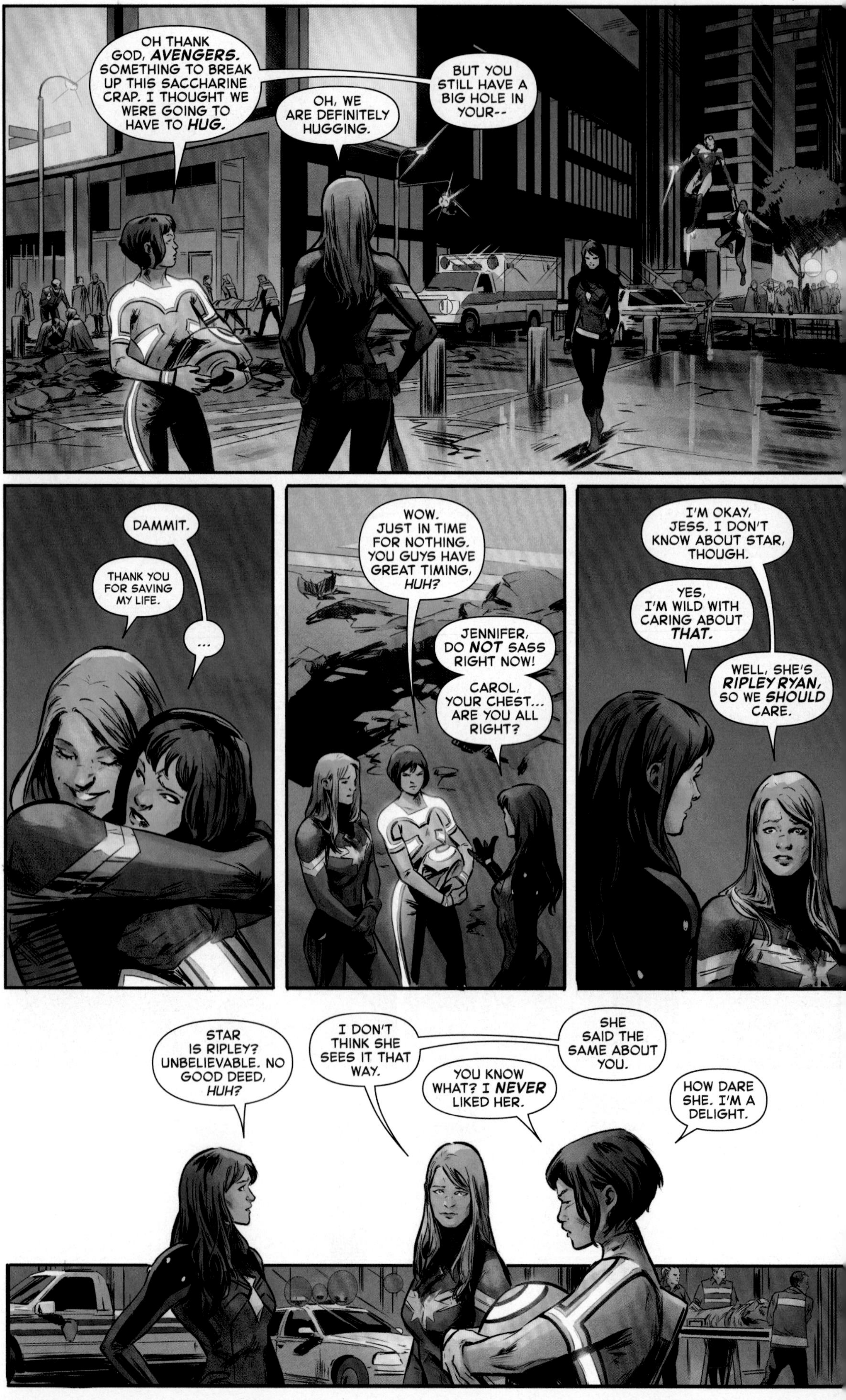
OH THANK GOD, AVENGERS. SOMETHING TO BREAK UP THIS SACCHARINE CRAP. I THOUGHT WE WERE GOING TO HAVE TO HUG.
OH, WE ARE DEFINITELY HUGGING.
BUT YOU STILL HAVE A BIG HOLE IN YOUR--
DAMMIT.
THANK YOU FOR SAVING MY LIFE.
...
WOW. JUST IN TIME FOR NOTHING. YOU GUYS HAVE GREAT TIMING, HUH?
JENNIFER, DO NOT SASS RIGHT NOW!
CAROL, YOUR CHEST... ARE YOU ALL RIGHT?
I'M OKAY, JESS. I DON'T KNOW ABOUT STAR, THOUGH.
YES, I'M WILD WITH CARING ABOUT THAT.
WELL, SHE'S RIPLEY RYAN, SO WE SHOULD CARE.
STAR IS RIPLEY? UNBELIEVABLE. NO GOOD DEED, HUH?
I DON'T THINK SHE SEES IT THAT WAY.
SHE SAID THE SAME ABOUT YOU.
YOU KNOW WHAT? I NEVER LIKED HER.
HOW DARE SHE. I'M A DELIGHT.

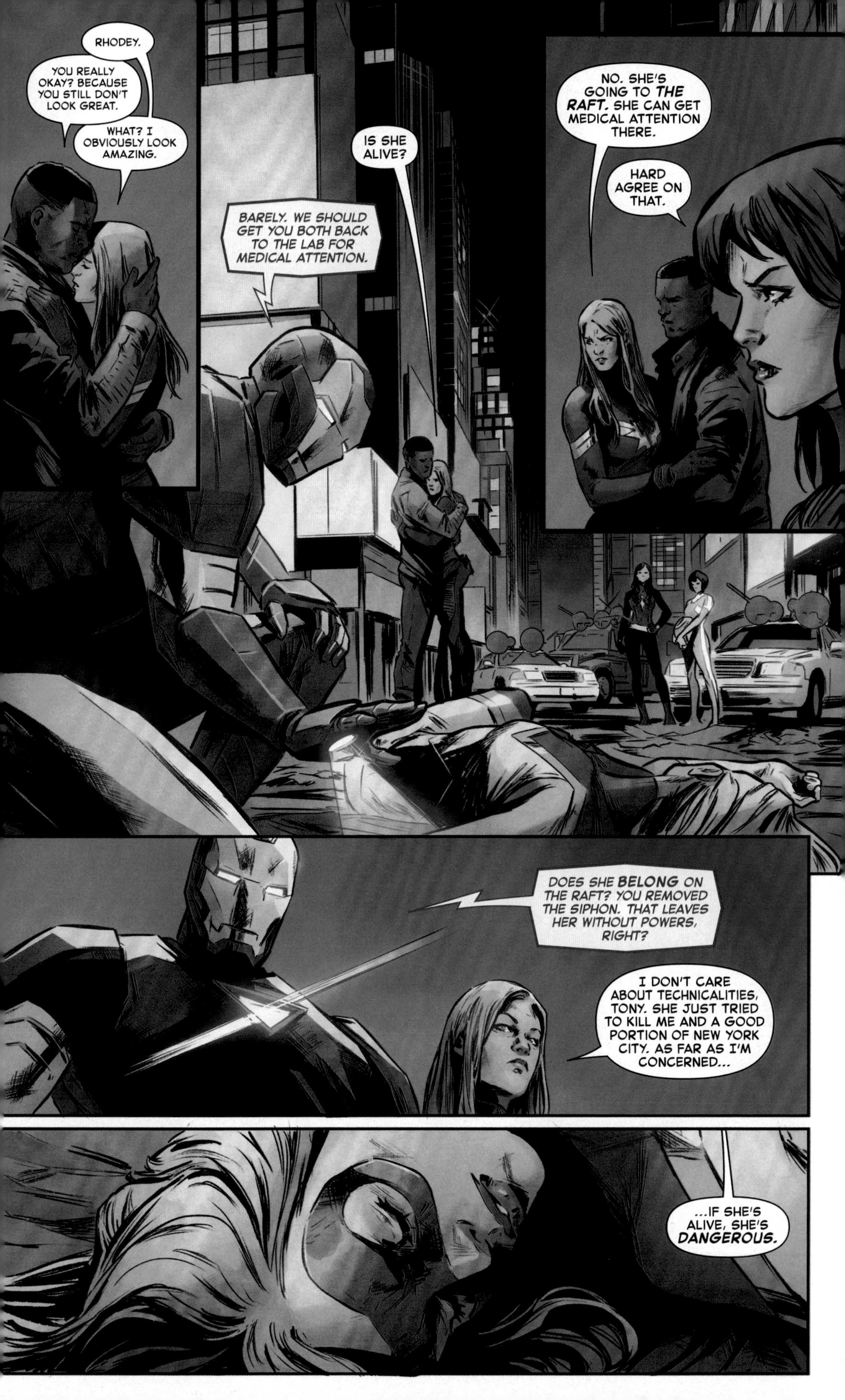
RHODEY.
YOU REALLY OKAY? BECAUSE YOU STILL DON'T LOOK GREAT.
WHAT? I OBVIOUSLY LOOK AMAZING.
IS SHE ALIVE?
BARELY. WE SHOULD GET YOU BOTH BACK TO THE LAB FOR MEDICAL ATTENTION.
NO. SHE'S GOING TO THE RAFT. SHE CAN GET MEDICAL ATTENTION THERE.
HARD AGREE ON THAT.
DOES SHE BELONG ON THE RAFT? YOU REMOVED THE SIPHON. THAT LEAVES HER WITHOUT POWERS, RIGHT?
I DON'T CARE ABOUT TECHNICALITIES, TONY. SHE JUST TRIED TO KILL ME AND A GOOD PORTION OF NEW YORK CITY. AS FAR AS I'M CONCERNED...
...IF SHE'S ALIVE, SHE'S DANGEROUS.

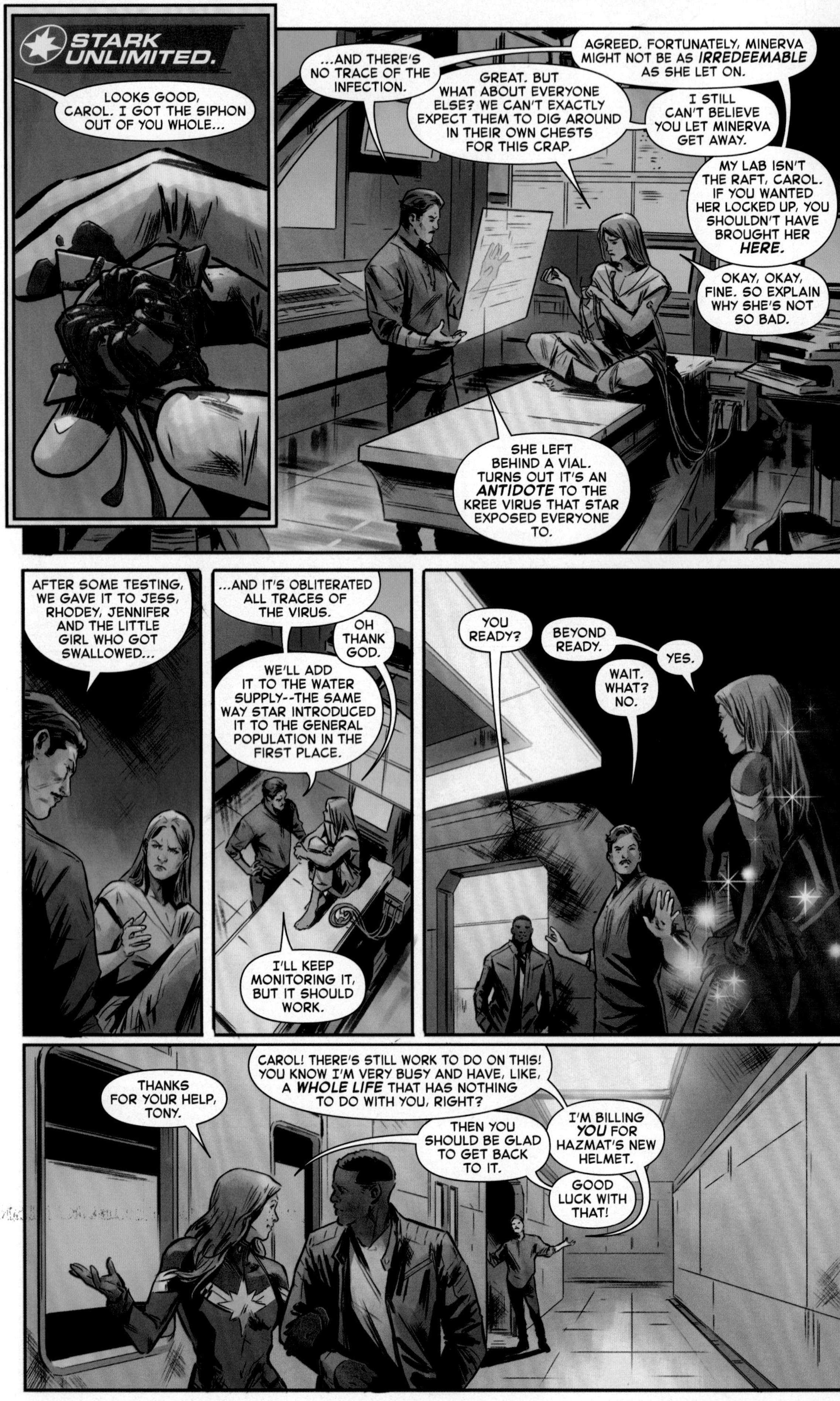
STARK UNLIMITED.
LOOKS GOOD, CAROL. I GOT THE SIPHON OUT OF YOU WHOLE...
...AND THERE'S NO TRACE OF THE INFECTION.
GREAT. BUT WHAT ABOUT EVERYONE ELSE? WE CAN'T EXACTLY EXPECT THEM TO DIG AROUND IN THEIR OWN CHESTS FOR THIS CRAP.
AGREED. FORTUNATELY, MINERVA MIGHT NOT BE AS IRREDEEMABLE AS SHE LET ON.
I STILL CAN'T BELIEVE YOU LET MINERVA GET AWAY.
MY LAB ISN'T THE RAFT, CAROL. IF YOU WANTED HER LOCKED UP, YOU SHOULDN'T HAVE BROUGHT HER HERE.
OKAY, OKAY, FINE. SO EXPLAIN WHY SHE'S NOT SO BAD.
SHE LEFT BEHIND A VIAL. TURNS OUT IT'S AN ANTIDOTE TO THE KREE VIRUS THAT STAR EXPOSED EVERYONE TO.
AFTER SOME TESTING, WE GAVE IT TO JESS, RHODEY, JENNIFER AND THE LITTLE GIRL WHO GOT SWALLOWED...
...AND IT'S OBLITERATED ALL TRACES OF THE VIRUS.
OH THANK GOD.
WE'LL ADD IT TO THE WATER SUPPLY--THE SAME WAY STAR INTRODUCED IT TO THE GENERAL POPULATION IN THE FIRST PLACE.
I'LL KEEP MONITORING IT, BUT IT SHOULD WORK.
YOU READY?
BEYOND READY.
YES.
WAIT. WHAT? NO.
THANKS FOR YOUR HELP, TONY.
CAROL! THERE'S STILL WORK TO DO ON THIS! YOU KNOW I'M VERY BUSY AND HAVE, LIKE, A WHOLE LIFE THAT HAS NOTHING TO DO WITH YOU, RIGHT?
THEN YOU SHOULD BE GLAD TO GET BACK TO IT.
I'M BILLING YOU FOR HAZMAT'S NEW HELMET.
GOOD LUCK WITH THAT!

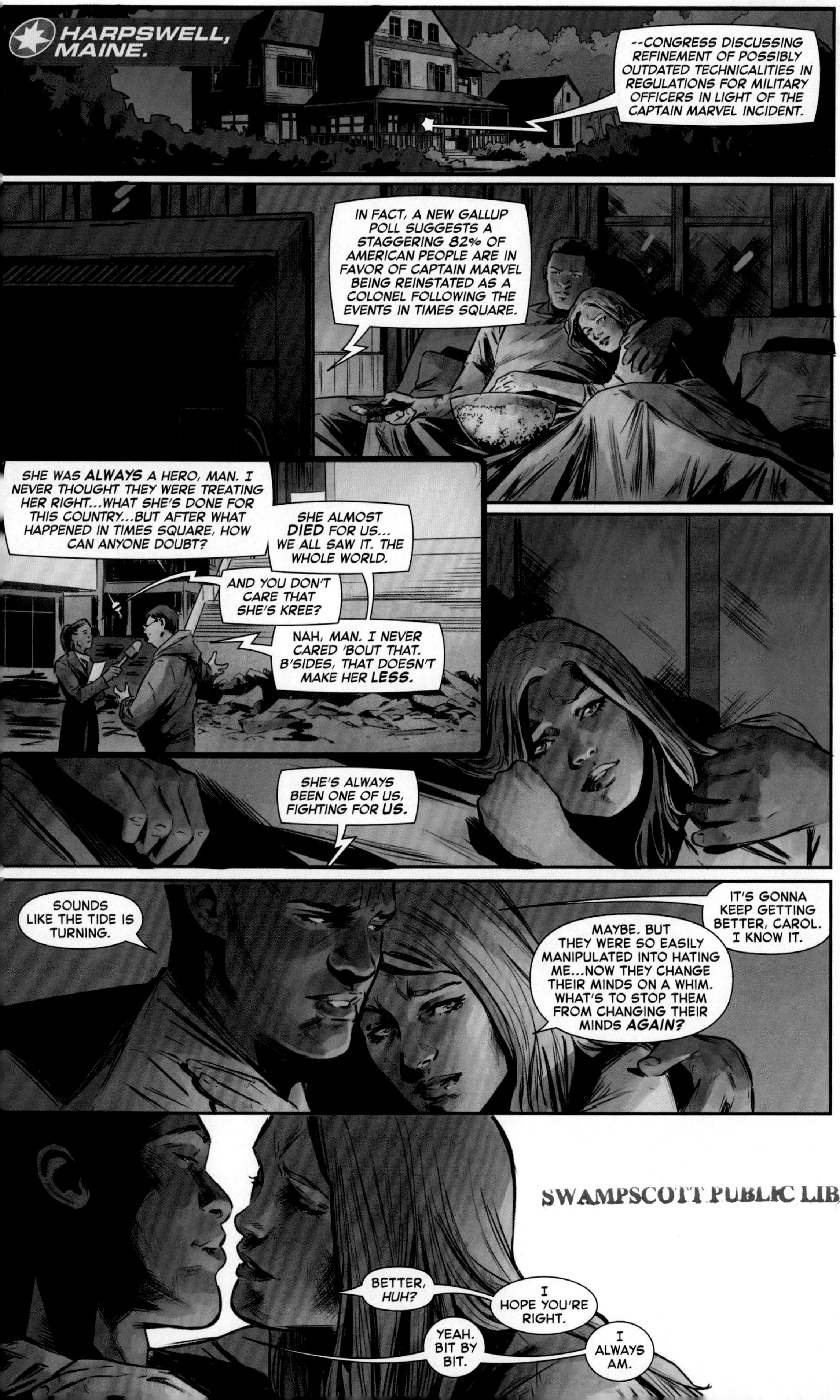
HARPSWELL, MAINE.
--CONGRESS DISCUSSING REFINEMENT OF POSSIBLY OUTDATED TECHNICALITIES IN REGULATIONS FOR MILITARY OFFICERS IN LIGHT OF THE CAPTAIN MARVEL INCIDENT.
IN FACT, A NEW GALLUP POLL SUGGESTS A STAGGERING 82% OF AMERICAN PEOPLE ARE IN FAVOR OF CAPTAIN MARVEL BEING REINSTATED AS A COLONEL FOLLOWING THE EVENTS IN TIMES SQUARE.
SHE WAS ALWAYS A HERO, MAN. I NEVER THOUGHT THEY WERE TREATING HER RIGHT...WHAT SHE'S DONE FOR THIS COUNTRY...BUT AFTER WHAT HAPPENED IN TIMES SQUARE, HOW CAN ANYONE DOUBT?
SHE ALMOST DIED FOR US... WE ALL SAW IT. THE WHOLE WORLD.
AND YOU DON'T CARE THAT SHE'S KREE?
NAH, MAN. I NEVER CARED 'BOUT THAT. B'SIDES, THAT DOESN'T MAKE HER LESS.
SHE'S ALWAYS BEEN ONE OF US, FIGHTING FOR US.
SOUNDS LIKE THE TIDE IS TURNING.
IT'S GONNA KEEP GETTING BETTER, CAROL. I KNOW IT.
MAYBE. BUT THEY WERE SO EASILY MANIPULATED INTO HATING ME...NOW THEY CHANGE THEIR MINDS ON A WHIM. WHAT'S TO STOP THEM FROM CHANGING THEIR MINDS AGAIN?
BETTER, HUH?
I HOPE YOU'RE RIGHT.
YEAH. BIT BY BIT.
I ALWAYS AM.

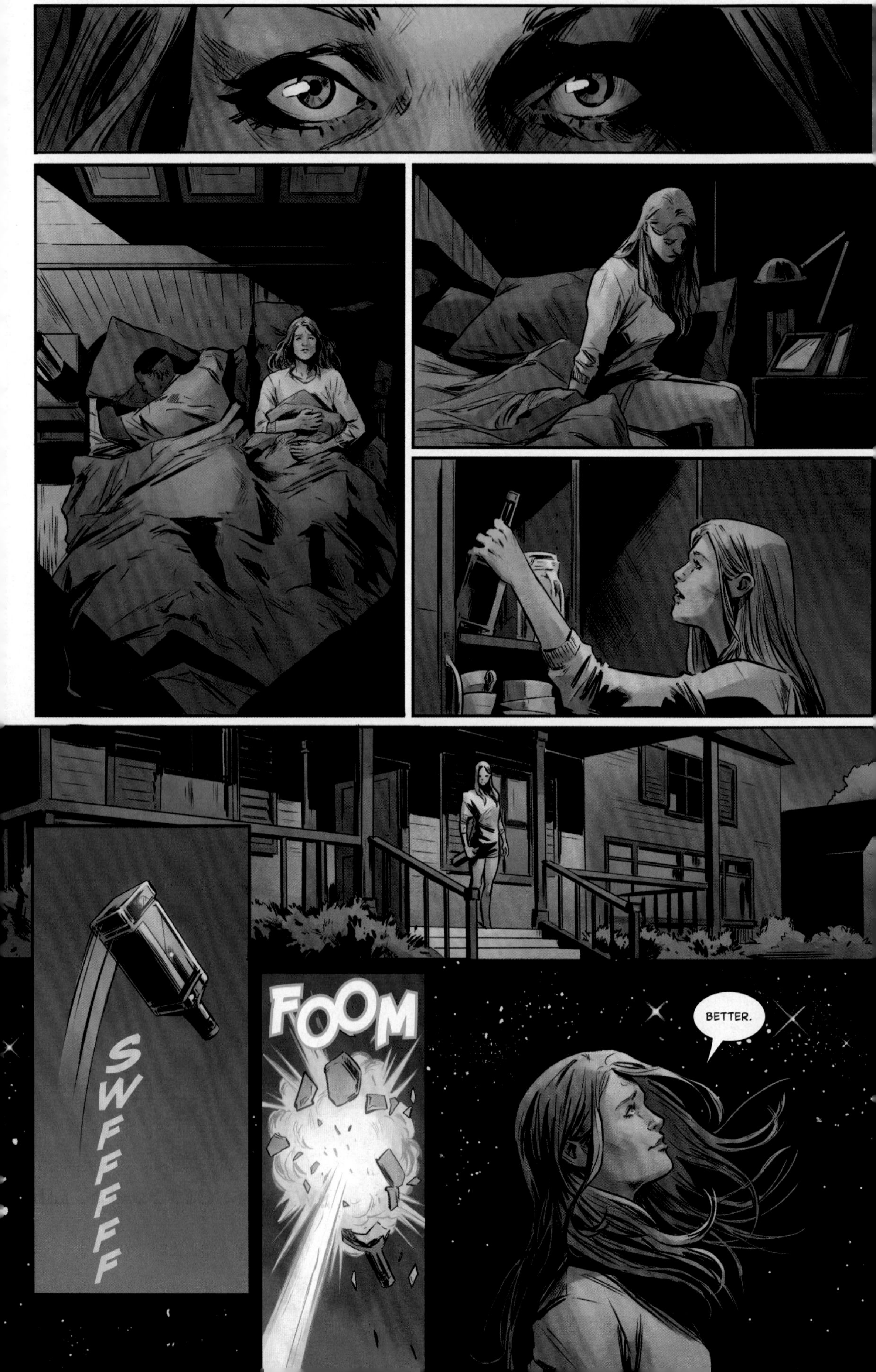
SWFFFFF
FOOM
BETTER.

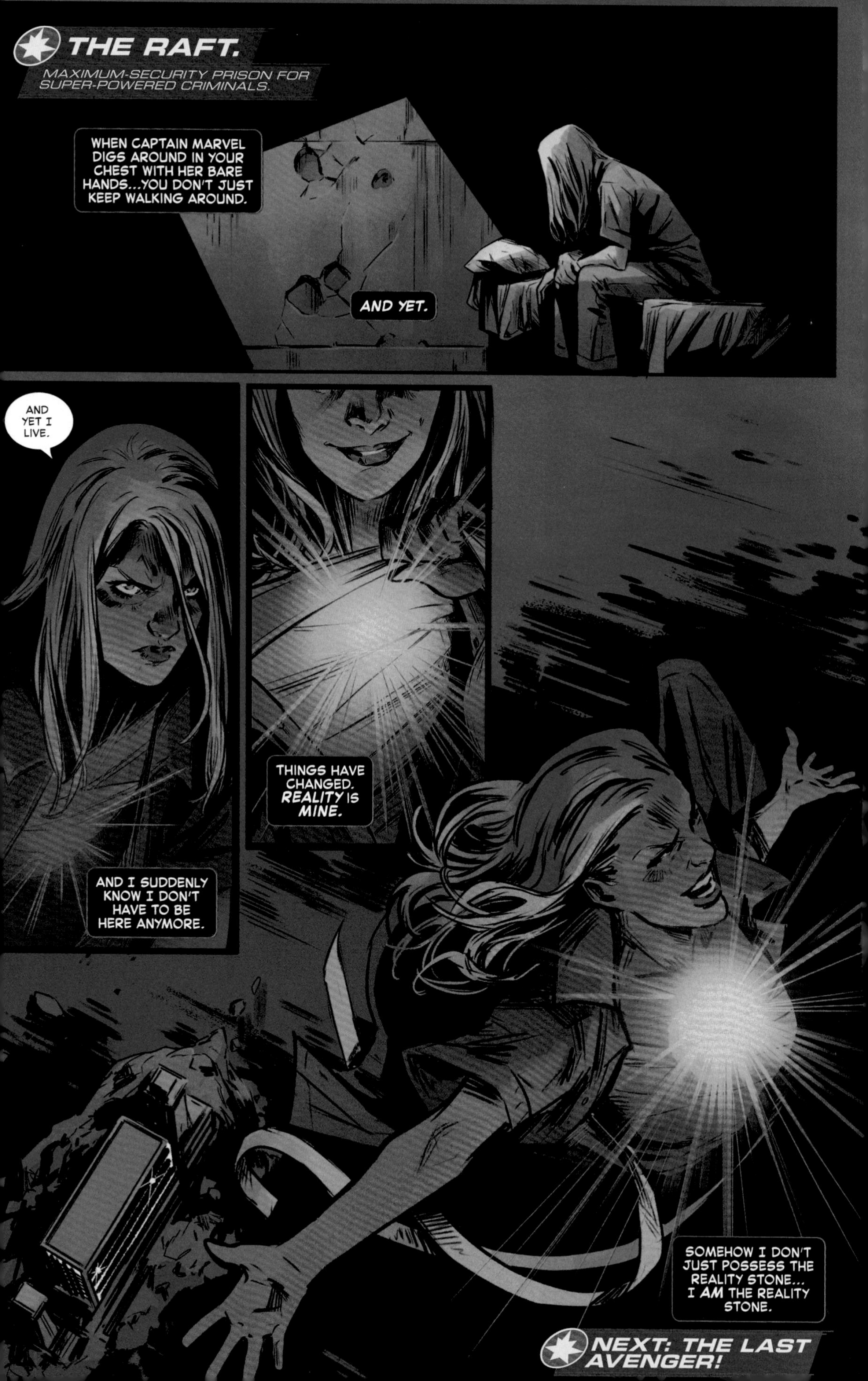
THE RAFT.
MAXIMUM-SECURITY PRISON FOR SUPER-POWERED CRIMINALS.
WHEN CAPTAIN MARVEL DIGS AROUND IN YOUR CHEST WITH HER BARE HANDS...YOU DON'T JUST KEEP WALKING AROUND.
AND YET.
AND YET I LIVE.
AND I SUDDENLY KNOW I DON'T HAVE TO BE HERE ANYMORE.
THINGS HAVE CHANGED. REALITY IS MINE.
SOMEHOW I DON'T JUST POSSESS THE REALITY STONE... I AM THE REALITY STONE.
NEXT: THE LAST AVENGER!

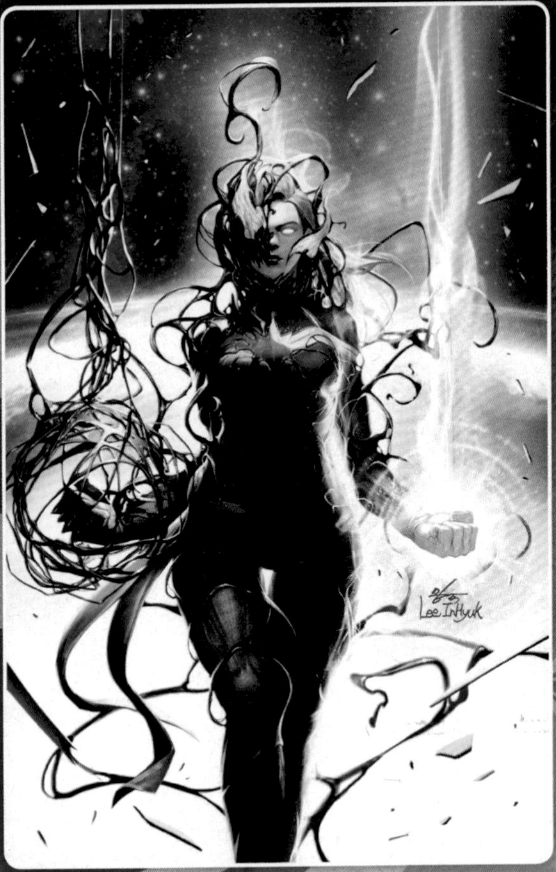
Lee InHyuk

INHYUK LEE
8 CARNAGE-IZED VARIANT

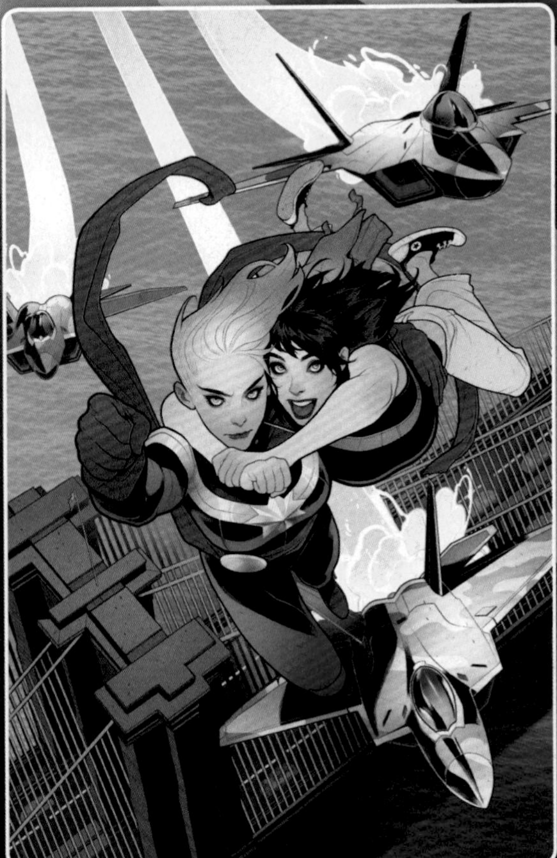

ELIZABETH TORQUE
11 MARY JANE VARIANT